Kay Zwerling

For KSCO: I'm Kay Zwerling

A Collection of Commentaries

Kay Zwerling

Published by FastPencil, Inc.

Published by FastPencil, Inc.
3131 Bascom Ave.
Suite 150
Campbell CA 95008 USA
(408) 540-7571
(408) 540-7572 (Fax)
info@fastpencil.com
http://www.fastpencil.com

First Edition

To:
My son and CEO Michael Zwerling,
who time and again urged me to ventilate my political frustrations using our own KSCO microphone. I finally did so, and was both surprised and delighted to find that so many listeners actually agree with me.

❧

CONTENTS

Acknowledgements

Melanie Flint for her assistance and professionalism helping me at the beginning of this new journey.

Michael Olson, KSCO General Manager and very good friend, who took much time to inspire and guide me through the long process. Without Michael, this book probably would not have been born.

My good friend and transcriber Marcia Miller for the countless copies of commentaries (at least four drafts of each one) until it was just right. We also often shared humorous and angry allusions which concurrently we would agree upon regarding the human condition.

Also, our very talented engineer Bill Graff, who records my many commentaries and patiently removes all my extra allergy breaths, and more importantly, makes sure we stay on the air loud and clear.

And finally, Carol Stafford, our very efficient station manager, who patiently edited all of this book, and who makes KSCO run so smoothly.

To all of you, my deepest appreciation. Thank you.

— KZ

EDITORS NOTE:

What you are about to read is a compilation of commentaries broadcast by Kay Zwerling in the period of 1999 through 2009. Kay Zwerling along with her son and CEO Michael Zwerling, own two radio stations broadcasting from Santa Cruz, California. KSCO AM 1080 has a 10,000 watt signal that is heard over one-third of the State of California during the daytime. The station has a 63-year history, having first come on the airways as KSCO in 1947. Since that time, there have been three owners. Kay, her husband, and son Michael bought KSCO in 1991, and it remains to this day one of the few independently owned and operated radio stations in the United States.

Because Kay wrote these commentaries over a ten-year period with no intention of compiling a book, there were some challenges for the editor. Original air dates were often difficult to establish with certainty. Also, over time, some final draft copies in digital form have been lost due to computer demises over the years. The original air dates of these commentaries were typically broadcast the following entire week. Kay broadcast more than 500 commentaries between 1999 and 2009.

We have done our best to include every original commentary up until the end of 2009. As Kay continues to write and broadcast this book has been a living document from the beginning. So, if you wish to know her latest thoughts on anything from the State budget to the situation in the Middle East, you will have to tune into KSCO and hear it for yourself.

We hope that this book is as enjoyable to read as it was to work on over the past year with Kay.

— Melanie Flint

PREFACE

Never in my wildest thoughts did I ever contemplate writing a book.

In January 31, 1991, my husband and I helped MZ buy KSCO – and I started following him around the station learning about the radio business.

For several months, I would complain about our ultraliberal City Council, and also about our County Board of Supervisors taking too much money for themselves when they met probably twice a month or so, and started giving themselves more money than they deserved – and finally MZ said "Mom, why don't you ventilate on the air – you have a free microphone."

I took his advice, and to my wonderful surprise, I began to receive many personal emails from listeners who were equally angry with our local government and totally agreed with me.

That did it.

I started writing and broadcasting weekly commentaries – many political, sometimes jokes, and other current interesting topics.

Many listeners started sending me materials they thought were especially interesting, and I used some of them – always giving credit to the person who sent it.

Now we are about to write a book with many of these commentaries – so any acknowledgments must be accurate.

When I wrote about Ben Stein and some other famous persons, of course, I gathered the information from their biographies.

If I accidentally used material from another writer not acknowledged, please forgive me. I believe that if it were the case, any one of our very bright listeners would have called it to my attention, but that never happened.

I hope you enjoy my book.

— Kay Zwerling

INTRODUCTION

While well into my eighth decade of life, I find myself pleasantly surprised for numerous reasons.

I never expected to be blessed with such a long life, and the notion that I could write enough material that might justify or warrant a respectable book feels delightful.

At this point in my existence, I do honestly believe that every day is a gift. Whoever thought my first boyfriend at age fifteen would turn out to be the one and only love of my life? And it was mutual.

He was a college graduate from New York University when we met. He didn't know how young I was, and I was awed by his knowledge and his delightful sense of humor. We were married for 58 years, and he was my boyfriend for four years before that. We did bicker occasionally, but he passed away ten years ago, and I miss him every day.

We were blessed with three wonderful children - then seven grandchildren. I became a grandmother at age 45, and now I also have seven great-grandchildren.

My husband was a self-employed optometrist for 48 years in Santa Cruz, and we were able to travel around the world and see so much while my mom stayed with the children.

A child of the Great Depression, I was able to go back to school at age 42 and get a Bachelors of Arts at University of California, Santa Cruz, and then a Masters Degree at San Jose State University.

When we helped Michael, our youngest son, to buy KSCO Radio, life took on another interesting dimension. I used to follow Michael, the CEO, around the station and complain about local politics constantly, so finally he suggested that I say it on the air. And I've been doing just that for over a decade now.

It has been a delightful, adventurous ride, and I have now recorded more than 500 commentaries. In addition to the joy of producing them, these commentaries have brought me something that I never expected – fans! I've been thrilled to find that so many listeners agree with my views. So I decided to collect some of my favorite commentaries together for them. The result is this book. I hope you enjoy it.

1

Part One: Santa Cruz, California

1

It all started about 40 years ago in our pristine, incredibly beautiful, and peaceful Santa Cruz, population about 15,000. While many rejoiced when the regents of the University of California chose Santa Cruz for their new campus, I felt uneasy, sensing that this quiet little piece of heaven would never again be the same, and that the changes would not be for the better.

Despite my opportunity to enter the new campus as a reentry student, the political environment I encountered confirmed my fears that in some ways UCSC would prove to be our deterioration – or even our nemesis.

The U.C. plan was to make the Santa Cruz campus a cluster of small colleges patterned after Oxford in England, where the free exchange of ideas between faculty and students would encourage inquiring young minds to flourish. The small colleges did become a reality, but the young minds were not allowed to flourish, at least not in the political sciences department. Conservative students taking part in KSCO programming confirmed that fact. They felt stifled, intimidated, and ostracized. Some professors in the political sciences called themselves the New Left and made sure that their students understood the Marxist philosophy, and they did not – I repeat, did not – encourage dialog from students with differing points of view. One Professor, Michael Rotkin, decided to run for City Council and make Santa Cruz a model for his doctoral dissertation, which was "How To Create A Socialist City". He was elected, became mayor at least twice, got elected again, and still makes policy for us. One could admire the tenacity of purpose of Rotkin and other leftist newcomers, who embraced Santa Cruz as their own and set out to make sweeping changes in our formerly conservative city. It should be noted that our previous leaders did not allow any pollution producing industries. They were sensitive to the environment long before the lefties thought they had invented that concept.

Among the new changes, Santa Cruz was declared a Nuclear Free Zone (whatever that means), and war was rejected because it was hateful (duh). Now, peace is patriotic (whatever that means). Our navy ships are denied permission to come to Monterey Bay, new businesses are discouraged, and the ultimate short-sighted foolishness, our leaders actually declined federal funds to widen Highway 17. It is deja vu all over again now. Our present city leaders – yep, still Rotkin and Cynthia Matthews, who are making careers out of serving on the City Council – have just declined to participate with adjoining counties to help widen the gridlocked Highway One. Santa Cruz has become a place not allowed to grow but growing anyhow, a place to bypass, a place run by liberal extremists who spend money foolishly and make many of us ashamed to admit that we live here.

Back to around 40 years ago... the New Left leaders let it be known to all the country's needy – that is, the real needy whom most of us will always be willing to help – and the by-choice, able-bodied needy, that Santa Cruz was a great place to live and that our leaders were happy to provide for all of their needs. In return, all that was expected from them was to continue to vote their benefactors into office. Word spread like wildfire and now, decades later, what do we have? A stroll on the Pacific Garden Mall will reveal the appalling answer. Dignity and self-respect have been robbed from the gullible able-bodied recipients still on the dole, a very large price to pay for years of accepting freebies. The deep satisfaction of independence and self-worth, these poor souls will never know.

Since 9/11, the world has forever changed. Global terrorism will have to be dealt with, probably forever. To deny that reality will be deadly, literally. Now our country is buckling under the years of state, local, and federal excesses, not the least of which are enormous salaries, pensions, and hidden perks which our leaders quietly give themselves – plus open borders, validation of illegals, and the rewarding of illegals with amnesty, driving licenses, and the right to vote. Our leaders are ignoring the Rule of Law and making a farce of our Constitution, all for the Almighty Vote. Corruption is acceptable, but where do we go from here? Our role models are unacceptable.

The prophetic parting words of my Cabrillo College history professor in 1967 continue to haunt me. His chilling prediction was that the United States will eventually become a third-world country. What can we do to stop the madness?

2

Ten years ago, immediately after the Loma Prieta earthquake, our city leaders decided they no longer wanted small, cozy buildings downtown. Instead, they wanted large-frontaged buildings, preferably three stories high.

With that plan in mind, my husband and I, who lost our two small downtown buildings in the earthquake, were forced to sell both of our parcels, one to the next door neighbor and one to the city through eminent domain.

Now, our City Council wants only small businesses downtown in order to maintain the pre-earthquake sort of cozy look. What a cruel joke Tell me, what is small about the many large three-story buildings which now cover downtown. Most are beautiful, but small and cozy? I don't think so.

The sad truth is, the City Council is manufacturing ordinances so that it can selectively control our free enterprise system of government. Never mind that it will stifle the rest of the downtown business community.

The sad truth is, the City Council does not want another large bookstore downtown, only because it wants to protect one politically correct local individual.

One thing about the politically correct: they are very protective of their own. They will fight to the death to protect their own, even if the larger community suffers for it. To them I say "This is wrong. This is manipulative. This is controlling."

Borders Bookstore should be welcomed downtown. Borders' taxes should be welcomed also.

To the members of the City Council, I say "Do not tamper with the free market. Let it prevail. It worked with Crown Books. Now, let it work equally with Borders."

There must never be permitted exclusivity or favoritism in a free democratic society. If we allow that to happen, we will become a fascist society. And, to the voters of Santa Cruz, I say "Now is the time to speak out. Stop this transparent assault on our free trade system from happening." We know from history that bad things happen when good people do nothing. It is called the Sin Of Omission.

3

Does anyone listening disagree that Gray Davis is possibly the slimiest Governor that California has ever had? He is a dismal failure as a leader. He is nothing more than an untalented bureaucrat at the right place at the right time. Do we want him to continue to lead us until 2006? Having spent a good part of his first term collecting funds for his campaign for a second term, he used the method of "You scratch my back, and I'll scratch yours" or "If you donate money for my reelection, I'll give you some very nice perks like maybe a cushy government job." His performance as state leader is the best argument for term limits, and I do mean one term only, but that's another story.

Now, thanks to Gray Davis and his cavalier way of spending We the People's money – remember the hasty, expensive decisions made during the energy crisis? – California is now on the verge of economic collapse. How is this possible? Could it be incompetent, corrupt leadership? While campaigning last fall for a second term, Davis assured We the People that the state budget deficit was no more than $26 billion (with a "b"). Shortly after safely being in charge for another four-year term, he confessed that the state budget shortfall was really more like

$38.8 billion. Clearly, he blatantly lied to get reelected. For that alone, he should be recalled. His credibility is zero, and we cannot afford his inferior leadership until 2006.

A recall effort is going on right now. Two hundred thousand signatures of registered voters have already been collected. A goal of one million signatures must be collected by August. With a state population of over 30 million, that goal is doable. Here at KSCO, we are calling for volunteers to donate time to accept drive-by valid signatures from registered voters at Steve Hartman's bus, which will be parked in KSCO's parking lot at 2300 Portola Drive. If you can help out, please call Rosemary at (831) 475-1080, and thank you very much.

Together, we may unseat this lying scoundrel.

4

About Measure B, it is no longer needed. On May 14th during the California State Budget Revision Meeting, Governor Davis announced that the original decision to drastically reduce funds to all California schools, which was discussed during the January budget meeting, has been reversed. Cuts to education are eliminated. Schools will continue to remain fully funded. The legislature will surely agree because the governor stated that the necessary funds are available now.

Measure B, a Santa Cruz city initiative, was created for one reason only, and that was to replace the state's shortfall to education. That need no longer exists. Measure B is no longer necessary. Our schools will remain open, and nothing will change.

Please be aware, however, that because of attrition, Santa Cruz city schools will continue to have fewer students. Young families are leaving Santa Cruz in droves. They can no longer afford to live here, and they realize that they may never be able to own a home in this area. So, fewer schools will be needed in the future.

The election for Measure B is only days away. Ideally, the City Council should cancel the June 3rd election. It is not necessary. Perhaps legally they are not able to cancel it, in which case, please vote no on Measure B. I repeat, vote no on Measure B.

In the event that it passes, be assured that the city leaders will keep and use that extra $6 million for other possible frivolous projects, or maybe even pad salaries and retirement pensions like the county does (and we will talk about them later).

About Gray Davis, he did give We the People his middle finger. In order to win re-election for another four years, he lied about the extra $12 billion state deficit. Way to go, Governor.

5

And now, the story of the elephant in the living room: When the 13 colonies became the United States of America, it was an honor and privilege to make policy for the new country. Those chosen to represent the colonies met together from distant areas several times a year, full of hope, idealism, and tremendous enthusiasm. For their efforts, they were paid expenses only. Now, our elected leaders pay themselves very well. In the highest levels, public service has become a most secure, lucrative career – really not a bad deal – four years, maybe eight, maybe even 12 years of elected service, then a hefty pension for life. We the People, who foot the bills, have no say whatsoever in decisions regarding lifetime pensions, salaries, cars, bonuses, and many other hidden perks. Our elected leaders decide for themselves what they should receive.

Now we learn that our state and all its counties are in perilous financial straits. Added to that news, we also learn of the recent unexplained loss of funds to county non-profits, because of careless lack of county oversight. There is no excuse for this sloppy administrating. Our leaders dole out our money and do not bother to demand accountability.

Last fall, County Supervisor Marty Wormhoudt stated that California's budget deficit is so critical that we must expect drastic cuts in most state and county programs – adding that the poor, elderly, physically and mentally handicapped will suffer first. She was right. Why is it that the weak who are the most needy are always targeted for cuts first? They should be the last denied help. Those who got us into this horrendous mess because of greedy, irresponsible leadership should take cuts first. Instead, they reward themselves.

A short time ago, a Sentinel editor wrote about the issue of California state pension giveaways, noting that local cutbacks are happening in the wake of irresponsible state pensions. He was only half right. He clearly chose to not take on the elephant in the living room.

Bad things happen when good people do nothing. Or, in this case, say nothing – it is called the Sin of Omission.

About the elephant… The Sentinel editor ignored the recent huge 30%+ salary and pension hikes which our own CAO and supervisors are taking for themselves and other upper level county employees. Like our governor, those leaders are giving We the People their middle finger.

This is happening while we must endure severe cuts in necessary services.

Where is the leadership, integrity, compassion for the needy – all the qualities they promised to uphold while running for office?

To my knowledge, only one supervisor had the sensitivity to decline the recent raise – Ellen Pirie. If that is still so, kudos to you, Ellen. About the others, there is no moral justification for this self-serving, callous behavior.

Checking that similar leaders of adjoining counties are in the same salary range does not make it right. If it's true, they must equally share in the blame for California's possible catastrophic collapse. These people should GIVE BACK THEIR RAISES. If not, there is always the justification and the possibility of a recall. The reason? How about dismal leadership and fiscal irresponsibility?

A few words of advice to Governor Gray Davis now: Sir, you have betrayed the people of California. You lied to get reelected to the tune of $16 billion. Your credibility grade is an F. The recall effort for your removal is moving along, and most probably will be successful. You have the power to redeem a measure of respect at this time. Help the state avoid the unnecessary expense of the recall election. Governor, go out with class. Do the right thing. Resign.

6

An Open Letter to the Santa Cruz City Council

Your recent action requesting the federal government to consider initiating the impeachment of President Bush on behalf of the citizens of Santa Cruz was once again the height of irresponsibility and chutzpah. How dare you decide that you have the right to speak for me or any other Santa Cruzan with regard to federal issues. You were elected to work for the City of Santa Cruz only, and nothing more. If a member of our community is unhappy with President Bush's performance, or with anything else outside of our city, that person should write to directly to the federal government as a private person.

It is surely not your place to make pronouncements on behalf of all Santa Cruzans.

With regards to the whereabouts of "weapons of mass destruction", it is naive to think that Saddam Hussein would be stupid enough to leave the evidence of their existence sitting around in Iraq. Those weapons may be well hidden in Iran, Saudi Arabia, Syria, Jordan, or any other country near Iraq. They may never be found. However, every logical-thinking person would agree that the megalomaniac Saddam Hussein had to be disarmed and made irrelevant, and the world is infinitely safer without him.

If, however, you continue to believe with every fiber of your being that there never were any weapons of mass destruction, despite the documented proof that he used poison gas on many of his own people, then I have a bridge in Brooklyn I would love sell you.

7

Because this issue cuts to the heart of public sector injustice, it won't go away easily despite the fact that a U.C. top gun, the University Vice Chancellor, was quickly dispatched to our local Sentinel to rationalize the recent public event. The result of his attempt was tepid. So, continuing the saga of the U.C. administrator's constant concern with budget issues and possible shortfalls, they still just approved salaries and bloated moving expenses for Denise Denton, new UCSC Chancellor, and her girlfriend, Professor Gretchen Kalonji.

As a result of her request, a new position was created at UCSC for Dr. Kalonji. It appears she has prestige in engineering circles, so now the Regents didn't want to lose her; in fact, they were honored and happy to pay her $193,000 per year and $50,000 for moving expenses. All this while university leaders were denying first-time raises in three years for UCSC clerks and other employees. As usual, the top dogs get too much, and those on the lower levels don't get enough. Even Professor Kalonji states "It's so expensive to live in California", so is it equally expensive – or more so – for clerks?

The inequity in salary is insulting and unjust, especially since this past year UCSC has been the recipient of a windfall of donations of $35 million from alumni and others. They used $5 million of that endowment to purchase a large industrial building in Westside Industrial Park with significant acreage for future buildings. Does that also mean that the university is exempt from paying property taxes? If so, We the People will have to pick up the slack.

Haven't we also lost the former Holiday Inn to the public and visitors? It was either purchased or leased to house UCSC students. When the University of California system in the 1960s received the 2000-plus acres from the Cowell Foundation to create a U.C. campus, the plan was to build housing for students and some for faculty on campus. That happened in the early years, but now it appears that the entire west side of Santa Cruz is being inundated with students and their cars. Parking is becoming a problem, rents are higher, and residential neighborhoods are crowded and deteriorating. Clearly, the university on the hill is opting to continue to grow but build minimally on campus and keep it pristine, and instead buy or rent facilities in Santa Cruz. Doesn't one get the uneasy feeling that UCSC is gradually taking over our city?

8

(February 25, 2005) Weighing in on the Santa Cruz Coast Hotel project, any real estate professional would agree that the three most important qualities in any real property are location, location, and location. The proposed site for this $100 million plus hotel and convention center I believe is wrong, skimpy, and in a crowded funky area with an overabundance of constant traffic. The one piece of land worthy of this expensive expenditure is Lighthouse Field. Had we proceeded 30-35 years ago with this same plan at Lighthouse Field, our city would have had a beautiful and profitable addition costing a fraction of what it costs today. However, the powers in charge, then spearheaded by attorney Gary Patton, local activist for Agenda 21 of the U.N., squelched that idea in favor of keeping Lighthouse Field pristine for strollers, bicyclists, and dogs.

Now, decades later, we have a large parcel of very valuable land overlooking gorgeous Monterey Bay full of scrubby weeds, careless pedestrians leaving garbage, and all sorts of dogs urinating, defecating, and fornicating – and that's pristine? It's malignantly stupid.

Michael Rotkin, UCSC instructor and City Council member on and off for many years, promised decades ago that he would make Santa Cruz into a socialist city, and he succeeded well in doing just that. Now, he urges that We the People of Santa Cruz must go forward with this project quickly, mainly because ten months have already been spent on researching this project, and that seven hours of public opinion input has been given, and that's enough. That's nonsense.

A $100 million expenditure deserves much more than seven hours input if that's what the public wants.

Since many city residents are polarized on this important issue, the logical solution is to have a special election no matter what it costs. It will be a pittance compared to wasting $100 million on a wrong location. So I say we should try to use Lighthouse Field for people and not for dogs.

Realistically, in view of the politics generated these last 3-1/2 decades in Santa Cruz by a relatively small group of well-meaning extremists, our area, like Berkeley, is viewed by the entire country as being eccentric, business unfriendly, weird, and scuzzy. One wonders if a fancy hotel can be viable and profitable in this environment. Will any business want to come and give us money?

So, if the project proceeds with a special election, several issues should be considered:

1. Should there be a $100 million hotel and convention center in Santa Cruz?
2. Should Lighthouse Field be the best location?
3. Should the Dream Inn be demolished and replaced by the new project?

Here's a reality check: Do we expect that out-of-town businesses and corporations will even want to have their conferences in an area that has literally chased business away for many years? Wouldn't they opt to go to business-friendly Monterey instead? Are our leaders prepared to make a fundamental change and invite new business here?

9

(May 17, 2005) Last month, on April 6th, I felt a sense of revulsion at the extent to which our country and Canada, and now all of Europe, have been poisoned by the intrusion of political correctness. That day last month, the front page headline in the Sentinel was "Student Protest Disrupts Job Fair". Two hundred UCSC student protestors loudly demanded that the military recruiters lawfully participating in the job fair on campus be forced to leave. University administrators actually validated the undemocratic student protest and forced the military recruiters to leave. What should have happened, at the very least, is that the protestors should have been forced to leave; at best, all of them should have been expelled. The loudmouth pipsqueak inmates are being encouraged to run the asylum, which We the People pay for.

In Sunday's May 15th Sentinel, we learned that our own twice-time mayor, Mike Rotkin, longtime UCSC instructor, and much too longtime Santa Cruz political activist, publicly complimented the student protestors for evicting the military recruiters. Is it any wonder that new businesses will no longer dream of locating in Santa Cruz? And is it any wonder that we are in a constant budget deficit, and our roads are full of potholes because of Mike Rotkin and his ilk running the show for so long?

This Saturday, May 21st, our city will have its first armed services parade initiated by parents of Vietnam veterans and all other veterans. Michael Rotkin, the mayor, has agreed to attend. Mayor, if you have integrity, you can't have it both ways.

Back to the student protestors. You should know that their behavior against military recruiters is being condoned and encouraged in all of the UC campuses where 85% of the professors are liberal and 15% are conservative. This is a fact. University instructor recruiting is in the hands of the left. Political indoctrination has no place in institutions of higher learning where all sides of issues should be permitted and encouraged in a mutually respecting environment. Our schools on all levels are now being highjacked by liberal extremists who among other things are brainwashing young fertile minds totally and irrevocably against any preparation for our country's defense. How many of these loudmouthed one-sided teachers and professors of military age will scurry to Canada if we are forced to initiate the draft again? Probably many of them: the same ilk which defends criminals and evildoers and ignores victims' rights and hates the U.S. but enjoys the benefits therefrom.

Finally, kudos to the Sentinel for describing fairly and in detail this deplorable situation where military recruiters continue to endure spitting and even bodily injury by student protestors. Why is this behavior permitted? Because not all, but many, high school teachers, university and college professors condone and encourage these actions and have the students do their dirty work for them.

10

(July 21, 2006) So when my husband and I, and our two little cherubs, came to Santa Cruz to live in 1947, my husband had recently been released from the U.S. Navy at Treasure Island.

Coming from New York, this little slice of heaven was unbelievable, peaceful, and beautiful – a welcome bit of culture shock after life in the Big City. The then two-page Sentinel News delighted us, because the most exciting item of news was that Mrs. So-and-so went over to San Jose yesterday. What a great place it was to raise a young family.

MZ was born three years later, virtually with a radio in his little hands. He has always loved radio. At that time, many homes had intercoms in their rooms, and I would wake the children with KGO, one of the early trailblazers of interactive news-talk radio.

The population of the city was 12,500. People from the very hot valley used to come here to retire and finally die, but they did not die easily because our climate was so moderate, and life was peaceful and happy.

In the 1940s, back east, many people died at the age of 62. So, here again, it delighted my optometrist husband when a 75-year-old woman came to be examined, and when she was finished she asked if he had time to examine her 95-year-old mother. All things considered, life was good then. People liked each other. Then came the university, and the educated elitists, and things changed. Some of the professors brought along their extended families, and once they came they wanted to close the gates of Santa Cruz. They also brought their new left philosophies and began to impose the same upon their students and the rest of us. Now, sometimes we endure vicious political polarization, and the fanatic left only have elitist sense. A community can function only with common sense. And the elitists do not like common.

So, they wanted to stop growth – all growth. Therefore, for the past 40 years, No Growth became the leaders' agenda. They became business unfriendly, and we have been going downhill financially ever since. Our reputation in the country and the world has become totally negative – and we are totally broke – and now our elitist leaders want business to come back to Santa Cruz. How simplistic. Their arrogant, unreasonable restrictions and regulations have chased business away for decades.

By the way, I never gave our City Council or county supervisors the right to speak for me in the world arena by saying that ours is a Nuclear Free Zone and that peace is patriotic, whatever that means. These leaders were voted into office to fix the potholes and not wax global. And what gives them the right to say that the U.S. Navy is not welcome here in the Monterey Bay area on the 4th of July or at any other time?

For years, they having been hiring experts for large fees to come and evaluate our problems. Well, the latest expert came and was paid $50,000 just to tell the city that the trouble with Santa Cruz is that it is business unfriendly. Duh! Many of us who live here have been telling that to our liberal leaders for years. So this is the saga of foolish, misguided Santa Cruz political leaders. And about growth… It becomes more crowded here every day.

11

(November 2, 2005) The University of California, for the past 30 years considered among the finest schools in the nation, is no longer a true place of higher learning where the exchange of ideas in all disciplines is encouraged and welcomed. It is evident that many students graduating from publicly financed schools like those in the UC system are being shortchanged. UC campuses have become one-sided political factories, graduating large numbers of leftist, brainwashed students, many of whom were taught to hate America, hate our government, hate God, and hate religion, any religion; and they are always offended. How could this happen?

I reported sometime back that the hiring of teaching personnel in all UC campuses for years has been 85% liberal, 15% conservative, by design. Who gets the blame for the imbalance? The answer is the highly paid elitists at the very top, the Board of Regents, the UC president, plus the various chancellors, all of whom make policy for the entire university and all of whom know how unjustly they are using their power.

Speaking of those top-of-the-heap policymakers, several weeks ago, newspapers reported that the regents et al – presently earning almost $400,000 each per year – claimed that they needed a raise, so they proposed a creative way to receive raises by asking the public to donate to a special fund. This went over like a lead balloon. Most newspaper editors were offended and responded negatively. These top-gun elitists, by this callous and crass proposal, added to their joint political biases and have lost respect and credibility as fair leaders of the UC schools. Many already receive enormous salaries, hefty pensions, medical coverage, free homes, and moving allowances. And this omission of the valid need to give raises to the poorly paid employees and staff in lower levels of the system magnifies the greed and absence of sensitivity of these elitists. It is an outrage. Are these the leaders we should trust to make decisions for our grown children? Think about it.

12

(March 12, 2006) About the forthcoming meeting at the Resource Center for Nonviolence (a nonsensical name for a group which revels in creating emotional violence all the time) leader Scott Kennedy chooses to invite speakers to spew their hate for Jews. Kennedy lost his credibility as a reasonable, non-biased person when years ago it was reported that he made several visits to Israel to have an audience with the Palestinian leader and terrorist Arafat so he could kiss his ring and, by implication, compliment him for killing Israelis.

Unlike many local Jewish community leaders, I am not outraged by the visit of Professor Norman Finkelstein. Probably I developed an early tolerance for bigots when as a little girl living in a Brooklyn, New York German neighborhood in the early 1930s, I was scared and bewildered when often I was called "a dirty little Jew girl".

I believe that Finkelstein, who minimizes the Holocaust and refers to Nobel Peace Laureate Elie Wiesel as a clown and the highly respected Simon Wiesenthal Center as a gang of heartless and immoral crooks, is himself an irrational self-hating Jew who grew up in a Palestinian area where from early childhood he was educated to despise Jews. Inasmuch as he became a professor, he should have known better, but he opted to spread hate.

Both Finkelstein and Scott Kennedy are to be pitied because both exist to disseminate venomous hate, the emotion which decays one's own soul. What a blessing it is to live in a country where free speech exists. Despite others' protests, Scott Kennedy and Professor Finkelstein will continue to spread their poison but will only infect bigots. While anti-Semitism is an incurable social disease, let us hope that those infected are in the minority.

13

(August 4, 2006) As residents of Santa Cruz for six decades, our family remembers it as a bit of paradise when people respected and were kind to each other.

It was a sad day many years ago when the so-called "Resource Center for Nonviolence" came and stayed. Led by its leader Scott Kennedy, the Resource Center set out to introduce, at every opportunity, unadulterated hate for the state of Israel.

In truth, the organization should be called instead "The Resource Center for Hate and Violence" because sooner or later, hate begets violence. Its modus operandi has always been to invite speakers who bemoan the Arab issue and blame Israel.

You should know that the name "Palestinian" is newly adopted. It's a made-up word. Israel was called Palestine for 2000 years. "Palestinians" sounds ancient, but it's really a modern invention.

Before the Israelis won the land in the 1967 war, Gaza was owned by Egypt, the West Bank was owned by Jordan, and there were no Palestinians. I borrowed the last paragraph from Dennis Miller, comedian turned researcher, and also the next two paragraphs which are awesome and priceless. "As soon as the Jews took over in 1948 and started growing oranges as big as basketballs, what do you know – say hello to the Palestinians weeping for their deep bond with their lost land and nation.

So, for the sake of honesty, let us not use the word 'Palestinian' anymore to describe these delightful folks who dance for joy at our deaths until someone points out that they are being taped."

Well said, Dennis.

To continue... under Arab leader Arafat, whose ring Scott Kennedy bragged that he kissed on his various visits to Israel, an Arab country of their own was offered and refused many times. The Arab agenda was, and still remains, the total annihilation of the state of Israel and all their Arab brethren from Saudi Arabia, Iran, Syria, etc., love using these displaced Arabs as political pawns.

So, the other night during another Resource Center sponsored talk by the Arab ambassador to the U.S., Ambassador What's-His-Name, once again lamented the condition of his stateless people. Give me a break.

At that meeting, our mayor gave the Arab ambassador the keys to our city, and by so doing joined the army of hate and bigotry, adding more shame to our city, and surely not speaking for many of us. All this from our proud Hate-Free Zone city.

Also, the Sentinel gave that recent get-together a big front-page spread. Why does it keep haunting me that our Veterans' parade and Not This Time Vets never even got even one word mentioned on the Sentinel front page. Wasn't it worthy enough?

14

(April 9, 2007) As an American Jewess, I find it painful, albeit necessary, to help expose the shocking truth that there are, in our midst, self-hating Jews (UC professors, no less) who are vigorously promoting the extinction of the state of Israel.

Also as we speak, the seeds of another Holocaust are being planted in the shameless godless country of France.

Kudos to Gil Stein, a local attorney, for making known the following condensed, impassioned protest. Also, kudos to Tom Honig, Editor of the Sentinel News for printing Gil Stein's entire comprehensive letter called "UC pays for political rally against Israel". I would also call it "Anti-Semitism Is Alive And Well On UC Campuses".

And I have added a few of my own remarks.

"On March 15th, UC Santa Cruz hosted a conference entitled 'Alternative Histories Within and Beyond Zionism'. The conference was organized by Lisa Rofel, a professor of anthropology at UCSC. The event was co-sponsored by other university departments such as Feminist Studies, Community Studies and Sociology.

There were five speakers, all Jewish, and all from different UC campuses, opposing Israel. This was presented as an academic conference. In fact, it was a political rally against Israel, sponsored and paid for by the University of California" and which We The People subsidized.

Why is this a concern? It is just one more example of the arrogance of power. Professors are educators and should teach and not exploit their power to promote their personal agenda. When university resources are used to promote a particular political point of view, it concerns us all, and those educators are brainwashing our children. It happened here with a deliberate attempt to promote and encourage an anti-Semitic agenda. All five anti-Zionist speakers had no contrary opinions.

The event organizer, Rofel, asked the chair of the Jewish Studies Program here at UCSC, Professor Murray Baumgarten to cosponsor the event and even asked for a financial contribution. This is like asking someone to help purchase the rope for his own hanging. To his credit, Professor Baumgarten volunteered to help secure other presenters who might add a more balanced viewpoint. This was declined; the political agenda was already set.

Israeli policy is simple. It only wants the right to exist in peace.

This conference was a deliberate attempt to indoctrinate students and others and to promote the concept that Israel has no right to exist.

The University of California has a responsibility not only to the students and faculty, but to all Californians, to refrain from promoting an ideology or personal agendas. The university belongs to all of us and should not be used for the private use of its employees. This is not an issue of academic freedom. It is an issue of academic integrity and honesty. Whether the indoctrination is from the left or the right, it is improper. It needs to be stopped now.

Way to go, Gil Stein.

15

(May 24, 2007) For many years, countless numbers of World War II veterans living in Central California, also veterans of subsequent wars, have yearned for the promised Fort Ord veterans cemetery to become a reality. These veterans, many now in their 80s, are referred to as the Greatest Generation – my generation – because we were all involved, we were together as a nation, and victory in war was more achievable then than now when our nation is very polarized and not together. And many have yet to grasp the danger of world Islamic terrorism.

Now, finally, after 14 years, AB3035, the bill to create that Fort Ord cemetery, has been passed, and for that, kudos to State Senator J. Denham, Assemblyman S. Salinas, and Congressman Sam Farr.

The Central Coast State Veterans Cemetery Endowment Fund is now charged with acquiring the initial $4,000,000 to proceed with this project. The yearly maintenance funding for the cemetery, however, will be the responsibility of the state.

So now, why don't We The People use our creative thoughts and see how soon we can raise the necessary funds?

Kudos also to World War II veteran Paul Ventura of Pebble Beach for caring so much for this project to become a reality that for years he kept the desire alive. Also, he has various ideas about how to raise the funds needed.

If you would like to be involved in this project, call Paul Ventura at (831) 626-0377, again, that's (831) 626-0377, or email Paul at pfuture@ pacbell.net .

Let's all get involved in this worthy and much wanted project. It is a way for us to say to those veterans who fought for our us, "With deepest sincerity and appreciation, we thank you for the huge sacrifice you have made by putting your lives on the line for our nation."

16

(February 26, 2002) On Tuesday, March 5, Santa Cruz County voters will go to the polls. The central issue of concern on the ballot is Measure L. Why? Please follow me carefully.

A 'yes' vote on Measure L will repeal and eliminate the abusive and illegally instituted, ten-year-old utility users tax.

It is illegal because the law states that only the voters can decide on the merits of such a tax. That never happened.

Instead, the supervisors in office at the time simply ordered the citizens to pay the tax. Un-American? You bet!

But they got away with it for ten years! This utility users tax is charged at the rate of seven percent on top of already huge actual charges for water, sewage, garbage, electricity, natural gas, cable TV, and telephone charges. This evil, unnecessary tax on necessities of life that people MUST USE on a daily basis, generates about ten million dollars per year, or, on a more personal level, it costs each family about 260 extra dollars per year. This money goes into the county's general fund and therefore may be used at the discretion of the county administrators.

Last year, the general fund was budgeted at 395 million dollars. After all county expenses were paid, there remained a surplus of 32 million dollars.

A 'yes' vote on Measure L will remove that ten million dollars generated by the illegal utility users tax, and STILL leave a surplus of 22 million dollars.

Now the supervisors are desperately mounting a well organized, well thought out SPIN campaign to defeat Measure L. They have gotten used to having this extra ten million dollars of surplus play money for the past ten years, so now they're having tantrums, crying poverty, shedding crocodile tears, and using scare tactics and threatening innocent and uninformed taxpayers that if Measure L passes, many much-needed programs will be eliminated.

This is a blatant lie! Once again, we are being snookered by these administrators and their ilk. And sadly, also much of the media, knowingly or unknowingly, are a party to this canard.

While these bleeding hearts, supposed do-gooders are righteously wringing their hands and scaring the people, AT THE VERY SAME TIME, they are busy voting themselves obscene salary raises and padding their retirement pensions, so that by the time they leave office, their pensions will be almost as large as their salaries!

How about a few documented examples? The County Administrative Officer, known as the 'CAO,' in February 2001 received a salary of $147,512. In February 2003, her salary will jump up to $190,500, an increase of $43,308 over a two-year period. Not exactly a reasonable yearly cost-of-living increase. Oh yes, the CAO ALSO will receive an additional BONUS of $7,056!

Over 160 county employees make in excess of $100,000 per year, and they retire at 95 percent of their pay? And our supervisors, they are voting themselves a $30,000 pay increase to $91,000 per year. And the list of excesses goes on and on. It's really sad and disheartening how power, especially long-time, entrenched power, can corrupt and make perhaps otherwise good people cruel, greedy, insensitive, and uncaring.

What is so tragic about the actions of these administrators is that they show no qualms about financing their obscene raises with the very same money they claim will be taken away from hungry children, the elderly, the poor, and the disabled. I hope by now you get the picture.

Let's go to the polls on March 7, and vote 'yes' on Measure L and eliminate the abusive, unnecessary, illegal utility users tax. Much of the material in this editorial was supplied to me by two very special local heroes in our community.

They are Steve Hartman and Ed Mazenko. These two gentlemen are a credit to us. We are DEEPLY indebted to them for working for us TIRELESSLY for years to try to keep our leaders honest, and keep the electorate informed.

If you wish to view details of the individual increases being paid to the top 35 county positions, log on to www.sccu tilitytax.com. To co nclude, KSCO and KOMY endorse a 'yes' vote on measure L, a 'yes' vote for Mark Primack for supervisor, and a 'yes' vote for Kate Canlis for District Attorney.

17

(2005) I am totally bewildered by the loud protests of those who object to the recent photo in the Sentinel of the eight-month-old little girl fatally injured in last week's tragic Highway 17 accident. I saw love, concern, and compassion in the picture of the fireman carrying the little victim away from the scene of the tragedy. It was poignant, human, and so sad – but offensive and insensitive? – nonsense. It was a picture of life, and life happens. We should feel comfort in knowing that our police, firemen, and medics are there to help when help is needed and time is of the essence. It is wrong to verbally assault the Sentinel or Nick Lovejoy for capturing a prize-winning picture of life. It is déjà vu all over again.

There will always be those in our midst who are selective in their human concern and compassion. Seeing pictures of graves full of hundreds of murdered innocents in Iraq elicits no public emotion from these critters, but a picture of an injured or possibly dead infant being carried to safety by a caring fireman being offensive blows my mind. Seems like misplaced and misguided political correctness is showing its foolish ugly head yet again.

18

(November 12, 2005) A number of years ago, when Fort Ord was divided, a 175-acre parcel was put aside for a veterans' cemetery. That was very appropriate. Thus far, nothing has happened to make that a reality. Despite the fact that there are over 40,000 veterans in this area, our lawmakers – federal and state – are in no hurry. So much for misguided priorities.

Veterans of World War II – my generation, the best and the bravest, often called "The Greatest Generation," – are now getting the shaft. A state cemetery would be easy to achieve. It's merely a question of money. Our state leaders say, "Sorry, there are no funds available at this time for a cemetery." I say, "Bull-pucky!" It's disgraceful and unforgivable to let down our vets, who put their lives on the line for the rest of us. Many died in combat, and if we had lost in World War II, we'd all be marching lockstep and saying "Heil!" today. "No money" you say? So, give up a part of your very bloated salaries, pensions and perks, plus your own hefty health benefits, all of which the rest of us, and the veterans of World War II, plus the veterans of subsequent wars, continue to provide for your comfort and your enjoyment.

Mr. Maldonado – you promised to faithfully represent our area, so we voted for you, and you have shown no interest whatsoever in this urgent project. So if you expect to remain in office, lean on your buddies in Sacramento and make the cemetery happen now, not later, because time is running out for The Greatest Generation. Many already are in their mid-80s. We're not talking useless pork. We're talking payback time. So, get on with it. Do the right thing.

And another thing – it would be nice to know exactly which of our lawmakers are keeping our warships out of the San Francisco Bay area on Veteran's Day (or any other day). That is a national disgrace. Shame on all of you, and you know who you are.

For all veterans, and for KSCO and KOMY, this is Kay Zwerling.

19

(January 21, 2005) Listen to this. Isn't there a disconnect somewhere? UCSC's new chancellor, Denise Dee Denton, will receive a salary of $275,000 per year plus moving expenses of $68,750. She also managed to have her longtime partner, Professor Gretchen Kalonji, hired at UCSC also for $192,000 per year. This while UC student fees have just been raised by about 29%, and that is a real hardship for many. This also while lower-bracket UC employees receive minimal wages and are having difficulty getting even small raises. UCSC this past year received gifts of around $35 million, probably from alumni, from whom they solicit all the time.

Likewise, one of our own county administrative officers, Susan Mauriello, when I looked several years ago, gave herself $192,000 per year, same as the vice president of the United States, plus a hefty pension for herself and the Board of Supervisors, who at that time were giving themselves close to $100,000 per year for two or three meetings per month. No doubt they give themselves yearly cost of living raises in addition. All this while many of our county needy like stroke victims are told that there are no longer funds in the county coffers to continue to give them free bus or cab transportation for shopping or doctor visits. This pattern of heartless, shameful greed by those on top of the public sector from the federal, state, county and local levels is occurring all over our country. Those on top take the cream for themselves first in the form of high salaries, high pensions, high health insurance premiums which We the People pay for, and at the same time, they all cry poverty and ask for more and more funds to get the job done. It is all so immoral. What is happening to fairmindedness and sensitivity in our society?

20

Printed in the Aptos Times, September 1, 2002

(August 3, 2002) In 1771, Samuel Adams wrote in the Boston Gazette, "Power makes men wanton – it intoxicates the mind; and unless those with whom the power is entrusted are carefully watched, such men will not govern the people, according to the known laws of the state."

It is clear that our county lawmakers are not being carefully watched, for while we have entrusted them with making laws and decisions which should benefit the people first and foremost, they benefit themselves!

The County Administrative Officer, called the CAO, sets yearly salaries for herself, the Board of Supervisors and other county employees. This is like the fox minding the chicken coop.

Soon, this CAO will be giving herself a 30% plus raise to approximately $191,000 per year, while the vice president of the United States receives approximately $170,000 per year. This, plus hefty pension plans, Social Security, bonuses, and other perks. Each supervisor will also receive a 30% plus raise and benefits to approximately $98,000 – all for attending about 35 meetings per year. Assistants do most of the gruntwork for them and bring them up to date on agenda issues. By contrast, San Francisco supervisors receive $36,000 a year, not $98,000.

These lawmakers tell us that we are facing serious budget deficits, so now they are cutting needed aid to the poor, the elderly, the mentally and physically ill, and the handicapped. What happened to the supposed budget surplus of $21 million we had only four months ago?

The Stroke Center budget has been cut. Also, the Center for Independent Living, which helps wheelchair-bound, handicapped, and convalescent people to become self-reliant. The latest outrage is that county managers want the supervisors to make 33% cuts to the medically indigent, who do not have any insurance. Bottom line: no more preventive care for the poor.

To Susan Mauriello, CAO, and to each of the supervisors I say, "In the face of these hardships, to so many constituents, who trust you for protection and guidance and wisdom, how dare you plan to give yourselves 30% plus raises? Or any raises? You have given yourselves too much already, with your lifetime benefits and perks! Your greed and callousness are irresponsible and unforgivable! You all deserve to be ousted from your cushy bureaucratic jobs!"

Recently, for one brief moment, Wormhoudt suggested to her colleagues that maybe they should forego the 30% plus raise, but that idea went over like a lead balloon. Jeff Almquist, poor baby, said that he needs that raise for his son's college tuition. Wormhoudt could have refused her raised, but she didn't. Heck, she made her gesture, and that was enough. Oh yes, she served on the Santa Cruz City Council for umpteen years, and now she is running for a third term as supervisor. So much for career politicians and term limits. But that's another story.

How do We the People stop these unconscionable excesses?

We could do what California state voters did in 1990. They became fed up with lawmakers' abuses, so they crafted an initiative which created a panel of citizens, not state employees, who meet yearly to set lawmakers' salaries from the governor on down. It was put on the ballot, passed easily, and is now law.

Because of budget constraints, for the past six years, no state salary increases have been approved. That panel is the California Citizens Compensation Commission and the Chairman is Claude Brinegar.

While it is too late for this November election, we could prepare an initiative for an upcoming election. If you would like to be involved, call KSCO at 831-475-1080 and leave your name and phone number.

KSCO will be happy to provide free airtime to help solve this issue of lawmakers' greed.

Once again, kudos to those who spend many hours to decipher obscure, convoluted county budgets, gathering financial facts for this editorial. They are Steve Hartman, Bob Suhr, Ed Mazenko, Harold Griffith, and Mike Schmidt – all heroic seekers for honesty and truth in government.

Let us not forget the powerful tool We the People have in the initiative process. It is the one way left for citizens in a free society to make right that which is wrong.

21

(September 18, 2002) Recently, I received a letter from someone needing to vent his frustrating experience with the County Planning Department. It's a sad story which simply underscores the arrogant, cavalier reception which citizens often receive when applying for a building permit.

Next to getting married and having a family, what should be the most important and happiest event in one's life is building one's dream home. Here, more often than not, it is an aggravating, oppressive, and very expensive nightmare.

This restrictive attitude by planners, who take their orders from their bosses – the supervisors – who allow the rights of the long-toed salamander to overrule the rights of taxpaying county citizens, is nothing short of incongruous lunacy.

This treatment is by design (no pun intended). A process which elsewhere in the state and country is expedited in a timely manner, here usually takes many months and sometimes years; one is forced to jump through many hoops, each time paying more and more fees.

Now for the frustrated applicant's letter:

"Dear Kay,

This letter commends you on your letter to the Aptos Times in the September 1, 2002 issue.

The county expenditures have indeed become outrageous and I agree 200% with you that things should be different. Hardly any citizen knows how high the employees' salaries have become, especially the management salaries.

Your attention is invited to the liberal benefits of such employees in our county, especially the retirement pensions. It is my understanding that if one stays around long enough, they can retire on about 95% of their salary. In the last year or so, I know of several people in planning who did just that. This is found nowhere in private industry.

Wouldn't you like to get 2-1/2 months vacation each year if you work only 15 years? Again, this is found nowhere in private industry.

The county's spending habits have irked some of us for years. The Board of Supervisors must take responsibility for this, for the Supervisors are the CEOs of the organization. We can complain about the proposed closing of libraries in recent years and everyone gets upset and holds car washes, bake sales, etc. to raise money for libraries. But no one looks to see what the county is spending money on instead of libraries.

While you properly described the sad story of the management greed, the Planning Department has caught the attention of many citizens. For many years, nearly anyone who has applied for any permit in the Planning Department has met with frustration. Why does the Planning Department have more employees per capita than any other county in California except L.A. County?

I can't sign this letter because I have an application pending. I am a simple citizen, not a developer. I know full well that if I become known as a resister, my name goes on a black list informally maintained in Planning and I will be hit with even more unreasonable demands to any of my plans. Many property owners have this problem, especially those with property which might be developed. We are at the mercy of the planners who hold all the authority over us. We can't negotiate but must submit to whatever they demand, which already costs us many thousands of dollars for no purpose.

Many of us will donate toward the cost of an ad or other actions if we are not identified. (Isn't this a sad state of affairs?)

Again, thank you for publicizing the facts as you did. The public needs such facts to judge our government. I'm sorry I can't stand up and identify myself.

~Unsigned for fear of reprisal"

So my friends, remember again, the planners take their orders from the supervisors, the ones on top. And when the fish stinks, it starts from the head down.

So now, what can We the People do about this sorry mess? For starters, come November 5th, let us express our anger and disgust by voting out of office each incumbent supervisor who is running – and hope that the new supervisors will be more reasonable and responsive to the needs of the people.

22

(October 25, 2002) For three decades, We the People have been held hostage to a political majority of extreme leftists who have ruined our business community and continued a destructive no-growth policy. Roads are in disrepair and in constant gridlock, rents are outrageously high, real estate prices are the highest in the nation, our beautiful downtown is now a scary and filthy disaster, people are afraid to go there — the whole city is a mess! And We the People are saddled with more and more taxes. All this because our leaders have been irresponsible, inept, totally lacking in any business sense, and their immature and foolish priorities have made Santa Cruz the laughing stock of the entire nation. Sometimes it feels like the inmates are running the asylum.

If you are satisfied to continue this same old charade, then bring back Mike Rotkin and Cynthia Matthews. They are both drooling to come back and rule us again. They also both know that this time, someone might challenge their right to seek office on the City Council because of a clause added to the city charter in 1948 which states, quote, "No member of the City Council shall be eligible for reelection for two years after the expiration of the second full term for which such person was elected." Rotkin and Matthews left office on November 28, 2000 and therefore would not be able to run until November 28, 2002.

Another council candidate, Aldo Giacchino, did challenge their right to seek office 21 days before the end of the two-year moratorium. The issue was taken to court because Aldo felt that the letter of the law should be upheld. The court, however, ruled that a few days more or less did not matter, so Rotkin and Matthews were permitted to stay in the race. I am sorry that the court saw fit to trivialize the letter of the law. Two years means two years and not one year and three hundred and forty-five days.

A similar issue came up in another California jurisdiction where the period in question was only one day short of the two-year ruling and in that case, the law was upheld. Here in Santa Cruz, it appears that the law was bent to accommodate two politically correct fixtures.

A resident of Santa Cruz for 24 years, Rotkin has ruled on the City Council for 18 of those years, twice as mayor. In his first term, his stated intention was to implement the subject of his doctoral dissertation and make Santa Cruz into a socialist city and he did just that. So, it can be truthfully said that Rotkin is the architect for the socialist mess which We the People have endured for so many years! And now he wants to serve again!

About Matthews, she served on the council for eight years. Jointly, they have been our local leaders for a total of 26 years, and look what we have now.

They point to their experience as being a benefit. I believe it is really a detriment. One who enters the political arena for the first time can vote honestly and responsibly simply by studying the issues.

One doesn't have to be a rocket scientist to understand how to implement laws. As novice lawmakers, they are not influenced by, or beholden to, the "old buddy network" which sooner or later infects incumbents and career politicians.

About Mardi Wormhoudt, running again for supervisor: she has been a total disaster. Her no-growth and anti-business philosophy has emasculated the business community and kept Santa Cruz in a time warp.

It is bewildering how she sustains a level of adulation from the foolish left while she cuts programs for the needy and handicapped. She still will take her 31% raise to $98,000 starting next year, plus an enormous pension, bonuses, health benefits, and Social Security, all of which We the People pay for! San Francisco supervisors get $33,000 per year, by contrast. Where is the outrage? This repeated information bears remembering on November 5th when you must remember to vote!

Wasn't it during the Rotkin, Matthews, and Wormhoudt watch on the City Council that the badgering and demonstrations against the Miss California Pageant were allowed? The unfriendly situation became so intolerable that the pageant was forced to leave Santa Cruz and move to San Diego. Now San Diego is the happy recipient of the yearly millions of dollars that we have lost! Thank you, Santa Cruz City Council for your continued stupidity and lack of business sense! And who suffers? 'We the people' with more and more and more taxes!

KSCO recommends a 'yes' vote on Measure P. It has been unfair for too many years for all taxpayers, especially the poor, to continue to pay for a never-voted-on additional tax on daily essentials.

Rather than threaten to eliminate police and firefighter services that they legally must provide, why not eliminate some of the many non-essential non-profits who should get their funding from private donations? The city leaders are resorting to lying and scare tactics instead of considering other viable solutions to raise money, like normal communities do.

KSCO recommends a 'yes' vote on Measure Q. That's a nobrainer. Hotel users will pay an extra one percent and it will provide a much needed infusion of money to business.

For City Council, a huge 'yes' vote for Aldo Giacchino, who will provide us with the leadership which we have been waiting for for a long time. He will be a true leader who has the ability and experience to plan, manage, and make tough decisions.

We also recommend Karen Woblesky and Connie Thomasser or Phil Baer, all of whom will bring a new and sane energy as council members.

And for supervisor, Mark Primack.

And finally, a few words to Mike Rotkin and Cynthia Matthews: If you win this time, please work for ALL of us, and not just the politically correct. Please work to create a robust business community, and help Santa Cruz to regain its self respect in the entire nation.

23

(October 2008) They say "Words have meaning." I believe it!

They say, "A picture is worth a thousand words." I believe that, too!

Imagine then, the millions of words that came to mind when I first gazed upon the cover illustration of the October 22nd edition of Metro Santa Cruz.

This cover featured an illustration of Barack Obama sporting a toothy, wining grin and a colorful Superman-like costume. The Obama caricature stood astride a black and white line drawing of Santa Cruz in the foreground, America in the background, and everyone locally and nationally crying out, "Help!"

Fair enough. Our candidate is here to help with "Hope for change" as the campaign touts.

Now, what captured the attention of all those who called our attention to this picture is that Superman Obama is standing hands on hips with one colorful boot squashing the Santa Cruz Sentinel and the other colorful boot squashing your local radio station, KSCO.

But wait. There, firmly affixed to the squashed KSCO is a Nazi swastika, and therein lies the reason a million words flooded my mind at the site of that cover graphic.

You see, as a Jewess who lost family members to Nazi concentration camps, I am all too aware of the significance of jack-booted caricatures bearing swastikas. To cope, I close my mind off to the millions of words that want to cry out and turn instead to our friends at Metro Santa Cruz to ask "Why?"

"Why did you affix a swastika to the squashed KSCO on the cover of your newspaper?"

Is Metro Santa Cruz telling us that a victorious Obama is going to squash all political dissent like the Nazis squashed the Jews?

If this is what Metro Santa Cruz is telling us, we ask, "What happened to the liberal ideals of inclusiveness, non-judgmentalism, and diversity?"

Words do have meaning. Pictures are worth a thousand words. And I am Kay Zwerling.

24

(October 26, 2001) Some months ago, we installed a separate comment line for listeners who chose to ventilate concerns or offer kudos regarding programming. On September the 11th, that fateful day when the unthinkable happened, our country lost its innocence when it was brutally attacked and thousands of innocent and brave people perished.

Their family's lives have changed forever. We have all changed forever.

Now we face a war, possibly a very long and costly war, to find and punish the cowardly monsters of this dastardly act to make certain that what they did to our country will never happen again.

President Bush and his advisors carefully and thoughtfully took three weeks to prepare what needed to be done and to identify the culprits.

Most Americans and most countries of the world are in support of his actions. However, there are some people who vigorously disagree. As pacifists, they want us to think about this issue very carefully, assume the dead roach position, study and understand why part of the world hates us - these pacifists believe that love and patient understanding will get us through this.

I see it as a recipe for annihilation. If, in our efforts to be humanitarian and help other nations, we may have harmed them —well, let's deal with that and fix it later, after we destroy the animals who are committed to destroying us. Now back to the station's comment line... Until about a year ago, we had Jim Hightower, a reasonable Democrat, on KOMY. Suddenly, Hightower was replaced by Peter Werbe, probably by the syndicator of both.

We had no contract with Werbe. But we kept him on for a year, and businesses did NOT want to sponsor him. Werbe is an extreme leftist whose mission is to tear down the opposition, and President Bush has been his favorite target for ridicule. In fact, many regular listeners complained about him and stopped tuning in to our station.

Well, Werbe's comments may have played well with some and may have been fair game in normal times, but these are NOT normal times. We're now engaged in a war.

So as of several weeks ago, Werbe is no longer on KOMY. Now he goes on the internet, states his case, in third person — is that cowardly or what? — spins it and screams foul and claims that his free speech rights are violated! Is this nuts? Now a number of angry listeners are using the station comment line to say some very ugly and menacing things. Others are sending angry e-mails and few have signed their names.

Please understand that we, the owners, have been the sponsors for Werbe's show for a year, and we no longer choose to subsidize him. Bottom line: Werbe has a right to his free speech and we have the right not to have him on our station.

Maybe these listeners could find a place for Werbe on public-supported radio. His kind of rhetoric is welcomed by some in peacetime, but now we are in a battle for the very survival of our way of life. And we do not wish to be an active party for political divisiveness which will give aid to the enemy and weaken our country's resolve! Our men and women in the armed forces, who are fighting this war for us and may be dying for us, must know that we are with them. We cannot withstand another Vietnam War fiasco, when the country was bitterly divided and torn apart.

The chilling truth is, this may be our only chance to get it right — we destroy the enemy or they destroy us. And make no mistake —this is their agenda! I believe our mission is clear. We must, as a country, come together.

To paraphrase the words of Benjamin Franklin, spoken at the signing of the Declaration of Independence: "We had better all hang together or we will surely hang separately."

Dear God, please bless America!

25

(October 31, 2001) A Lying Opportunist Peter Werbe, leftist talk host on KOMY, was dropped from our schedule several weeks ago. As a result of that action, he never did lose his right to "free speech," despite his rantings on the subject. In addition to public radio, there are about thirty-five stations in this market, most with more powerful signals than our little one thousand watt station. Surely one of those stations would have carried his program.

BUT.....that was not Werbe's plan ... he chose to use his departure from KOMY to go online, present himself as a victim, obtain worldwide FREE publicity, and claim that his first amendment right of free speech was denied. (Pretty smart, actually, if he wasn't so dishonest...) He deliberately fomented hate against us, the owners of KOMY, under a false premise simply to promote himself. The first amendment has nothing to do with a person's right of free speech, and Werbe has known that all along.

As owners of a commercial radio station, it is our legal right to offer programming that we believe a majority of our listeners would enjoy. Werbe certainly did not fit that description. Many listeners used the station comment line to characterize him as arrogant, rude, mean-spirited, and other various expletives. There wasn't one advertiser willing to sponsor him.

Even if this were not wartime, we were about to let him go ... too many listeners were tuning us out.

Last Saturday, 10/28, Werbe agreed to be a guest on the two-hour weekly Saturday Special. Unable to handle the criticisms of several callers, he walked out of the show after the first hour. As a result if this incident, we received an astounding number of emails full of hate and indignation because we "deprived" Werbe of his free speech rights.

If you are one of those gullible souls who bought into his big canard, your anger at us is misplaced. Your anger should be directed to Wormy — I mean Werbe — the lying opportunist. You have been snookered ... and we have been the victims of deliberate character assassination.

26

Local attorney Gil Stein wrote a letter to the Santa Cruz Sentinel recently, saying that anti-Semitism is alive and well at UC

Santa Cruz. The Sentinel, on November 18th, also reported that anti-Semitism is increasing on college campuses throughout the country. How is this possible in institutions of higher learning where parents of college students pay as much as $ 100,000 for four years so their children can become educated, fair-thinking members of society? Because Gil Stein's letter is very worrisome, I will repeat portions of the letter along with my own thoughts so that many others in this area can be made aware of the ugly situation, which, if not confronted, will escalate just as it did in Germany in the early 1930s. Please listen, then register your outrage with the local chancellor and those irresponsible members of the faculty. Remember: When good people remain silent and do nothing, bad things happen and evil takes hold. It's called 'the sin of omission.'

Gil's letter refers only to this campus where anti-Israel faculty and students intimidate Jewish students who express support for Israel. You won't believe the following, but it's true. Tenured professor Nancy Stoller, who teaches at this campus, was caught red-handed, removing flyers posted by pro-Israel students. This incident happened last year, but the then-chancellor just looked the other way.

Pro-Palestinian speakers receive university sponsorship, while pro-Israeli speakers are denied sponsorship by those same departments. The university promotes diversity, but not diversity with which they disagree. This policy of looking the other way when certain speakers spout racist venom needs to stop. Academic freedom should not be a cover for bigotry. All campuses should also be open to speakers who do not represent the views of the "politically correct."

Kudos to Gil Stein for uncovering this ugliness. I say shame on the biased and gutless faculty and leaders who encourage prejudice to fester in places of higher learning. We The People must vigorously protest to those accountable. Our publicly financed universities must no longer become institutions of hate and selective discrimination.

27

Looking back, a really sad aspect of California's budget disaster has been the behavior of too many self-serving state and county lawmakers. These officials, who betrayed us, were elected in good faith. They must share the blame for the reckless decisions which have taken our Golden State to the brink of bankruptcy.

They knew they were spending more than was in the coffers, yet that did not stop them from voting themselves raises in salaries and pensions plus untold bonuses and perks like personal cars. When the extent of the deficit became public knowledge, these same lawmakers warned We the People to expect to endure tough and serious cuts. First hurt - who else? - the defenseless, that is the poor, elderly, sick, and handicapped, while those responsible for creating the deficit shortfall are getting off scot-free. Has even one of them displayed any remorse, guilt, or been willing to give up anything personal? They could propose to roll back their raises, but that won't happen — they rationalize that the law is very clear that they must take their already-voted raises regardless of the state of the economy.

I say, "Bull-pucky! They made the laws, so they have the power to change the laws." The recourse for We the People now is to use the initiative process while it is still available. Let's pass a law stating that all salaries and pensions of state and county lawmakers must be voted upon by the people, and no more sneaky hidden perks which chip away at the peoples' money.

With our dynamite daytime signal covering one-third of California, KSCO ownership will pledge to make available a substantial amount of free air time to any serious organized group of citizens with an aggressive leader willing to pursue this democratic process.

Kudos to our new governor, Arnold Schwarzenegger, for being willing to take on an astonishing challenge (and it must be added, we sure could use more state and county leaders with the caliber of a Tom McClintock). And to those irresponsible lawmakers who should be voted out of office, to paraphrase a fitting quote, "Cheat us once, shame on you; cheat us again and again and again, shame on us."

28

What a happy surprise it was to open the Sentinel this morning and read the following front page headline: "Unions Forego Salary Boosts." This gesture could create a groundswell of good things to happen. Kudos to our Santa Cruz city police and firefighters who will give up a portion of their pay increases to help reduce the city's deficit. Kudos also to City Manger Dick Wilson for making the suggestion to them. This move will save the city approximately $1 million over the next three years.

I do believe that all government cost of living increases should be suspended until our budget is in balance. However, now, if all Santa Cruz city leaders would willingly take cutbacks in their wages, the city deficit would get smaller, or maybe even disappear. Then, if the Santa Cruz County Supervisors would willingly take the cut in their high yearly salary of about $94,000 for approximately 35 meetings per year, plus a pension, and personal cars and perks, and if our CAO Susan Mauriello would willingly cut back on her close to $200,000 per year, plus pension, etc., our county deficit might even disappear.

Talk about a wonderful ripple effect. Remember, the fish always stinks from the head down, and if our state lawmakers would willingly take cuts in their salaries etc., our state deficit would also shrink or disappear.

Finally, that move might inspire our lawmakers in the U.S. Congress to give up their exclusive retirement fund of $14,000 per month per congressperson, and instead, join the more reasonable Social Security retirement system with the rest of us schleps. Just think, instead of a countrywide deficit, we would probably have a large surplus. So much good could come from this voluntary generosity. The poor, handicapped and mentally ill could have their desperately needed benefits restored to them. And, best of all, every willing participant would feel an indescribable warm glow of joy for making this joint goodness happen.

29

What I am about to tell you could easily be referring to our own beautiful Santa Cruz. It is a city that is in Los Angeles County, and it has 97% Hispanic population, more than half foreign-born, and 40% illegal. It has achieved quite a goal. It is now as lawless and chaotic as anyplace in Mexico. It is called Maywood, California. This is a warning to every city and town in America.

The Maywood City Council announced recently that after years of radical policies, corruption, and scandal, the city was broke and all city employees would be laid off and essential city services contracted out to neighboring cities or to L.A. County government.

How did this happen?

Maywood was the first California city with an elected all-Hispanic City Council, one of the first sanctuary cities for illegal aliens. The first city to pass a resolution calling for a boycott of Arizona after that State passed a law to enforce federal immigration laws, because the federal government chose to not enforce them. Instead the federal government is now suing Arizona for enforcing them. This is nuts!

Maywood was the first California city to order the police department not to require drivers to have licenses to drive. It is the first America city to call on Congress for amnesty to all illegals.

Council meetings were conducted in Spanish.

The City of Maywood started out quite differently. Back after World War 2, Maywood was a booming blue collar town with good jobs, a multi-ethnic suburb of L.A.

But, the early 1970s saw these industrial jobs in aerospace, auto and furniture manufacturing, and food processing evaporate under higher taxes, increased regulations, and cheaper land and cheaper labor elsewhere.

The multi-ethnic Maywood of the post war years was transformed in the 1980s and 1990s by wave after wave of Hispanic immigrants, many of them illegal.

Today, Maywood is broke. Its police department is dismantled along with all other city departments and personnel. Maywood is a warning of what happens when illegal immigrants resisting assimilation as Americans bring the corruption and radical politics of their home countries.

Kudos to Roger Hedgecock for alerting us via the weekly newspaper, Human Events.

I say clearly, the key issue in this typical U.S. dilemma is assimilation. Ideally, illegals should be sent back to where they came from, and those immigrants who come here legally must understand that English is our only dominant language. They must learn English, function in English, vote in English. No more catering to their native language needs, and voting ballots should only be in English.

And, those in charge of our federal government must close our borders or be impeached.

For KSCO, this is Kay Zwerling.

2

Part Two: United States of America

1

(February 29, 2004) Well isn't there always something to fill us with angst? This time, it's the gays confronting the traditionalists, and the issue is becoming more hairy, and the gays are behaving like anarchists. With the help of certain lawbreaking mayors and judges, and other jurisdictions who are getting into the act, many gays are celebrating their so-called marriages. Almost everyone agrees that same-sex partners will and should have same legal rights as a married couple, that is, a man and a woman. Now gays, unhappy with the wording "legal partnerships", want their union to be called a "marriage". Since forever, marriage has been between a man and a woman, and nothing more. When children come into a marriage, they have one mother and one father, and in no way ever can two fathers or two mothers be a marriage. So it looks like there is a stalemate.

There is, however, a reasonable solution. Remember Shakespeare's "Romeo and Juliet", when Romeo said "What's in a name? A rose by any other name would smell as sweet"? To satisfy everyone, unions between gays could be called a garriage, with a "g". That would sound the closest to the word marriage without trivializing the institution of marriage. Just change one letter, an "m" to a "g", and if gays say the word fast enough, it sounds like marriage – even though it is not. Gays could get garried, hopefully have stable garriages, and celebrate long and happy years of gatrimony together. Isn't that a really good King Solomon-type solution?

As a pedestrian observer of the human condition, and of the attitudes of society toward the two most widely used recreational substances, alcohol and marijuana, otherwise known as pot, one wonders why alcohol is universally accepted, condoned, and promoted, while marijuana is maligned and, in some places, forbidden. The U.S. Government has declared pot to be illegal, so many caught with it are fined, stigmatized, languish in prison, and are otherwise made miserable. There is documented medical proof that pot can relieve the pain of terminally ill patients and afford their last days a measure of mellow peace. Despite this positive use of the substance, the federal government continues to declare it illegal, even though some states do allow its use for medical purposes. Alcohol, on the other hand, gets a free ride, despite the fact that its legal use has caused, and continues to cause enormous human misery with the breakup of families, neglect of children, loss of jobs, accidents and killings by drunken drivers, and the overall drain on society. One could argue that while both substances are considered bad, alcohol causes more grief in the world than pot does.

During a trip to Jamaica many years ago, our tour guide pointed out the abundant marijuana bushes growing wild alongside the roads, and he attributed the longevity and good health of most Jamaicans to their daily drinking of a tea made from the marijuana leaves. So one could wonder... if alcohol, with nothing good to justify its use, is federally legal, shouldn't pot, with some significant proven good, likewise be legal? Or, put another way, if pot is illegal, surely shouldn't alcohol also be illegal? Hmmmmm.

2

(February 20, 2003) Political correctness emerged in the late 1960s as the brainchild of the academic left, born of emotion. That is to say, feelings – not facts, not reality. It was decided by the left that to be politically correct, one must no longer use the word "handicapped". Instead, that word was replaced by the words "physically challenged". Nothing really changed. The handicapped person was still handicapped, and probably came to terms with that situation a long time ago.

Anyhow, the word "challenged" came into vogue, and any condition remotely negative or sad became hyphenated followed by the world "challenged".

KSCO's Russian talk host perpetuates this charade, no doubt jokingly, by explaining his lack of proficiency in English by starting each program saying that he is linguistically-challenged, another manifestation of political correctness bordering on the absurd.

About five years ago, a local high school accustomed to honoring the student graduating with the highest grades by naming them the valedictorian, had to withdraw that traditional singular honor because eleven students had the same grade average. Had the administrators factored in other individual accomplishments, one student would have stood out front, but rather than hurt anyone's feelings, that year there were eleven valedictorians. So much for the joy of achievement.

Likewise, in the 1960s, UCSC initiated a pass/fail grading system to replace letter grades, primarily because it was more compassionate for students who were unable to attain As and Bs. The pursuit of excellence was no longer rewarded – in fact, it was disdained. In the name of feelings, there came a settling for mediocrity.

Political correctness heralded the dumbing down of our educational system. Competing has become politically incorrect. Students are no longer expected to be high achievers. Everybody's comfort level must be equal. Nobody must have hurt feelings —nobody except maybe the innocent victims of Affirmative Action. The best and the brightest have to defer to the less able. Many brilliant students have been locked out of medical schools, law schools, dental schools, etc.

There must be a way to implement Affirmative Action without punishing those with the most potential. The feelings of everyone affected should be considered.

Because of political correctness, children are not being properly disciplined, not at home and not at school, because that might stifle creativity. Parents were admonished to avoid saying "No" or "Do not" to their kid for fear that those restrictions might damage Junior's psyche. Feelings have replaced discipline and common sense. Children are being cheated out of having parameters. As a result, respect for parents and teachers has eroded. In some schools, teachers are being cursed, assaulted, and in extreme cases, some have even been raped by students. Because of political correctness, many parents have abdicated their roles as guiding influences. And instead, have opted to be their kid's buddies – not all parents, only those who have allowed themselves to be seduced by the misguided notion of political correctness. So, if the shoe fits, wear it.

3

Moving along – political correctness has fostered a nation of wimps and victims. People do not take responsibility for their behavior. It is much easier to let someone else or the government bail them out. How about the elderly woman who held her cup of hot coffee between her thighs while driving, scalded her legs, then took McDonald's to court, sued for damages, and won? Also, the lifetime smoker who developed lung cancer, blamed, and then sued the tobacco company and was awarded millions? Victimhood has become a lucrative art. Now greedy, unethical lawyers are initiating frivolous lawsuits, all with the help of politically correct juries and especially condoned by politically correct judges who lack the backbone to rule rationally. Liberal and extreme judges must take responsibility for enabling our judicial system to become political and grossly unfair. These extreme judges and lawyers are surely in the minority, but it only takes a few rotten apples to ruin the entire barrel.

One could go on and on about the abuses and havoc generated by political correctness. It is really tiresome how these p.c. lefties are always offended. Now the word "Christmas" can no longer be mentioned in the public school system. Can't say "God" either. And the Ten Commandments are banned from all schools and all public buildings. Our national moral fiber is wearing very thin.

In a subsequent commentary, we will discuss more about the excesses perpetrated by political correctness and finish with the full text of the amazing Bill of No Rights. Stayed tuned.

4

What you are about to hear came to us recently in an email written by a very credible, famous person.

There is now a groundswell of interest around the country about this issue. KSCO and KOMY are privileged to be a part of disseminating this vital information which directly affects every taxpayer in the United States. The issue of how our own county supervisors are ripping us off Big-Time while directing the rest of us to take cuts and tighten our belts because of the budget deficit has been my own favorite and frustrating vendetta.

The author of the following takes the same issue to the federal level. Please stay with me. Together we can change laws that are wrong. Now for the email:

"I think the vast differences in compensation between victims of 9/11 casualty and those who die serving the country in uniform are profound. No one is really talking about it either, because you just don't criticize anything having to do with September 11th.

Well, I just can't let the numbers pass by because it says something really disturbing about the entitlement mentality of this country. If you lost a family member in the 9/11 attack, you're going to get an average of $1,185,000. The range is a minimum guarantee of $250,000, all the way up to $4.7 million.

Now, if you are a surviving family member of an American soldier killed in action, the first check you get is a $6,000 direct death benefit, half of which is taxable. Next, you get $1,700 for burial costs. If you are the surviving spouse, you get $833 a month until you *remarry. And there's a payment of $211 per month for each child under 18.*

When the child hits 18, those payments come to a screeching halt. Keep in mind that some of the people who are getting an average of $1,185,000 (up to $4.7 million) are complaining that it is not enough. Their deaths were tragic, but for most they were simply in the wrong place at the wrong time. Soldiers put themselves in harm's way for all of us, and they and their families know the dangers.

We also learned over the weekend that some of the victims from the Oklahoma City bombing have started an organization asking for the same deal that the September 11th families are getting. In addition to that, some of the families of those bombed in the embassies are now asking for compensation as well.

You see where this is going, don't you? Folks, this is part and parcel of over 50 years of entitlement politics in this country. It is just really sad.

Every time a pay raise comes up for the military, they receive next to nothing of a raise. Now the green machine is in combat in the Middle East while their families have to survive on food stamps and live in low-cost housing. Does that make sense?

However, our own U.S. Congress just voted themselves a raise, and many of you do not know that they only have to be in Congress one time to receive a pension that is more than $15,000 per month, and most are now equal to being millionaires plus. They also do not receive Social Security on retirement because they didn't have to pay into the system.

If some of the military people stay in for 20 years and get out as an E-7, they may receive a pension of $1,000 per month, and the very people who placed them in harm's way receive a pension of $15,000 per month. I would like to see our elected officials pick up a *weapon and join the ranks before they start cutting out benefits and lowering pay for our sons and daughters who are now fighting. When do we finally do something about this? If this does not seem fair to you, it is time to forward this to as many people as you can.*

Now, a little bit about Social Security.

Perhaps we are asking the wrong questions during election years. Our senators and congressmen do not pay into Social Security. Many years ago they voted in their own benefit plan.. In recent years, no congressperson has felt the need to change it. For all practical purposes, their plan works like this: When they retire, they continue to draw the same pay until they die, except it may increase from time to time for cost of living adjustments. For example, former Senator Byrd and Congressman White and their wives may expect to draw $7,800,000 - that's Seven Million, Eight Hundred Thousand), with their wives drawing $275,000.00 during the last years of their lives. This is calculated on an average life span for each.

Their cost for this excellent plan is zero dollars. These little perks they have voted for themselves are free to them. You and I pick up the tab for this plan. The funds for this fine retirement plan come directly from the General Fund – our tax dollars at work.

From our own Social Security Plan, which you and I pay (or have paid) into —every payday until we retire (with matching payments by our employer) – we can expect to get an average $1,000 per month after retirement. Or, in other words, we would have to collect our average of $1,000 monthly benefits for 68 years and one month to equal Senator Bill Bradley's benefits.

Social Security could be very good if only one small change were made. And that change would be to jerk the Golden Fleece Retirement Plan from under the senators and congressmen. Put them into the Social Security plan with the rest of us, then watch how fast they would fix it. If enough people receive this email, maybe a seed of awareness will be planted, and maybe good changes will evolve. WE, each one of us – can make a difference.

Kudos to Rush Limbaugh for this fascinating email. For a copy, log on to www.ksco .com

5

As a longtime resident of this planet, and a lucky native-born of this incredible country, I need to speak out about why our United States, once the hope and promise of the world, is rapidly becoming weaker and unable to live up to its past expectations. It is our own goodness, generosity, and trusting nature which is destroying us. The topic is: Assimilation Versus Diversity. Let's roll back the clock to around 1913 when my own European extended family was part of the greatest influx of immigrants to the United States. In the late 1920s, as a child, I saw how proud and grateful my family was to be here in America where they saw the hope and opportunity nonexistent in their native country. The one abiding desire of all immigrants at that time was to quickly learn to speak, read, and write in English – in short, to become truly American. It is called assimilation. That desire to be American in no way diminished the love that newcomers had for their own culture, history, and native language. They knew it was their responsibility to keep their own heritage alive, and they never expected their newly adopted country to do that for them.

Let's fast-forward now to the early 1960s or thereabouts, when immigration surged again, from Mexico, Korea, Japan, China, Vietnam, and many other countries. It was then that the notion of diversity became very popular, and it was celebrated ad nauseam by the politically correct left.

Always motivated by feelings, never reality, the left felt that it was wonderful to have this mixture of cultures in the United States, and in many ways it is true, it was; however, the left, in its enthusiasm, felt that as a country, We The People were responsible for helping these newcomers keep their respective languages and cultures alive. Big big mistake So what happened? At that time, most new citizens came from Mexico and spoke only Spanish. Our public education system, led by leftist educators, created the program of "English As A Second Language", whereby Mexican children receive most of their education in Spanish, so their parents and they did not have to learn English, so they remained primarily Mexican, but lived in America. That's is called diversity? I call it disaster.

Now, let's fast-forward to 2002, like now. As a result of 40 years of diversity, and the rejection of assimilation, many immigrants still do not understand English, but they do have the right to vote, so our voting ballots are now in many languages. This is stupid and wrong, and it is weakening and destroying the identity of our country. It is time to demand that to vote one must read, write, and understand English, and all ballots must be in English only, because English is our national language. What we have now is mass chaos and ghettos of different cultures. I say, tell political correctness and diversity to take a hike, because diversity divides, and assimilation brings unity. What we have now is a nation of babble. Let's take back our country, now.

6

"A fool and his money are easily parted." That was an expression I used often when my children were growing up and sometimes made foolish expenditures using their own money.

On a related subject, it was a creative idea cooked up by credit card issuers who saw a unique way to make more money. Even they didn't realize the enormity of their potential windfall. The plot involved them, retail businesses, and the general public. It was a win-win situation for all involved. For the participating public, it was a nobrainer because for the first time people could make purchases without paying up front. For retailers, it was worth up to 3% cost to get their money up front. Except for the always valuable and appreciated real estate mortgages and automobile loans, this mattery scheme was new and exciting.

For over 50 years now, public credit cards have become a way of life, and in retrospect, one could believe it was liberating and good that the ordinary consumer lacking big savings no longer had to wait to acquire things they wanted. Impulse buying, especially of big items, became easy, but there was – and is – a dark side to the new "buy now, pay later" idea. That little plastic card had the potential to seduce one into acquiring luxuries one might otherwise have done without or waited until one had the cash first. That same little plastic monster has made debtors out of many people who suddenly find they cannot ever seem to pay their monthly bills, and this is where they get sucked into monetary quicksand for all the nebulous pleasures of acquiring more stuff. It's called Instant Gratification. So often we let stuff own us. The most dangerous time of year is the Christmas season, when countless otherwise restrained people experience an irrational exuberance and overextend themselves. They foolishly purchase much too much, then take months enslaved by outrageous interest rates, sometimes upwards of 25% on the unpaid balances, and these rates are imposed by the credit card issuers. Some people don't ever get out from under.

Now, for some motherly advice: for starters, our lawmakers should put reasonable ceilings on credit card interest rates, but that won't easily happen. Nothing will change until people stop overcharging on their credit cards and pay up their dangling balances once and for all. If that's not possible, then it's better to say "Thanks, but no thanks" to credit cards and live within your means on a case basis. You will then experience an indescribable peace of mind by not being in debt. It is well worth it.

7

For decades, liberals have been celebrating diversity, which is a more polite way of tolerating human differences. However, when these same champions of diversity are confronted with beliefs diverse from theirs, they become offended and engage the ACLU because their beliefs are being challenged. Here's the drill: the ACLU initiates a lawsuit and a hand-picked liberal judge rules in their favor. Recent case in point (this may contribute to the Democratic Party's eventual demise): because the mention of God publicly is offensive to many on the left, the entire Ten Commandments have been removed from all public buildings and public schools. How mean-spirited. Couldn't those offended respect and tolerate the diverse wishes of others who appreciate the priceless knowledge in the Ten Commandments? These so-called "enlightened" promote diversity, but only selectively. Hypocritical? You bet!

How come highly educated elitists have forgotten that our wonderful and enduring democracy was founded on Judeo-Christian values that include God?

As a little Jewish girl in elementary school, every day when the teacher read a portion from the New Testament, I sat quietly and listened to beliefs contrary to my own about the divinity of Jesus. My parents were not offended, and I was not offended. I learned to respect the viewpoints of others, and it was good for my character.

These short-sighted liberals are making intolerant wimps out of their children, who will grow up always being offended, denied the right to grow backbones and deal gracefully with all diversities.

The Democratic party is reeling from their recent political defeat. In order to regain their former respect, they should heed the wake-up call, shape up, and grow up. They must discard their oppressive brainchild, "political correctness", in which competition is denounced, protecting feelings is primary (even though it diminishes achievement and high standards), parental respect is disdained, and the word God is a no-no. If they do not finally get the message loud and clear, they will surely cease to be relevant as a viable political party.

8

(December 20, 2004) First, here is a short open letter to a small, very loud group of Americans:

You are always offended by some bullpucky or other. Now, the rest of us are getting angry, because now your incessant complaining is taking the joy out of our beautiful holiday season.

For about 150 years, our government has peacefully acknowledged the existence of God with the words "In God we trust" on our money, and we have enjoyed reciting the Pledge of Allegiance and singing God Bless America at ball games and other public functions, and we like to say "Merry Christmas", and some of us are happy honoring Christmas with small public displays of baby Jesus in the manger, or a display of a Menorah saying "Happy Hanako". So what's the big deal? You'd better get over it, because we the silent majority will no longer cater to your offended sensibilities. Control yourselves, and put up with it. If you are momentarily bothered, cover your ears or go to the john, or go hug a tree, or better still, go to Canada where there are so many more like you. You will be happier there.

So much for the negativity.

Now, to those who listen to KSCO and KOMY, as matriarch and on behalf of the Zwerling family, local residents for 57 years, I say thank you to our bright and loyal listeners, thank you to our delightful and incredibly informed callers, thank you advertisers for your very much appreciated support, thank you to our great radio staff for working happily and enthusiastically, and it shows in the programming. We feel good knowing that we are a conduit for various points of view. I for one am grateful for the privilege to make commentaries and hope they make a positive difference. Let us all make an effort to be good to each other and respect our differences. My family and I wish all of you good health and peace of mind in the year ahead, the two most important blessings, without which life would not be worth much. We pray for our troops in action, and we pray for wisdom in our leaders, and God please bless America.

9

A Scottish friend from Edinburgh, Scotland, sent the following unique version of a commentary I did two years ago on the topic of political correctness. I truly believe that political correctness has been and continues to be the most compelling factor in the moral deterioration of our country during the past 35 years. Our Scottish friend obviously feels that this same sickness is overcoming all of liberal Britain and Europe. It's called "Obituary Notice".

"Common Sense died 24/7/365 in North America's Heart, USA. Today we mourn the passing of a beloved old friend by the name of Common Sense, who had been with us for many years. No one knows for sure how old he was. His birth records were long ago lost in bureaucratic red tape. He will be remembered as having cultivated such valuable lessons as knowing when to come in out of the rain, why the early bird gets the worm, and that life isn't always fair. Common Sense lived by simple, sound financial policies (don't spend more than you earn) and reliable parenting strategies (adults – not kids, are in charge). His health began to rapidly deteriorate when well-intentioned but overbearing regulations were set in place. Reports of a six-year-old boy charged with sexual harassment for kissing a classmate, teens suspended from schools for using mouthwash after lunch, and a teacher fired for reprimanding an unruly student, only worsened his condition. It declined even further when schools were required to get parental consent to administer aspirin to a student; however, the schools could not inform the parents when a student became pregnant and wanted to have an abortion.

Finally, Common Sense lost the will to live as the Ten Commandments became contraband, churches became businesses, and criminals received better treatment than their victims. Common Sense finally gave up the ghost after a woman failed to realize that a steaming cup of coffee was hot, spilled a bit in her lap, claimed McDonald's did not warn her, and was awarded a huge settlement. Common Sense was preceded in death by his parents Truth and Trust, his wife Discretion, his daughter Responsibility, and his son Reason. He is survived, however, by two stepchildren, U. A. Victim and Ima Whiner. Not many attended his funeral because so few realized he was gone. If you remember him, pass this on. If not, join the majority and do nothing."

10

(March 29, 2005) About the Terri Schiavo case, what is about to happen is a grotesque miscarriage of justice. For anyone to be slowly and painfully starved to death is barbaric. When husband Michael Schiavo ten years ago took himself a common law wife with whom he now has two children, he abdicated his right to be Terri's legal guardian, because Terri is no longer his priority, yet he adamantly refuses to relinquish his power which logically should be in the hands of her parents and immediate family.

Michael wants Terri dead, and one wonders why. There are now documented, signed affidavits from nurses who cared for Terri years ago when Michael verbally admitted during hospital visits that he was conflicted because he did not know what her wishes were. Now, his personal circumstances are different, and he remembers for sure that Terri preferred death in this situation.

There are still unanswered questions, so why are the judges unwilling to listen? With criminal murderers, their sentences of death can be commuted even minutes before scheduled execution if there is newly introduced evidence. Why is Terri's death pushed along without the same care and scrutiny? What about her unexplained broken bones? How come in 15 years, Michael has refused for Terri to have any treatments or rehab? And, the addendum, today – two weeks since her forced starvation – Terri died, and Michael Schiavo will know in the deep recesses of his being that what he did was evil, and he may not have peace of mind as long as he lives.

And, about the possible partisan judges, and the Florida Supreme Court, and Federal Supreme Court – they are all delinquent in their duties for refusing to listen to evidence not previously presented. The creators of our American justice system never wanted politics to enter judicial decisions, and perhaps now the laws of the judiciary should be revisited.

No judge should ever remain on the bench for life. They should be evaluated by We the People, and voted into office for a finite number of years. State and federal Supreme Court justices should be voted in also by the people, and not by the political party in power. I know this sounds like it is going to be complicated and difficult; however, if judges were made accountable, they would be more hesitant to inject politics into their decisions, and they would be more humane about hearing new evidence. Terri is an innocent victim, and the handling of this tragedy will forever remain a stain on our national character.

11

(June 23, 2005) The Democratic party is self-destructing. It has been highjacked by the extremist Left. It continues to make irresponsible, reckless decisions. They had a fair chance to win the recent election. Except for Fox news, 100% of the media promoted the Democrats. They hated President Bush so much, they made their political mantra "Anybody but George Bush". Such hysterical thinking made reasonable voters uneasy, so they left the Left. If the foolish liberals had put forth candidates with credibility, someone like a Joe Lieberman or a Zel Miller, they may have won. Instead, they settled for a pompous empty suit with a dismal 20-year senatorial record, who refused to expose his own military or health records, and, for V.P., a pretty-faced but politically inexperienced corporate attorney.

The Democrats' fatal mistake was to underestimate the intelligence of the average voter. They embraced the extremist Michael Moore, and now Howard Dean is their official spokesperson. After 3-1/2 more years of Dean, the Democratic party will be rendered totally irrelevant.

There did not appear to be much mourning by the Left extremists after 9/11 when 3,000 innocent Americans died. By comparison, these same leftists are going crazy ballistic about a handful of American soldiers using bad judgment and badgering Gitmo detainees by putting ladies' underpants on their heads and other demeaning antics. Never mind that those same prisoners, when given the chance, cut out tongues, chopped off hands, and sliced off heads for the smallest infractions, the stuff they learned from their role model Saddam Hussein.

About those few prisoners really badly punished by our interrogators, that is the standard practice in wartime, to force the enemy to talk in order to save American lives. Wild accusations about the detainees' treatment, using words like "Nazis" and "gulag", by a liberal senator and condoned by other liberals may add another nail to the possible coffin of the Democrats' demise. Gitmo is the best thing that has happened to these detainees. They never had it so good. Many are gaining weight. Where else are terrorists given their own prayer rugs, a copy of the Koran, Islamic approved gourmet meals, hot showers, and calls to prayers five times daily? Still, the liberal extremists continue to complain and obstruct, which will be their agenda for the remainder of Bush's term, and which may also become their swan song. Call me mean, but I believe we are overdoing the Gitmo hospitality.

About Saddam Hussein, found in a rat hole like a scared rat, I would have given him a shower, clean washed clothes, food, and a cell – nothing more. So, what is with the beauty shop treatment and the designer clothes? From a scared rat, now he believes he is still the leader of Iraq. He deserves a quick military tribunal followed by a long slow painful death, the kind he inflicted on millions of his own people.

12

(August 17, 2005) Weighing in on the national current debate of random searches vs. profiling, I emphatically cast my vote for profiling. Random searches, used at all airports and subways, where every fifth person is searched, are an exercise in stupidity. For example, person #4 may fit the profile of a human bomb – young, between 18-35, dark skin, hair, and eyes – while person #5 turns out to be an asthmatic slow-walking, fat 88-year-old female – she gets the thorough inspection while the suspicious-looking #4 walks away right into the possibly ill-fated plane or train.

It is way past time to stop fighting a kind and gentle war. We refuse to target traveling Islamic-looking Americans, while we are willing to put all Americans in danger. That is idiotic. I believe the Islamic Americans without any evil agenda should be willing to put up with selective body examinations under the present circumstances.

Whoever said that life is fair? The vocal Left say that they are against the war in Iraq, but they are for supporting the troops. That's bull-pucky. Their constant whining and complaining are giving aid and comfort to the enemy and hurting the morale of the very troops they claim to support. To them I say, "You can't have it both ways." Please understand that for us winning is a must and it is not negotiable, so put aside your personal rights and personal privacy for the time being. Please, even if you are against this war, stifle your protests, and let us close ranks and fight as a united country. I want my grandchildren's children to have a life worth living. The world is watching us. The stakes are high. The outcome will decide whether it will be a dark world, or a free world. We can't not win.

13

(January 26, 2006) Considering the recent exposure of the shady shenanigans of a certain Mr. Abramoff, a high-powered Washington DC lobbyist, a quick internet search tells us that the lobbying business is alive and flourishing. This industry has doubled in the past five years, mainly because large corporations have discovered that since hiring lobbyists at starting salaries of

$300,000 per year, those corporations have seen their business increase significantly, in some cases as much as fourfold.

Now, five years later, well-connected lobbyists are commanding and getting $750,000 per year, and one is getting $1,000,000 per year. A lobbyist in Washington may have once been in, and understands the workings of passing laws, and can and does persuade lawmakers to legislate laws that directly benefit the corporation which hires the lobbyist. It has become commonplace for members of corporations to actually sit in on lawmakers' meetings and help with the creation and wording of the law which the corporation wants passed. Outrageous? You bet But this practice has been around for so long and it has probably never been challenged.

A recent case in point – the just passed and implemented Medicare Part D law to help seniors pay less for their medications actually was written by the pharmaceutical industry. This is a perfect case of a fox minding the chicken coop.

Another tidbit of political incest – a number of lawmakers' wives are lobbyists, also. Imagine their pillow talk.

It is unknown when this lucrative business of political persuasion or culture of corruption began. Our Founding Fathers would surely have nixed the notion of private business paying obscene sums of money to certain powerful persons to get laws passed in their favor. Anyhow, it smells. In fact, in stinks. The laws of the nation should not be made and bought by big corporations. It is inherently dishonest and wrong, and the little guy never gets a chance at a level playing field. But nothing will change. The lobbying business is too entrenched, it is a big industry in Washington DC, and I believe it is here to stay.

There are 30,000 registered lobbyists operating in our capital today.

Is it too much to expect our elected officials to work diligently and honestly to thoroughly study the issues then pass laws which benefit all of us, the poor and the not poor, and do so without outside influence and bribery? The answer is yes, it is too much to expect. In a perfect world, that could happen. But this is not a perfect world. Because of the dark side of human nature, power will always corrupt.

14

(April 15, 2006) Weighing in on the present immigration mess – first, close the borders; ignore the marchers who wish to undermine our laws. Those here illegally must obey the laws, must learn English, vote in English, apply for citizenship, and wait the same amount of time as those who come in legally. No drivers' licenses, no voting rights until they become legal citizens. That's what I think. No more amnesty. Furthermore, no more voting ballots in any language other than English. (That's idiotic.) No more pandering to foreign newcomers.

All of these related troubles stem from weakling leaders in both political parties whose main concern is, and has always been, reelection and vying for newcomers' votes. Those leaders willingly left the borders open. Both political parties, for over two decades, are responsible for the eleven million illegals here. Thank you President Ford, thank you George Herbert Walker Bush, thank you President Clinton, and George W. for your deliberate failures. Since the word felon has been used so loosely, and then crossed out, I submit it is our delinquent leaders, presidents, and congress, who by their inaction in upholding the laws of our land are the real felons. There is only one special political leader, like a voice in the wilderness, who stands out, who for years pleaded with the legislature to protect our borders from illegals, criminals, and terrorists, and to him we must say "Kudos to you, Tom Tancredo " because you cared and you tried.

And another thing, the tail must stop wagging the dog. About the UCSC student protests re: the military recruiters being on campus – the students should be expelled for leaving their classes, and We The People should withdraw our public funds helping them. They are in school to learn their subject matter and not to make policy for the university and the country. And the wimpy delinquent faculty better shape up or they should be fired. About the regents who approve enormous salaries and bonuses to upper employees while denying raises to the lower employees who keep the university functioning, that's wrong. The regents should be replaced.

Better still, maybe the public universities which We The People support, who have 85% liberal professors brainwashing our children, should be closed.

15

(May 13, 2006) As a once longtime Democrat, I remember proudly voting for the first time at age 21 and thereafter never missing an election. Aware that the ability to vote is the greatest right we Americans have, I have felt frustrated often hearing certain peers and young people say that they're so disenchanted with government corruption, whichever party is in power, that they don't vote at all. That is a copout. Bad things happen when good people do nothing. And we usually get the government we deserve.

In the 1940's, when the Democratic party was led by strong leaders like FDR who created national programs to pull us out of the Great Depression, I felt proud to be a Democrat. FDR engaged the country on a regular basis with his famous fireside talks – and families gathered together to listen to him on the radio. We all cared.

The Republicans then didn't like – in fact, some of them hated – FDR because he was a successful leader and he continued to remain in power after the traditional two terms when he was elected to a third. The Republicans then, like the Democrats now, were miserable because of jealousy. And when we closed ranks and joined England and France to finish off Hitler and Germany during World War II, FDR and Winston Churchill, the dynamic leader of Great Britain's war effort, were an awesome, and in many ways a beloved, twosome.

Many Americans were shocked and appalled when President Roosevelt at that time chose to deny a ship full of Jewish immigrants from Germany to land in New York Harbor. He sent them back to Germany to die in Hitler's ovens. Ironically, now we have room for 11 million illegals from Mexico. That episode of Roosevelt's was unforgivable. And it may have, and should have, haunted him forever.

About the Democratic party of today, it has been self-destructing since Bush won. It is desperate for power, vindictive, and it makes no positive contributions, only complaints and obstructions. Many Democrats, and the media for sure, want us to fail in Iraq. Democratic leaders claim that the American people want them to win in November. How presumptuous and how arrogant. Now they talk about impeaching President Bush because he MADE us go to Iraq. This is becoming tiresome. Our Congress (minus two or three votes) unanimously voted to go, as did the United Nations. We've all been through this before. And I still believe that the Weapons of Mass Destruction are still there or in Syria or someplace else, but very well hidden.

My prediction for the election in November is this: With pathetic leaders like Nancy Pelosi, a silly woman who is in way over her head, and Howard Dean, infected with diarrhea of the mouth, running the Democratic party, their future looks bleak. Because they continue to obstruct and discredit the government, the Democrats will remain out of power indefinitely.

I am now and have been for many years an Independent because both dominant parties are very flawed. But the economy is good, Iraq is becoming a democracy, and right now the Republicans, even with their mistakes (of which there are many) have more brains and focus than the Democrats who blew a chance to win the last election. If they had chosen a credible candidate, like a Joe Lieberman instead of the empty suit and contriving John Kerry who took his own photographer with him to Viet Nam for photo ops, signed up for four years and left after four months, with many photos of himself, and as the Democratic candidate for president gave the people no valid reason to choose him for president. Won't the foolish Democrats ever learn that the biggest mistake arrogant people make is that they underestimate the intelligence of the public?

16

(May 26, 2006) The first priority for President Bush during his second term was the need to repair Social Security, but it became clear early on that the Democrats would rather not deal with this pressing issue until they are in power, whenever that happens, so this issue is on hold.

Therefore, it doesn't matter if you're a Republican or a Democrat. Let's get a bill started to place all politicians on Social Security. Our National lawmakers do not pay into Social Security. This program was not suitable for them. They were too important to settle for the meager benefits that are good enough for the rest of us. They felt that they should have a special program for themselves, so many years ago they quietly voted in their own benefit plan.

No congressperson has felt the need to change things. After all, it's a great plan, for them. It works like this: When they retire, they continue to draw the same pay until they die, except it may increase from time to time for cost of living adjustments. Even if one serves only two years in Congress, he still gets a salary of about $4000 per month plus benefits for the rest of his life. For example, Senator Bird and Congressman White, who are elderly, may expect to draw $7,800,000 each with their wives drawing $275,000 each during the last years of their lives. This is calculated on an average lifespan for each of those two dignitaries. Younger dignitaries who retire at an early age will receive much more during the rest of their lives.

Their cost for this excellent plan is zero, nada, zilch. This little perk they voted for themselves is free to them. You and I pick up the tab. The funds for this fine retirement plan come directly from the general fund, in our tax dollars. From our own Social Security plan, which you and I pay, or have paid, into every payday until we retire, with payments matched by our employers, we can expect to get an average of $1000 per month after retirement. Putting it into perspective, we would have to collect our average $1000 monthly benefit for 68 years to equal the benefits of our congresspeople.

This thievery has been happening because We The People have allowed it. There's no way in hell or heaven or Earth that this blatant inequity is justified. Frankly, Congress was voted into power to make laws to benefit all the people, not to help themselves to enormous perks at our expense. It's dishonest, it's wrong, and it needs to be challenged.

Social Security could be very good if only one small change were made, and that change would be to jerk the extravagant retirement plan from under the senators and congresspeople, put them into the Social Security plan with the rest of us, then sit back and see how fast they would fix it. I wonder if this could be done with a national initiative. If enough people receive this message, maybe a seed of awareness will be planted, and maybe good changes will evolve. Pass this around to everyone you know.

Kudos to Sherman Weitzman, whoever and wherever he is, for exposing this issue with a solution. People Power can make powerful changes. Nothing ventured, nothing gained.

Again, please pass this around. It will become an issue in the 2008 election.

Let's all mobilize and do this because we're mad, and we will not take it any longer.

17

(2006) For as far back as I can remember, eminent domain did not elicit many complaints from the general public. After all, it sounded and felt reasonable. The parameters which American cities had to abide by were fair.

Those leaders who made decisions concerning eminent domain had to be very specific that the law could be used only if it was for the betterment of the entire city or community and not for any one business or individual. For example, if a private parcel was in the way of a proposed highway which would be for the betterment of the entire community or a certain parcel and its location for a public hospital was to better serve the community at large, then certain private parcels may fairly come under those parameters, but only if the owners received fair market value.

However, what has been happening since the summer 2005 is that the U.S. Supreme Court, because of the swing vote of retiring judge Sandra Day O'Connor, made the shocking, and not well thought out law that cities or other municipalities could take away private property at fair market value so that property could be used by private developers to generate more revenue for themselves and for the city involved.

This outrageous and insensitive treatment of property owners forced to give up their beloved homes for developers of communities to make more money is not proper for a free society. It is not the American way. It is unadulterated stealing.

Supposedly we have the finest minds in America serving as justices on the U.S. Supreme Court. How could they let this happen?

Numerous eminent domain issues are now surfacing, and the private property owner is on the losing end every time. The U.S. Supreme Court justices have opened an enormous Pandora's box, and the developers and certain cities are salivating because now they can make tons of money legally at the expense of a private homeowner.

Greed is overpowering fairness and creating pain and grief for the innocent property owner, and this is wrong.

We citizens must shout loud and clear and tell our U.S. Supreme Court justices that they have made a grave error and must reverse this disgusting law at once. I don't doubt that the recent appointees will surely agree to rescind this ruling.

Every citizen should get involved. Even if your property is safe today, tomorrow or sometime later, your home may be taken away. If it's a referendum we need, let's do it. Who would like to lead the way?

KSCO AM 1080 has a dynamite signal which can be heard during daytime hours over a third of California, and we will gladly donate air time to urge the public to help get involved and reverse this wrong.

18

(September 8, 2006) This is called "Bush Haters Find A Way To Kill The President Vicariously". I have learned recently of the movie about the assassination of an American president. The reporting of this new film left no doubt whatsoever that it is about President George Bush, with the author using wishful thinking re his right to free speech.

How much lower can we go because we pride ourselves on having free speech which includes the right to burn the American flag in public and stomp on it, and we allow illegals here to do the same?

How far have we stooped to diminish our president and the presidency for some to not only be proud of what a great idea this film is, but what big profits can be made out of discrediting our country's leader?

This same ilk of miserable sorehead extremists both here and abroad are tearing down the respectable fabric of our brave and beautiful country. Many U.S. liberals are obsessed with hate because they are not running the country, and because they really did lose the last two elections. I predict that they will fail in November because they offer no solutions for their endless complaints.

They and the media made a big to-do about Abu Ghraib, which pales in comparison to what the enemy does (i.e., slicing off hands and heads, hiding behind women and children in hospitals, and dressing as civilians when in combat). Such a lopsided war has never been fought before, and our liberals keep harping on us not being compassionate.

In my lifetime, it has always been an unspoken rule that past presidents do not criticize the current president publicly. That rule has been discarded by Clinton and Carter, two of our weakest leaders. Leave it to our low class though charming President Clinton, the one who dirtied the Oval Office, the one who lied under oath, the one who left the White House taking every piece of furniture not nailed down, all with the help of Hillary, who now wants to be our president (God help us). They were forced to return the stolen property, which they did shamelessly. Nice résumé, right?

Clinton and Carter both make speeches discrediting the president and the Administration, all of which comforts the enemy. Carter was a one-term president, the one who gave away our national protection, which the U.S. built, the Panama Canal, which is now run by the Chinese. Our troops, wherever they are, feel shame and embarrassment about this display of national disloyalty.

How can we hope to win in Iraq and help it become a democracy when our own media presents the blackest pictures and withholds all the good things happening in Iraq – of which there are so many? How disloyal, how unpatriotic, how demoralizing, how treacherous, how clear that our own media wants us to lose in Iraq.

When the time comes that we must have a draft to defend ourselves against the Islamic fascists here at home and abroad, how many of these miserable loudmouth citizens who criticize every Republican move yet provide no solutions will stay and defend our country, and how many will scurry away to Canada or elsewhere? I dread to know that answer.

19

(October 4, 2006) What a political twilight zone these past weeks have been, with our Congress agonizing about the degree of torture our military should be permitted to inflict upon captured enemy combatants who, as we speak, are doubled up with laughter along with the rest of the world. Our leaders were arguing about taking the moral high ground and dispensing with any torture whatsoever (that's called political correctness) vs. employing some tough interrogation to force valuable information from the enemy which will save countless lives. It is a twilight zone because if being p.c. is in the picture we can never win this war in Iraq or anyplace else.

There are wimps among our lawmakers who do not grasp the seriousness of this war.

The Al Quaeda chief in Iraq, Abu Musab Zarckari, has said often "Killing the infidels is our religion, slaughtering them is our religion until they convert to Islam or pay us tribute" (whatever "pay us tribute" means).

Senator John McCain, a good guy and main proponent of using the high moral ground, is politically damaged. He can no longer be seen as a presidential candidate since he puts his moral high ground above the safety of our troops fighting a barbaric enemy, who will stop at nothing and does not care if winning takes decades or forever because they love death and we love life.

Too many legislators are politicizing this global war, and the world can see every move and therefore, we remain weak and vulnerable.

Realists in Congress have prevailed and now our troops have permission to use some terror in interrogating captives. How demeaning that those who put their lives on the line for us every day must be put on the defensive also and are not trusted to do the right thing on their own.

The two elephants in the room could shorten the war in our favor, but are not being dealt with because of political correctness.

#1. Profiling is necessary. Loyal Muslim-Americans must resist being offended when questioned at airports, borders, or other public places. The enemy now can slip by easily and cause thousands of innocents to be annihilated.

#2. It is time to initiate the draft. Too many volunteer military, both male and female, are forced to do multiple tours of duty in Iraq and Afghanistan, and that is wrong, and it is unfair. Clearly we are in this mess for the long haul, and every able-bodied American has the same vested interest in maintaining and protecting our freedom. That includes college students and professors who evict military recruiters from all publicly funded teaching institutions while they themselves enjoy the benefits of democracy.

Israel handles this issue best. There, every 18-year-old male and female serves in the active military for two years, then remains in the reserves, I believe until close to age 50. The draft is fair, and being physically involved will make all Americans have a personal interest in the outcome. Bona fide conscientious objectors can serve in a noncombat capacity.

Certainly the Bush team has made mistakes, but for us, winning this war is imperative, and our public bickering is deadly. Now, more than ever, our country must come together. Forget politics and close ranks, because we all deeply love our nation despite our differences. Nobody is happy about Iraq. However, if we pull out now, the vacuum created will suck in thousands of terrorists, and we will be in greater danger here at home.

My generation in World War 2 were all willingly involved and we saw a similar unthinkable alternative. Again, if we love our country, we must be willing to fight for it. So let's close ranks, and let's roll.

An unrelated thought: the U.N. should move out and go live in Venezuela.

20

(January 4, 2007) Our Congress has been very remiss in their treatment of our military. I refer to the amount of pay our troops receive and the amount received by their families. The words are pathetic, or miserly, or outrageous, or obscene. Take your pick. Military families have to struggle constantly to make ends meet, and that is unforgivable.

Conversely, the same lawmakers take very good care of themselves. Let me tell you about it:

As of 2007, rank and file congressional lawmakers will earn $165,200 per year, while the Speaker of the House, Nancy Pelosi, will receive $212,100 per year, and the majority and minority leaders of both the House and Senate each will receive $183,500 per year.

Added to that, each member of Congress may wind up with as much as 80% of their final salary, that is, their own special member retirement annuity. Pretty nice - right? Many congresspeople come into office with modest savings and leave as millionaires.

I thought they were put into office to make fair laws for all of us. Who gave them permission to make separate laws to benefit only themselves?

Now, how about the salaries of those who join the military willingly, without the draft, to fight for all of us and our freedoms? Willing to die or maybe be physically handicapped for life – and what do our lawmakers give them? Basic salary for newly enlisted soldiers in the Army as of 2006 has been $1,459 per month, or yearly, less than $18,000, plus a small addition of $250 per month for family separation, and double salary of about $36,000 per year if in combat. There are other little categories for small amounts of money for the military.

There is quite a discrepancy between lawmakers' wages and benefits, and military wages and benefits. I submit that there should be a level playing field between the military and the Congress.

The military should receive as much or more than our lawmakers, and military families should not have to struggle financially for anything, and if it is not already the case, children of military should be given free university educations.

If we all separately demand of our lawmakers to give the military at least what they give themselves, maybe it will happen. It is not enough for Congress to say we support the troops. It is time for them to really support the troops with the same living wages they take for themselves. Of course, that won't happen.

21

(February 15, 2007) It's the big elephant in the room this time. It keeps needling us constantly since 9/11 and especially after our war in Afghanistan. We realized then that the Islamic terrorists had already infiltrated the entire world, many living among us here in the U.S.

It's four years since we entered Iraq, and we can see now that our military effort was too little too late.

What a mess we have created. We were too weak. We were never strong enough, and the Iraqis finally didn't care enough to want to be a democracy. We didn't have the wherewithal to stop their infighting.

The one thing that would have made all the difference in Iraq, and may have prevented the civil war there, is so noticeable by its absence, and it's called the draft. D-R-A-F-T.

The courageous young Americans who signed up to fight in Iraq did not expect to be called upon to go back again and again and again. That was not the expected deal. That was not fair. But our leaders opted to do that rather than to establish what was fair, and that was the draft. And, if it's so, why after 60 years do we still have occupation troops in peaceful Germany and peaceful Japan?

Where is the government outrage when daily, military recruiters are physically thrown out of publicly financed universities around our country?

All Americans benefit from living in our glorious nation, so all able-bodied Americans should be serving in the military. That terrible word that no elected official from the president down has the cajones to mention has been missing for the past four years. What are we waiting for?

Our enemies are laughing at our self-imposed impotence.

Poisoned and crippled by political correctness like all of weak and useless Europe, our leaders are afraid that they will be committing political suicide by promoting the draft. I think the opposite would be true. They would finally be considered honest, courageous, and serious instead of self-serving.

Like it or not, 9/11 was the dawn of a different world. Realistically, we may be fighting world terrorism for 20 years or even more. To defend ourselves and our allies, we must all be totally prepared and strong, like my generation was in conquering evil in World War II. We were all involved. We all cared. We all had a vested interest. We all had meat rationing and other restrictions. Women took over the factories when our men were fighting the enemy. Because we were together, we won.

Every able-bodied man and woman should serve willingly in the military for two years at age 18, then be in the reserves until age 50. That is the law in Israel, which always has a strong, prepared army. If our entire society was invested in our safety and security, many of the polarized situations politically would be neutralized.

Again, for the past four years, most Americans have been only spectators and critics of the war, but personally involved? Unthinkable. To them I say, "Wake up. If you want freedom, you must be willing to fight for it."

Every American must be involved. Every American must care. Our country cannot fight cheap and win. The world observes and sneers at our stupidity and at our military weakness.

There are those cowards who will scurry away to Canada or elsewhere, but they will be in the minority. To reiterate, if we initiate the draft, never again will it be too little and too late.

22

(February 23, 2007) This is in response to the hornet's nest I stirred up with the most recent "Initiate the draft" commentary. You, Gary Ransone, and others with the same parental knee-jerk reaction, went ballistic at the notion of your child having any military involvement whatsoever. You're right that I did not want MZ to have to fight in Vietnam, but had he been called to serve, he would have gone. The alternative of abandoning his country was unthinkable.

My oldest son Lou served in the U.S. Army for three years, part of it in occupied Germany. My husband Bernard served three years in the Navy in World War 2 and was on his way to help finish off Japan in 1945 when VJ Day happened.

But this is a different world now. Islamic terrorism is real and barbaric, and will not stop, and has permeated every part of the globe, so we must have a strong military which will inhibit and discourage the enemy much more than if we remain weak and vulnerable.

The reaction of those of you who are appalled at the suggestion that we must be militarily strong is always that there are ways to deal with our enemies other than war, but like the far left now in power, they have yet to propose a peaceful solution, or any solution, and meanwhile the enemy becomes stronger.

It's tragic and idiotic that the four-month-old, liberal-led Congress is now busy micro-managing the Iraqi war with their foolish destructive non-binding resolutions which only serve to tell the enemy that we are buckling and about to give up.

So, to Pelosi and Murtha and the others involved in those political shenanigans, I say, "You have probably blown it for 2008, proving you're incapable of true and honest leadership."

To all caring Americans, I say, "Get real."

We are in the midst of fighting for our very existence. If we do not confront the enemy as a nation with a formidable military, we will lose our freedom and everything that is dear to us.

Bullies don't fool with those who are strong and prepared.

Two years of military training and its attending discipline will not hurt your sons and daughters, or my grandchildren and great grandchildren. It will make them stronger and more involved citizens. Only by being together and militarily prepared will we ever hope to overcome this evil and very organized enemy.

23

(March 2, 2007) My recent two commentaries dealt with the suggestion that clearly Islamic terrorism must be dealt with for many years to come. Therefore, the draft should now be resurrected. That news generated strong, sometimes hysterical reaction from some listeners. So let's pursue this issue further.

Foolish me. I took a risk, and thought I was talking to an audience of Americans who were very aware of the present danger to our freedom and way of life and could see that it is OK for each of us to care enough to participate in the preservation of our own national safety. It is wrong to expect a voluntary military to do it all indefinitely for the rest of us. If we were asked to serve in some capacity, I thought most would agree. Guess what – I was initially wrong, and then after a while, I was right.

One proverb keeps haunting me as a reaction to the negative emotion regarding universal military preparedness. "As you sow, so shall you reap." The permissive generations of the past 40 years chose to not discipline their children, to never say no to them, to be overly protective of their emotional well-being, and those parents did a grave disservice to their children, many of whom are now totally self-absorbed and selfish. Even more important, they, the children, were cheated out of the sense of joint responsibility and loyalty.

Many listeners who at first were angry at the mention of the draft thought about it and decided that after all, it would help our nation and our own self-worth to participate in our national military preparedness. And our able-bodied young people would then have a personal reason to love and protect their national home.

Even the man who called a local program and threatened to move to Poland with his son in the event of a draft, I honestly believe would finally agree to stay and participate in our own defense.

By way of emails and voice mails to me and other local programs, this topic has brought up many other creative ways of serving our country. Very appealing, especially to conscientious objectors, are working in forestry, road building, housing for the poor, dealing with pollution, etc. These were mentioned by the same listeners who at first were angry about the draft. Also mentioned was the fairness of a lottery along with the draft.

All of these suggestions are wonderful. And best of all, instead of remaining mildly interested, critical spectators of whatever our elected officials decide to do about terrorism, we all could be personally invested, and we all would be stronger.

The final thought: it is good to be willing to look at and confront unpopular situations which, in the final analysis, bring us together and surely would help to conquer the evil in our midst because in unity, there is strength.

I have a good warm feeling because this has been a moment in time when the best came out of those who confronted their own inner fears, and selves, and responsibility to their fellow Americans prevailed. If we remain on this track instead of being mired in political divisiveness, without a doubt we will eventually conquer the enemy and be safe and home free.

24

(June 9, 2007) Here's a story I received recently regarding the Social Security program. Kudos to my friend Michael Olson for some of the material.

President Franklin Roosevelt, a Democrat, introduced the Social Security FICA program in 1935. It promised the following:

1. That participation in the program would be completely voluntary.

2. That the money the participants elected to put into the program would be deducted from their income for tax purposes each year.
3. That the money the participants put into the Independent Trust Fund rather than the General Operating Fund therefore would only be used to fund the Social Security retirement program and no other governmental program, and finally –
4. That the annuity payments to the retirees would never be taxed as income.

Since many of us have paid into FICA for years and are now receiving a Social Security check each month, we are finding that we are getting taxed 85% of the money we paid to the federal government to put away for us. You may be interested in the following questions.

Which political party took Social Security from the Independent Trust Fund and put it into the General Fund so that Congress could spend it whenever they felt like it? The answer: It was President Lyndon Johnson and the Democratically controlled Congress.

Which political party eliminated the income tax deduction for Social Security FICA withholding? It was the Democratic party.

Which political party started taxing Social Security annuities? The Democratic party, with Al Gore casting the tie-breaking vote as president of the Senate while he was vice president of the U.S. And the Democrats, to this day, continue to raid the trust fund and leave IOUs – which they will repay when Hell freezes over – and they all use that money for their own states' pet projects, like a bridge that goes nowhere.

So let's see, which political party decided to start giving annuity payments to immigrants? Jimmy Carter and the Democratic party. Immigrants moved into this country and at age 65 began to receive Social Security payments. The Democratic party gave these payments to them even though they never paid a dime into it. Why did they do that? For their votes, of course. That's why Democratic politicians are so charitable with our money to all newcomers, so they the politicians can remain in power.

Recently, to add insult to injury, the Democratic Congress began allowing illegals to receive Social Security.

Then, after doing all this lying and thieving, and violating of the original contract of FICA, the Democrats turn around and tell you that the Republicans want to take your Social Security away. The worst part of it is that uninformed citizens believe it.

Do you really want the government to take care of everyone, including 12 million illegals, from the cradle to the grave? What about individual initiative and dignity and self-respect?

Do you really want a Democratic leadership in 2008?

25

(May 21, 2007) About the new Senate immigration Bill, it is very bad. It will change the U.S. security and economy forever.

It is another disastrous amnesty Bill.

It tells the world that anyone can come here illegally, sweat it out for awhile, then become emboldened because our irresponsible leaders give perks and privileges like our Social Security for free, and health care for free, to 12 million illegals. Already these illegals are marching for their "American rights". If this amnesty giveaway is finally voted on by our entire Congress, possibly in five years our no longer sovereign nation may be called Meximerica and our dollars may be called Ameros, and the upcoming super international highway linking the U.S. with Canada and Mexico will make us one country instead of three separate countries.

Amnesty will surely speed up these plans about which our leaders have not consulted We The People.

We must tell Congress that this amnesty bill could finally lose us our country. The Republican party would barely or no longer exist, and the Democrats will make all our decisions, and God help us then.

Wake up, America! Tell the House of Representatives to vote NO on this convoluted, messy bill.

Of course, the American business community loves this bill. They are salivating about the available cheap labor but couldn't care less about the negative effects on our economy.

It's the same problem about our leaders condoning our free trade policy whereby those we trade with are getting stronger, and we are becoming weaker and acquiring bigger and bigger trade deficits.

Final thought: Why is President Bush fighting so desperately to instill democracy in the Middle East, which would be good for the world, while at the same time he is willing to give up our own sovereignty to a tri-country alliance with Mexico and Canada?

Another final thought: The U.S. population is now 300 million, probably not even including the 12 million illegals.

Wouldn't it be wise at this time to put a moratorium on all immigration, both legal and illegal, for the foreseeable future, until such time when we could absorb more people without wrecking the American economy altogether?

26

(June 1, 2007) I am tired and weary of those gullible Americans who are buying into this global guilt trip, saying things like "The world disapproves of United States being belligerent and starting wars with different countries," and "We need to improve our image in the world community," and the arrogant left repeatedly tell us what the American people want.

All that is pure bull pucky.

These complaining righteous countries who sit on their derrieres and beg us for foreign aid and then have the gall to criticize us – what would they do if they were attacked and lost 3,000 innocent citizens? They would probably assume the dead roach position.

The truth is – our country is the most compassionate and the most generous in the world. What other nation, being at war with Germany and Japan, wars that they had initiated, conquered them and then went back and helped them to become robust democratic societies, spending billions of tax dollars to repair their destroyed lands? The answer is.. probably none.

Let's not buy into this type of insidious guilt our enemies here and abroad are using to demoralize and weaken us and our military.

Coincidentally, the following gem floating around underscores my remarks. Here it is:

"A movie called Flags of our Fathers depicted the radio broadcast of Tokyo Rose.

During World War 2, the Japanese developed a way to demoralize the American forces. Psychological warfare experts created a message they felt would work.

They gave the script to their famous broadcaster, Tokyo Rose, and every day she would broadcast the same message – packaged in different ways. These Japanese hoped it would have a negative impact on American GI's morale.

That demoralizing message has three main points:

1. Your president is lying to you.
2. This war is illegal.
3. You cannot win. Does this sound familiar? It is because we are being bombarded by Tokyo Hillary, Tokyo

Harry, Tokyo Teddy, Tokyo Nancy, Tokyo Murtha, etc. They have picked up the same message and are broadcasting it to our troops on Tokyo CNN, Tokyo ABC, Tokyo CBS, Tokyo NBC, etc.

The only difference is that they claim to support our troops before they demoralize them. They believe the lies are okay because the end will justify the means. That's why the liberal Left lies so much.

27

(July 27, 2007) Why the Fairness Doctrine is Anything but Fair

Legislation is currently before Congress that would reinstate an FCC policy known outright as the "Fairness Doctrine". It is being sponsored in both the Senate and the House by the Democrats, who are determined to resurrect this foolish and unfair law.

It would codify a 1949 FCC regulation that once required broadcasters to afford reasonable opportunity for the discussion of conflicting views of public importance.

The Fairness Doctrine was overturned by the FCC in 1987. The FCC discarded the rule because, contrary to its purpose, it failed to encourage the discussion of more controversial issues.

The American Left is totally comfortable with the current politically unbalanced liberal media, that is, the print media and much of the radio and TV media excepting for Fox news. Newspapers, magazines, and TV like ABC, NBC, CBS, and CNN deal primarily with concerns and opinions of the Democrats and omit opinions and issues of concern to the Republicans.

The Democrats are uncomfortable with successful radio news talk programs, like Rush Limbaugh's and those of numerous other conservative radio talk hosts, and radio is primarily the one media outlet which the conservatives have. The liberals failed in radio because they whined and complained about everything, and never presented solutions. Their conversation was toxic.

The only way the Fairness Doctrine could be fair would be if the conservatives would also be given the right to respond in print to newspaper stories and give radio and TV responses to liberal news interpretations. But that will never happen.

Clearly, the Democrats want to reinstate the Fairness Doctrine so that they can control any opposition from the conservatives by receiving equal time on all conservative programs.

One wonders why the liberals are always threatened by different points of view. Can it be that their opinions are often impractical, illogical, or unable to withstand scrutiny?

It is rightfully argued that the Fairness Doctrine can interfere with the First Amendment. And my hope is that despite the Democrats' desire to reinstate the Fairness Doctrine, this one-sided politically conceived law will be voted down because it is unfair.

28

(August 30, 2007) Sanctuary cities in the U.S.? Where illegals and other lawbreakers are allowed to live freely, receiving many freebies that legal Americans do not get? Where breaking our national laws is okay, and our leaders condone this? Bullpuckie. Suppose every city in the United States decided to become a sanctuary city.

This is sheer insanity. It's time for We The People to rise up against President Bush, whom I supported in the past, whom I'm so disappointed in now, who continues to leave our borders open, who by his actions is dissolving our country's sovereignty without our approval, and who is working diligently to connect us with Mexico and Canada, and to construct an international highway linking the three countries, with toll roads which some other countries will own on our land.

We The People never ever were consulted, unless we were connected to some international corporations. Never – I repeat, never – would we give up the sovereignty of our U.S. and replace it with being accountable to Mexico and Canada or any other entity.

Tell your congressional representatives who never got to vote on this issue that we were against that sneaky outrageous plan called The North American Union.

It appears that within the last few days, when President Bush received close to 200,000 protests against the North American Union, his only response was that he was amused. He intends to double-cross us into liking this as a good thing for our country just like Clinton pushed through NAFTA which has made other countries richer but not us.

If we don't make noise now, we will forever lose our beloved country as our original lawmakers created it. Some higher-ups in the government have figured out a way to bypass the American citizens' votes by creating commissions and appointed groups to make all the decisions for us.

This is not acceptable. Once again, We The People must now rise up and say "NO NO, NO North American Union to supersede our own sovereignty"

Mr. President, you were duly elected, and now you are acting like a dictator. That's not acceptable. Mr. President, are you out of your mind? Clearly, big corporations with which you must be connected, and their profits, must be more important to you than the sovereignty of our country. You have betrayed us.

29

(November 24, 2007) It has been several months since I have been able to comment on KSCO. Since last August, I have had two spinal operations. The first was a failure. The second was a success. So I am very grateful, and I am recuperating nicely, and learning to walk again, and I am deeply humbled and grateful for all who have prayed for my recovery. Thank you very much.

Something blessed also happened to leave me awed as a patient while at Dominican Hospital.

The people who care for patients personally are not wealthy, and I have asked most of them why they chose this profession, and all said they love people and want to help them get well. I see them as angels sent from God. So thanks to them for making my three weeks after surgery so loving and comfortable. And, thanks to Dominican Hospital. I highly recommend them to anyone who must spend time in a hospital facility. Dominican is indeed a Class A facility.

Now, let's talk about an issue which most Americans think about – Social Security. Political leaders stay away from that subject because through the years Social Security, as originally created by Franklin Delano Roosevelt in 1935, has been hijacked by the Democrats. For example, FDR said that participation in the program would be voluntary, and that the money the participants put into the Independent Trust Fund rather than into the General Operating Fund would only be used to fund the Social Security retirement program and no other government program, and that the annuity payments to the retirees would never be taxed as income. You may be interested in the following tidbits:

1. Which political party took money from the Independent Trust Fund and put it into the General Fund so that Congress could use it, which they have been doing abundantly, for things like the bridges that go nowhere? It was Lyndon Johnson and the Democratically-controlled House and Senate who can take credit for that thievery.
2. Which political party started taxing Social Security annuities, at the rate of 85%? The Democratic party, with Al Gore

casting the tie-breaking deciding vote as president of the Senate while he was vice president of the U.S.

This is my favorite: which political party decided to give annuity payments to immigrants? That's right – Jimmy Carter and the Democratic Party. Immigrants moved into this country and at age 65 began to receive Social Security payments.

The Democratic Party gave these payments to them even though they never put a dime into the system. Why? For their votes, of course.

Then, after doing all this lying and thievery, Democrats tell you that the Republicans want to take your Social Security away, and uninformed citizens believe it.

So, think about it – will you still vote for the Democrats – and God forbid, Hillary – in 2008?

30

It is really time for Hillary to leave the political arena. Besides her being a pathological liar, the country and the world have already had enough of the Clintons.

Only those like the Clintons, with enormous arrogance, continue to discard the judgment of the voting public. The Clintons should, but won't, go gracefully and quietly. Didn't Bill embarrass our country enough for so many years?

About sanctuary cities ignoring the federal laws, it is bewildering that they exist.

What justifies an American city picking and choosing which federal laws they agree with and which they reject?

Sanctuary cities created themselves to shelter illegals.

Presently there are probably close to 21 million illegals here in the U.S., many receiving perks that anger American citizens, especially those new Americans who endured the lengthy process to become legal.

Those people feel penalized and cheated because among other things the illegals are being offered free education and possibly Social Security, which they never paid into.

The message to those who cross our borders illegally is that they will be rewarded. Most may be good people who want to find a better life for themselves and their families, but allowing them to do so illegally makes our laws a farce.

How many sanctuary cities are in the U.S.? New York City is one, for sure. Chicago is probably another. And, maybe even Washington D.C. And many others.

If thousands of cities become sanctuary havens, sheltering illegals, they undermine our federal government. And, doesn't federal law supersede state law?

Our past four or five presidents deliberately allowed our borders to remain open. So, what about our sovereign country and what about those presidents' agendas? Our forefathers would be heartsick to see our leaders giving up our sovereignty for globalization.

Whatever the pundits with vested interests say, we will be weaker while other nations become stronger.

And now, because it is timely, and floating about, author unknown, let's listen to 15 ways to be a good Democrat.

First, you have to be against capital punishment, but support abortion on demand.

Then, you have to believe that businesses create oppression and governments create prosperity.

You also have to believe that guns in the hands of law-abiding citizens are more of a threat than nuclear weapon technology in the hands of Chinese and North Korean communists.

If you want to be a good Democrat, you have to believe that global temperatures are more affected by soccer moms driving SUVs than by scientifically documented cyclical changes in the earth's climate.

You also have to believe that gender roles are artificial, but that being homosexual is natural.

Also, to be a good Democrat, you have to believe that the AIDS virus is spread by a lack of federal funding.

Then, you also have to believe, if you are a good Democrat, that the same teacher who can't teach fourth graders how to read is somehow qualified to teach those same kids about sex.

You also have to believe that self-esteem is more important than actually doing something to earn it.

And again, you have to believe that the National Rifle Association is bad because it supports certain parts of our constitution, while the ACLU is good because it supports certain parts of the Russian communist constitution.

You also have to believe that Hillary Clinton is normal and a very nice person who lies all the time but cannot help it.

Also, to be a good Democrat, you have to believe that conservatives telling the truth sometimes belong in jail, but a liar and one who is obsessed with sex belong in the White House.

You have to also believe that illegal Democratic party funding by the Chinese government is somehow in the best interests of the United States.

And, finally, if you are a good Democrat, you have to believe that this message is part of a vast right-wing conspiracy.

31

(April 6, 2008) About my most recent commentary – some listeners were unhappy with a few of the descriptions in the piece entitled “How to be a good Democrat”.

I am changing the title to more accurate and calling it “How to be a fanatic, extreme, or unreasonable Democrat.”

I am truly sorry if I offended or caused pain to anyone for the following section: “To be a good Democrat, you must believe that gender roles are artificial but being homosexual is natural.”

I don’t really know if being homosexual is natural or not, and I don’t really care. As a mother, I have thought that if I had a child who was a homosexual, which I don’t, I would still love my child dearly, but my heart would ache knowing that dealing with our present society mores, life would be more difficult for my child. I believe that whatever their lifestyle, many people are decent and wonderful humans beings.

There are, however, two things about that lifestyle which I cannot respect or agree to:

#1 The parades that some homosexuals participate in hurt their image and their cause, which is “demanding to be accepted.” One cannot demand acceptance; that comes only with respect and integrity.

#2 Their insistence that a union between two men or two women should be considered legally a marriage. It can never be considered a marriage because God created the union between one man and one woman, which is called a marriage, and that must never be tampered with.

I further believe that a union between two men or two women should be legally accepted with a title of “legal union,” or something similar, with the same rights as a marriage.

32

(June 17, 2008) Recently I attended a Flag Day celebration to honor American veterans from World War II, Korea, and Vietnam. The ceremony was touching, and it was beautiful to see their pride when each veteran got up and said a few words.

The program opened with a young girl singing God Bless America, and she concluded the ceremony with the Star Spangled Banner. When the words "The land of the free, and the home of the brave" were sung, my eyes filled with uncontrollable tears.

Because I'm bummed out, because there is this gut feeling that We the People are losing our beloved country.

Our president and our congress, without our knowledge and approval, are giving away our nation as it was planned by our forefathers. We are, and still should be, a sovereign nation beholden to no one, but there are changes ahead.

Effectively, our borders with Canada and Mexico will be erased.

They call it globalization. But we never voted on this change. We have been betrayed by our leaders.

We are in the process of becoming an alliance with Mexico and Canada called the North American Union. Our nation and our wishes eventually will become subordinate to the union, and as we speak, the international superhighway is already becoming a reality, where certain other countries will be bidding to buy portions of the highway, and they will institute tolls to make money for themselves. We the People never approved this.

How do you feel about other countries owning part of the U.S.? Why weren't we consulted? Now it is clear why President Bush broke our laws by leaving the borders open deliberately all these years. It's because he's a globalist who wants to enlarge NAFTA, which has been a disaster for the U.S., but good for the other countries involved.

What can we do to stop this abomination? Undoubtedly, the greed of a few powerful people who stand to benefit from this sneaky alliance is involved. And the kicker is that the despicable, corrupt United Nations intends to be in charge of the North American Union, and eventually, in charge of the world. It's insane, and we are allowing it to happen. How can we stop this takeover?

33

(June 26, 2008) Pretty soon, We the People will be voting for the political party which will lead us for the next four, or eight, years.

The outcome is crucial.

Do we want big government, or small government?

When Clinton's big government was in charge, he got rid of most of the military, as Obama will probably do. Obama will raise taxes, and continue to expand social welfare so that the weaker – or less motivated to work – can be taken care of.

Without going further, let's all agree that no matter which party is in power, the elderly, handicapped, and the truly needy should always be helped unconditionally.

I would like to focus on the moral changes where citizens in big government know that no matter what, the government will take care of them. That attitude is morally destructive, and it produces physical and mental weaklings.

It takes away self dignity and self respect.

Clearly the liberals in office like big government because of the enormous and powerful perks that it has for them. Those who receive welfare vote for the liberals to remain in office because liberals are their saviors.

But those gullible dependants are trading in their own pride and self-respect for government security. How sad.

Less government is best because every able-bodied American must be responsible for himself, or herself, and the pride and dignity maintained is a million times more valuable than big government handouts.

Currently we see the moral decay taking place in Gloucester, Massachusetts, where 17 girls from age 15 through 17 have chosen to become pregnant and are proud of it. Where is the shame? Why the proud arrogance?

These girls plan to raise their children together. Who will pay the expenses? It will not be their parents who did not give them the moral parameters and backbone to abstain.

Since big government via social welfare has gladly given other young unmarried mothers free apartments and free money, their parents have been off the hook. That is because We the People are supporting the delinquency. What's to worry? I think the situation stinks.

When high schools are providing nurseries for the loose teenage mothers so they can stay in class and have other schoolmates envy them, while the government picks up the tab, society is condoning something terribly wrong.

Our once proud and responsible country is going into the sewer, all of which is the fault of big government — or Big Daddy.

That reason alone underscores why these misguided, shameless girls and parents prove we must vote for small government, and that means John McCain.

He is not the perfect choice offered, but he is infinitely better than Obama, who is a carefully chosen, extremely liberal puppet who is not running the show. The fact that he is black is a plus for our democracy, but I believe, like good wine, he has not yet mellowed enough to lead the nation.

34

(August 6, 2008) There is much justified concern about the Social Security system possibly not existing in the foreseeable future for those who have been putting into the system for many years.

It is a national disgrace that members of our Congress have been raiding the system. Arbitrarily, they chose to take money out of the Social Security fund, which was specifically set up for those who were paying into the system with the expectation of receiving monthly payments starting at age 65.

Congress ignored the rules and transferred that fund into the General Fund so that they could help themselves to millions of dollars for projects in their own constituencies, often ridiculous projects.

For many years, they have taken the money and left instead IOUs.

Now those leaders are crying crocodile tears because the Social Security funds are almost gone, and the system will be broke in the near future.

The congressional thieves are totally responsible and should be forced to put back what they stole, from their own personal bloated salaries and pensions.

Will it happen? Of course not. We the People, as usual, will pick up the tab because Social Security must continue to exist for all those Americans who, in good faith, trusted the government with their money.

Isn't it way past time to have term limits in Congress? Presidents and vice presidents have term limits. There are too many scoundrels who make being in Congress a lifetime job.

Their own foolish constituents continue to vote them into office, thinking that their experience makes them valuable. Bull pucky!

It is the opposite. The longer they remain in Congress, the more entrenched, cockier, and more corrupt they become.

A two-year term is adequate. After that, they become callous and sneak in earmarks. Term limits for Congress should be a priority, but it will never happen unless We the People demand it.

35

One could submit that political correctness, born in the late 1970s, is alive and well and has been destructive to our society. It has traveled to the European countries where, because of the pre-existing elitism there, it took hold rapidly.

I believe most of Europe, minus Britain – and possibly other countries where there is still hope, though they are rapidly being invaded by an extreme religion called Islam – is lost as a world democratic partner.

Europe stands back and criticizes all the great efforts that we attempt in the name of world humanity, and Europe criticizes and dislikes us and does little or nothing in the name of democracy and world peace. They are only interested in protecting their own fannies. They send troops to Iraq and Afghanistan, a token amount, but not for combat.

Because of political correctness, historical happenings are being assaulted Big-Time. In England, for example, the Holocaust has been eliminated from history textbooks because it was so barbaric. Despite that, the Holocaust still destroyed millions of innocent lives. Not only has world media been corrupted and become political, but history no longer is authentic or honest.

Very recently, George Archibald wrote in the still credible Washington Times that social studies textbooks in elementary and secondary schools are mostly a disgrace, that in the name of political correctness and multiculturalism, there is failure to give students a true account of American history. Academic historians and educational advocates agree.

It is insane, but going back to the 1970s, textbook publishers and teachers said "Do not cast adverse reflections on any gender, race, ethnicity, religion, or cultural group."

Publishers added further anti-bias guidelines which banned words, phrases, images, and depictions of people deemed unacceptable such as the words man, mankind, manpower, and men – said to be sexist. Also banned are: able-bodied, aged, babe, backward, chic, fairy, geezer, idiot, imbecile, redskin, sissy, and waitress."

This is so foolish. And doesn't this nonsense make our children weak and sensitive wimps who will never learn honest history?

Kudos to Joseph Terranco for shedding light on the despicable, deliberate attack on the authenticity of true historical facts in children's textbooks. Our younger generation is being misled, and we can no longer trust history. Will it be lost forever?

36

(September 25, 2008) With regard to the relationship between We the People and our national government – we have become estranged. We the People dropped the ball because our government had slowly learned to dumb us down with distractions like little emergencies.

Like pesticides and chemicals in our food and water sources, toxic spraying, flu shots and vaccines, fluoride in our drinking water.

They do that so they can do whatever they want without our involvement or interference.

You know the analogy of putting a live lobster in a pot of cold water on the stove, turn the heat up gradually, and by the time the lobster realizes it, he is being boiled to death, and it is too late.

So, our scoundrel leaders, led by our President George Bush, illegally kept our borders open these last eight years, was hell-bent to get our country involved in making us part of the new world government. He never bothered to consult us or let us know to decide whether all of us liked the idea of subordinating our country or giving up our own sovereignty to become part of the forthcoming three-way alliance with Canada and Mexico. The latter is a corrupt, trouble-filled country who leaches on us regularly and sends their criminals and unsavory citizens to come here illegally. Yet if we enter Mexico illegally, we may be put in jail.

I must say at this juncture that the Mexicans that come to our country legally are some of the most wonderful people that I have ever met.

Why in our right mind would we want that coalition as a pathway to the alliance with other countries, all led by the miserable corrupt United Nations? Why would we want to be a party to such a coalition?

Our leaders are betraying us, and somehow we must put a stop to this abomination.

Go to your computer and Google the North American Free Trade Agreement, and see what you think.

Let's hope it is not too late.

A different pressing issue – ten years ago, my husband and I entrusted AIG with a large portion of our hard-earned money. AIG has betrayed us, and I am in danger of losing a large part of that money.

Now those greedy skunks want We the People to bail them out for many billions, no questions asked, and with the same people still in charge, and the irony of it is my answer would be "Hell no! Not on those terms."

37

The sad current fact is that there no longer is a true media in this country. The news that We the People are getting is no longer honest and balanced. It is a planned liberal machine now committed to making Barack Obama president. And it furthers the motto of leftist extremists, which is "The end always justifies the means, no matter what."

The McCain campaign is barely covered, and then mostly to ridicule Sarah Palin. The public is not getting the real truth. The deck is stacked.

Obama never held an executive job in his life. As a member of the Illinois Senate, he voted "present" – but not "yes" or "no" – over 100 times.

As president, who must make clear, often fast decisions, Obama would be a dismal failure. He cannot make quick decisions.

Please, listen to this urgent request by Tom Winter, president and editor in chief of Human Events, a credible conservative Washington D.C. weekly.

Dear Conservative Friends, They say the truth hurts – in Obama's case, it is devastating. Not surprisingly, the BIG media has kept the American public blind to the truth about Obama including: The fact that a corrupt Chicago machine politician "made a U.S. Senator out of Barack Obama". How Obama won his first election by having his lawyers knock all his opponents off the ballot on technicalities – a great tool for shady lawyers – and this guy really plays hardball. Obama's support for a grotesque "infanticide" law which was even too extreme for Nancy Pelosi. The Tony Rezko connection "I have never done any favors for him", says Obama, about convicted developer Tony Rezko. Oh, but yes he has. Then, Obama's connection to ACORN, the ultra liberal tough organization, which started many years ago with good intentions and which supposedly bullied banks recently to make subprime loans to unqualified people. And, Obama's wife's salary tripled the year he became Senator and started earmarking funds to her employer. Then, Obama has repeatedly steered legislation to pay off campaign donors. And, there is much much more about Obama which has been carefully hidden.

Tom Winter and his Human Events Weekly want to expose the many skeletons in Obama's closet by sending, specifically to young people, especially those on college campuses, the editorial supplement called "The Truth About Obama, what every citizen needs to know."

He focuses on college campuses because liberal educators fill their students with liberal beliefs only. And 85% of professors hired for the University of California are liberals.

We the People should be grateful to Tom Winter for his passion in trying to let the public – and especially the young college students – know the truth. Kudos to you, Tom Winter.

Because Human Events is struggling financially, if you want to help, or even just buy a copy of The Truth About Obama, call 1-888-467-4448, repeat, 1-888-467-4448.

These are critical times in our country. We must not allow these BIG MEDIA LYING SCOUNDRELS and liberal college professors to succeed in placing one of the most extremely liberal and most inexperienced candidates ever in the White House.

Just like the swift boat exposure of John Kerry in 2004, The Truth About Obama, even at this late stage in the campaign, could stop his victory.

38

(November 2008) This is an open letter to our president-elect.

Without a doubt, many Americans are reflecting on the elections and how it all worked itself out.

Our country is ill, and we are apprehensive and worried – for numerous reasons.

The wonderful thing about this beautiful nation is that we can be passionate about our wishes and feelings, and can freely express our thoughts, and then have a say in choosing our leader.

We the People have spoken, and you will be our president for the foreseeable future.

I for one acknowledge that you are my president and hope that you will lead us in as democratic a manner as we have been accustomed to since the inception of our country.

I sincerely hope you will surround yourself with thoughtful people to help you understand what must be done to heal our nation.

There have been voting irregularities, which have not been dealt with yet, and from your handlers some very troublesome actions which you must not allow to happen again. We must remain a free country, and if you change it, we will rise up against you.

In point of fact, when Joe the Plumber asked you a perfectly normal respectable question, your staff within 24 hours scrutinized his life by way of the FBI hoping to diminish him as an example to not ask the president uncomfortable questions.

That is not the American way It was despicable.

These tactics will not work in our democracy, so please don't let it happen again.

To end on a happy note, to me, with emotional tears, the highlight of the election evening was to see you and your beautiful family come out and rejoice with our nation in finally having a black president. It was a wonderful historic moment.

President-elect Barack Obama, please don't blow it.

39

(February 13, 2009) Madame House Speaker Nancy Pelosi may have been rightfully outraged along with the rest of us when those CEOs of auto manufacturers came to Washington DC recently in their private jets and then had the gall to ask for public help for their troubled companies.

On the other hand, Madame Pelosi was not happy with the small private jet that comes with her own job.

Some Speakers accept the jet, and others, like Newt Gingrich, do not. Pelosi was aggravated because this little jet had to stop to refuel, so instead she ordered a big fat 200-seat jet that could get her back home to California every week without stopping.

In these bad times, what is wrong with her taking a first class, nonstop flight in a commercial jet? Both planes land in the same airport in San Francisco.

She only works three days a week, and this gas guzzling jet gets fueled and she flies home to California at the cost of $60,000 one way.

As Joe puts it – and Joe must be loose mouth VP Joe Biden – "Unfortunately, we must pay to bring her back on Monday night." The cost to We the People is another $60,000.

That means $120,000 per week to transfer Nancy from home to work. Folks – that is $480,000 per month, and times 12, it is $5,760,000 per year for Madame Pelosi – the leader of the most do-nothing Congress in the history of our country.

Nancy asks you and me to conserve our carbon footprints and wants the rest of us to buy small cars and ride bicycles. Is she really worth it? She also gets a hefty salary, a hefty pension, and special health insurance that you and I do not have access to.

Notice how difficult it has been for some of Obama's Cabinet and Congress to remember to pay their own private income taxes, but how easy for them to plan to spend billions (with a B) as we speak – billions which we do not have, which we must print, and which our new leaders cannot promise will do our country any good.

Is it possible that our new leaders are being dangerously irresponsible?

40

(November 30, 2005) Local attorney Gil Stein wrote a letter to the Sentinel recently saying that anti-Semitism is alive and well at UCSC. The Sentinel, on November 18th, also reported that anti-Semitism is increasing on college campuses throughout the country. How is this possible in institutions of higher learning, where parents of college students pay as much as $100,000 for four years so their children can become educated, fair-thinking members of society?

Because Gil Stein's letter is very worrisome, I will repeat portions of the letter along with my own thoughts so that many others in this area can be made aware of the ugly situation, which, if not confronted, will escalate just as it did in Germany in the early 1930s. Please listen, then register your outrage with the local Chancellor and those irresponsible members of the faculty. Remember: when good people remain silent and do nothing, bad things happen and evil takes hold. It's called "The Sin of Omission."

Gil's letter refers only to this campus where anti-Israeli faculty and students intimidate Jewish students who express support for Israel. You won't believe the following, but it's true: tenured professor Nancy Stoller, who teaches at this campus, was caught red-handed removing flyers posted by pro-Israel students. This incident happened last year, but the then Chancellor just looked the other way. Pro-Palestinian speakers receive University sponsorship while pro-Israeli speakers are denied sponsorships by those same departments. The University promotes diversity, but not diversity with which they disagree. This policy of looking the other way when certain speakers spout racist venom needs to stop! Academic freedom should not be a cover for bigotry. All campuses should also be open to speakers who do not represent the views of the 'politically correct.'

Kudos to Gil Stein for uncovering this ugliness. I say shame on the biased and gutless faculty and leaders who encourage prejudice to fester in places of higher learning. 'We the People' must vigorously protest to those accountable. Our publically financed universities must no longer become institutions of hate and selective discrimination.

41

(May 2, 2004) John Leo, prolific writer for U.S. News and World Report, calls it "a really ugly shade of green." I call it political correctness gone mentally haywire. Here's the story.

The Sierra Club leadership, preparing for its upcoming club elections, is blasting irresponsible accusations at three individuals with respectable credentials who are running for office as Sierra Club directors. They are Dick Lamb, former Democratic governor of Colorado, Frank Morris, former Executive Director of the Congressional Black Caucus, and David Pimentel, Cornel University professor of entomology, who has been studying the impact of population growth on the Earth's carrying capacity. The platform of this threesome is to limit immigration to protect the world environment. Protecting the global environment has been the mission statement of the Sierra Club since its inception more than 30 years ago. What is bewildering now, according to Leo, is that since 1996, the Sierra Club has backed away from its initial aim and instead it has adopted an opposite policy of neutrality on the problem of immigration. As a result of its current views, Sierra Club leaders are attacking these candidates for directors, calling them environmental racists, neo-Nazis and right-wing extremists. Governor Lamb responds to these verbal assaults, calling it environmental McCarthyism. The situation is very ugly.

One wonders what could be the reasons for the Sierra Club's total about-face on population control, which for many years has been the reason for its very existence. I believe the answer is that the Sierra Club now feels it is politically incorrect to place any restrictions whatsoever on fellow human beings. They want a level playing field for everyone in every aspect of life, despite any negative consequences to our own country.

The leftists, who are the architects of political correctness, and have been for four decades, have brainwashed astonishing numbers of American, most of Europe, and certainly a large part of Canada, where (and you will find this hard to believe) an anti-free-speech measure called bill C250 is on the brink of becoming Canadian law. Among other hard-to-believe oppressive provisions of bill C250, it will impose punishment and fines for those who voice any derogatory allusions to the gay or lesbian lifestyle. So much for free speech and rational thinking in Canada. Are we all lemmings, afraid to speak out about the crazy p.c. nonsense? Granted, we are unable to control gullible Canada and gullible Europe, but as Americans, we must stop the apathy and intimidation here at home. Those of us with our self-respect still intact must vigorously reject the destructiveness of political correctness. Please, let us reclaim our backbone and find our way back to being "the land of the free and the home of the brave."

42

(October 13, 2003) Your right to choose supplements is under attack. Senate bill 722 will be voted upon shortly. If it passes, it will threaten the freedom choice for every citizen of our country. This issue was discussed on a recent KSCO Saturday Special, but because of its seriousness and urgency, we feel this information must be exposed to as many people as possible, and our signal can be heard over one-third of California. Clearly, the pharmaceutical industry is feeling the impact of people making decisions about their own health. More and more of us are choosing nutriceuticals – that is, natural vitamins, minerals, and herbs – for healing and health maintenance in lieu of prescription drugs, which are often toxic and very expensive, and often the negative side effects of the drug are worse than enduring the ailment.

Since the 1920s, the pharmaceutical companies gradually have become very powerful and very rich. Surely, they are the architects of SB 722, which if it passes will significantly undermine health freedoms we now take for granted. This oppressive and sinister bill states that manufacturers of health products would have to submit to the Food and Drug Administration reports of any adverse reaction to any product. Furthermore, if even one consumer called and said, for example, that vitamin B complex gave him a stomachache, the FDA could ban the sale of all B vitamins. Even worse, it would not be possible to check the validity of these voluntary complaints. Further, if even one product is singled out for even one complaint, the FDA might have the power to remove entire classes of supplements from the market. Pretty scary and pretty outrageous, right?

Putting it bluntly, it looks like the pharmaceutical industry wants to crush the nutriceutical industry, render it impotent, then move in and take it on for themselves.

Isn't it ironic that the toxicity in some prescription drugs takes the lives of over 100,000 Americans every year, but seldom are those drugs removed from the marketplace despite their known danger to health? After their initial testing and approval to market their products, there is almost zero accountability from the pharmaceutical companies.

Are you beginning to smell some political hanky-panky and some expensive involvement from lobbyists? If SB 722 passes, products which have been used safely for many decades will be scrutinized and made subject to the arbitrary discretion of the FDA.

Suppose you take a nutritional supplement, say glucosamine, because it helps you maintain bone and joint health. Perhaps certain plant nutrients help you maintain a reasonable cholesterol level, which you would choose instead of the drug Lipitor, which is known to create serious side effects but makes millions for the pharmaceutical companies and so, still remains on the market. If SB 722 is passed, the nutrients you depend upon may be taken away from you.

Now, here is the kicker. Contact our Senator Dianne Feinstein. She is the co-sponsor of this onerous political bill, which, if passed, might lead to further legislation requiring you to obtain a doctor's prescription for any dietary supplement. Why is she doing this to us? Can it be that she has a vested interest in the pharmaceutical companies and is possibly leaving the Senate and has nothing left to lose? Nevertheless, register your outrage. Call the Capitol Hill switchboard at (202) 224-3121. Again, that is (202) 224-3121. Ask to speak to Senator Feinstein's office. Then, ask to speak with a staff member in charge of health issues. Or, access the internet, visit www.cong ress.org, enter your zip code, and proceed from there. We are asking our own senator to vote against a bill which she has cosponsored. Dianne Feinstein was elected senator to work for the good of all Californians. Instead, she chose to go with special interests and betray the rest of us. Is this grotesque or what?

43

(October 28, 2004) This is an open letter to reasonable liberals. From a Democratic memo, recent media reports warn that if the two Johns lose the election, even by a large margin, an ugly fight may ensue. The Democrats announced that they have 10,000 lawyers ready to scrutinize voting records in every voting precinct in the country. The reason for this nationwide probable quagmire is to search out Republican shenanigans. The Republicans have their contingent of lawyers ready to check out voting irregularities too, but they do not threaten similar action unless they lose by a large margin. This is disturbing. Liberal extremists know all about political shenanigans. They approved the Michael Moore documentary filled with half truths and lies, which has been shown in theaters around the country unrestricted. Now those same liberals are threatening some of the same theater owners with property destruction if they show a documentary response exposing John Kerry. Some of these bullied theater owners are backing off. The situation becomes even uglier. Liberal extremists have highjacked the Democratic party with Kerry's approval, rationalizing that the end always justifies the means – no matter how dirty.

Remember during the 2000 presidential campaign when then Vice President Al Gore engineered the plan of registering illegals to vote through drive-by precincts, no questions asked? Thousands of illegals cast their votes Democratic, and Gore still lost. He probably never even won the popular vote. He spent the next three and a half years crying foul along with many other sore loser Democrats.

Desperate now, the Kerry group is calling the president a liar and worse, using scare tactics. They want to win so badly that they are willing to do anything, all of which could backfire. Sadly for them, the two wannabes, Kerry and Edwards, are not leaders. Kerry equates global terrorism with someday becoming a mere nuisance. Dream on. Is this the kind of leadership we need or want for the next four years, and do we want Teresa Heinz Kerry to be our First Lady?

This time around, reasonable, clear-thinking, honest Democrats should distance themselves from this ilk and vote either Republican or Libertarian, precisely to preserve the future integrity of the once proud and honest Democratic party.

44

(October 28, 2004) This one is called "It All Doesn't Make Any Sense."

Putting it bluntly, it is mind-boggling that perhaps half of the voters are willing to discard President Bush in favor of John Kerry. How can so many people get snookered by a man whose dismal 20year record in Congress shows that he hates the military and voted against almost every issue to strengthen the military? How is it possible that any citizen would feel comfortable with Kerry becoming Commander in Chief?

President Bush knew instantly and decisively that 9/11 had changed our world forever. Bush has proven that he has courage and conviction, and his decisions have kept our country free of terrorist acts since that fateful day. Kerry, even after three years, still has a pre-9/11 mindset. He looks to the corrupt United Nations to make our decisions. He doesn't get it. How is it possible that half the electorate is willing to take a risk on a proven lightweight empty suit who describes his Monday morning quarterback plans but does not explain how to implement those plans, almost all of which he borrows from the present administration?

He signed up to serve in Vietnam for one year, then changed his mind after only four months and asked to be released from his military commitment to run for Congress instead. If it was really true that he left Vietnam eight months early because of serous battle injuries, why then is he not willing to make his medical records public? Think about it. And what serious, thinking person would choose to replace Laura Bush, our gracious and bright First Lady, with Teresa Heinz Kerry, a crude and arrogant loose cannon, who along with her husband Kerry, denounces outsourcing while, at the same time, does outsource at least 50 of her own Heinz factories around the world.

45

(October 18, 2003) In 1771, Samuel Adams wrote in the Boston Gazette, "Power makes men wanton – it intoxicates the mind; and unless those with whom the power is entrusted are carefully watched, such men will not govern the people, according to the known laws of the state."

It is clear that our county lawmakers are not being carefully watched, for while we have entrusted them with making laws and decisions which should benefit the people first and foremost, they benefit themselves!

The County Administrative officer, called the CAO, sets yearly salaries for herself, the Board of Supervisors and other county employees. This is like the fox minding the chicken coop.

Soon, this CAO will be giving herself a 30% plus raise to approximately $191,000 per year, while the Vice President of the United States receives approximately $170,000 per year. This, plus hefty pension plans, Social Security, bonuses and other perks. Each supervisor will also receive a 30% plus raise, and benefits to approximately $98,000 – all for attending about 35 meetings per year. Assistants do most of the gruntwork for them, and bring them up to date on agenda issues. By contrast, San Francisco supervisors receive $36,000 a year, not $98,000.

These lawmakers tell us that we are facing serous budget deficits, so now they are cutting needed aid to the poor, the elderly, the mentally and physically ill, and the handicapped. What happened to the supposed budget surplus of the $21 million we had only four months ago?

The stroke center budget has been cut. Also, the center for independent living, which helps wheelchair-bound, handicapped and convalescent people to become self reliant. The latest outrage is that county managers want the supervisors to make 33% cuts to the medically indigent, who do not have any insurance. Bottom line, no more preventive care for the poor.

To Susan Mauriello, CAO, and to each of the supervisors I say, "In the face of these hardships, to so many constituents, who trust you for protection and guidance and wisdom, how dare you plan to give yourselves 30% plus raises? Or any raises? You have given yourselves too much already, with your lifetime benefits and perks! Your greed and callousness are irresponsible and unforgivable! You all deserve to be ousted from your cushy, bureaucratic jobs!"

Recently, for one brief moment, Wormhoudt suggested to her colleagues that maybe they should forego the 30% plus raise, but that idea went over like a lead balloon. Jeff Almquist, poor baby, said that he needs that raise for his son's college tuition. Wormhoudt could have refused her raised, but she didn't. Heck, she made her gesture and that was enough. Oh yes, she served on the Santa Cruz City Council for umpteen years and now she is running for a third term as supervisor. So much for career politicians and term limits. But that's another story.

How do We the People stop these unconscionable excesses?

We could do what California state voters did in 1990. They became fed up with lawmakers abuses, so they crafted an initiative which created a panel of citizens, not state employees, who meet yearly to set lawmakers salaries from the governor on down. It was put on the ballot, passed easily and is now law.

Because of budget constraints, for the past six years, no state salary increases have been approved. That panel is the California Citizens Compensation Commission and the Chairman is Claude Brinegar.

While it is too late for this November election, we could prepare an initiative for an upcoming election. If you would like to be involved, call KSCO at 831-475-1080 and leave your name and phone number.

KSCO will be happy to provide free airtime to help solve this issue of lawmakers' greed.

Once again, kudos to those who spend many hours to decipher obscure, convoluted county budgets, gathering financial facts for this editorial. They are Steve Hartman, Bob Suhr, Ed Mazenko, Harold Griffith, and Mike Schmidt – all heroic seekers for honesty and truth in government.

Let us not forget the powerful tool We the People have in the initiative process. It is the one way left for citizens in a free society to make right that which is wrong.

46

(April 13, 2007) Let's call this Random Thoughts.

One must believe that the liberal Left in Congress is so intoxicated with its newly achieved power that they're making reckless decisions. They are killing their chances of taking political control in 2008.

To micro-manage the war in Iraq and demand to bring the troops home on a specific date, regardless of the opposite opinions of the American military commanders in Iraq, could be political suicide for Pelosi and her friends.

They are so drenched with hatred for President Bush and the administration that they are acting irrationally.

These irresponsible edicts are tied to a law to approve getting supplies to the troops quickly, which now will be held up by the president's sure veto. Are Pelosi and Murth, et al., so bent on going on record for us to deliberately lose in Iraq? The answer is yes.

Suppose they prevail and bring our 100,000+ troops home when many of the troops would rather stay and try to win in Iraq. What then will happen? Surely Iran will take over in Iraq.

What about the billions of dollars of pork in the bill to appease many Democrats in order to obtain their vote for this particular issue?

Our country is spiraling out of control.

Speaker Nancy Pelosi was in Syria recently, negotiating against the wishes of our leaders. She is giving the U.S. the middle finger and damaging our intelligence and disrespecting our field commanders.

Another issue – shortly before the presidential election of 2000 between Gore and Bush, some public relations person on the liberal left XXX the expressions, "The American people want this" and "The American people believe this" and the public ate it up. How can anyone presume to say exactly what the American people want? It was dishonest, but it was a great gimmick. The uninformed American people – of whom there are many – took that nonsense to heart and believed the pablum. Gore lost the election in 2000 anyway.

Another thought – thanks to Presidents Bush, Clinton, and Bush Sr. and all the other leaders who for over four decades have ignored our borders, now we have 12 million illegals here to support and who are making it difficult for Americans to keep their jobs, straining our schools and our entire infrastructure.

Our hospitals are buckling under the burden of caring for illegals for free while the rest of us who pay our way must wait many hours in the emergency rooms while the illegals are cared for first on our nickel. Shame shame shame on you, leaders. You sold us down the river just for votes. And you also betrayed those Mexicans who went through the process to become legal Americans. You have betrayed all American citizens, and Mexico is laughing at our stupidity, as is the rest of the world. Why should the world respect us?

47

(September 13, 2008) There is a new book out called "The Audacity of Deceit" by Brad O'Leary. It is about Barrack Obama and how he plans to implement his promise of change for the American people.

O'Leary discusses some important changes that Obama wishes to implement.

He will raise taxes from the low rate of 28% under Ronald Reagan to a whopping, economy-destroying 60% as under Herbert Hoover. Obama claims that only the rich who now pay 40% of their income will have to pay the higher 60%.

Because the rich and corporations supply most of the jobs, the country will probably spiral into a deep depression.

Obama will wage a trade war that will eliminate 10 million American jobs.

He will choke off America's domestic energy resources and send gas and electricity prices through the roof.

He will implement a government program designed to transfer infant and child raising responsibility from parents to the federal government. That is socialism.

He will establish a government agency to approve what types of medical procedures and operations senior citizens will be permitted to have. That is also socialism.

He will increase the liberal base by allowing felons to vote. This is the same reason liberals like open borders.

Then, O'Leary says, he will hand out federal medical insurance to more than 12 million aliens.

And did you know that, as a state Senator, Obama blocked emergency medical aide for babies who survive abortion? Instead, he would rather leave them in a room to die.

This is just a sample of the many issues which Obama will address if he becomes president.

You can buy this book through Amazon.com. Otherwise, you might visit www.AudacityofDeceit.com (all one word). If you go to that website, you can choose one chapter of the book to read online.

Also, the author says that Obama will restore the inheritance tax and implement a retirement tax.

And finally, there will be new taxes to pay for socialized medicine so that we can receive the same medical care as other third world countries do.

Now remember, these are not my words; these are the words of Brad O'Leary in his book called "The Audacity of Deceit."

If all this can possibly be true, do you really want a socialist to be your president?

48

(September 19, 2008) Last week I spoke about the book "The Audacity of Deceit" which is about Obama and his plans for change.

It was written by Bradley O'Leary, a leading respected conservative strategist and fund- raiser, who has taken election year tactics to a new and powerful level. This is really exciting, so please listen.

O'Leary has developed an online tool to put into the hands of voters who want to persuade friends and family to look deeper at the Obama values before voting for him.

The test, which may be found at barackobamatest.com, is a 39question test where voters can compare their views to the true Obama positions that are seldom revealed by the mainstream media. And there is a good reason for that.

For example, pro -life voters, unaware of the radical nature of Obama's views, can now learn how he would withhold medical care to babies who survive abortions and allow them to die in so-called "comfort rooms."

Also, voters who have no knowledge of Obama's economic vision can learn how his tax, trade, and spending agenda will destroy growth and opportunity and how his healthcare program will provide taxpayer subsidized healthcare for illegal aliens.

O'Leary concludes "The next president will determine the destiny of our country. That president should be a person whose values are yours." Take the barrackobamatest.com and learn the truth before it is too late. I took the test and learned that my values differ from Obama's by 98%.

Abundant kudos to Bradley O'Leary for his wisdom in creating such a unique and authentic way to learn about the values of a prospective leader of the United States and indeed the world.

49

(August 28, 2008) During some recent polls of frustrated voters, we learned that our present liberal Congress has received approval ratings as low as 9%.

The previous, conservative Congress was called the Do-Nothing Congress, but this present one is even worse.

When running for office, all these wannabes cater to We the People and turn themselves inside out dying for the cushy positions, promising sincerely to fix everything.

Once they are voted in, they forget their promises. Instead, they enjoy excellent salaries and pensions, which they vote for themselves (the pension is for life, even if they serve only one term, and that is outrageous).

They enjoy superb medical coverage, and – best of all – no term limits.

So, like Democrat Ted Kennedy and most of the others in Congress, they make a lifetime career of a dream job with no accountability whatsoever. Most recently, with the approval of the House Speaker Nancy Pelosi, they had the gall to take a five-week vacation, leaving urgent issues like energy in limbo. What can we do?

We must demand term limits. I like one four-year term, like the limit for president. Four years, and no more, and definitely no life pension.

We must demand easy access to live audio and video of each session of Congress – and public announcements of exactly what happens in each session, like who says what.

51

(October 22, 2008) The U.S. Supreme Court recently made the astonishing decision to not check into voter fraud in Ohio, where thousands registered to vote and then voted the same day; some may have voted several times because some admitted to registering several times. There was no proof of American citizenship – and that incident was condoned by the Democratic supervisor in that voting place in Ohio.

All this was engineered by the corrupt Acorn organization which was subsidized recently by Obama for well over $800,000.

Obama was also at one time their legal advisor. Acorn is now being investigated by the U.S. government, but it is already too late to fix the voting damage they have done to our country. Their irregularities are now being examined in 14 states. We the People are living in a Twilight Zone. It's like a bad nightmare. Also, when an average American had the opportunity to ask Obama personally why he, Joe the Plumber, would have to give money to another American if his profit is over $250,000 from the plumbing business he hopes to buy, Obama told him that as president, he expects to "distribute the wealth." That being the case, we no longer will be living in a democracy. It will be a socialist society where the wealth is shared if you work or if you do not.

When Joe the Plumber, within hours of his innocent question to Barack, had his entire past scrutinized by the FBI as if he were a criminal – and it was broadcast across the world, We the People began moving toward having an oppressive socialist administration.

When the American media gives full positive exposure to Obama, and only little and mostly negative, dishonest exposure to McCain and Sarah, We the People are being lied to daily.

The American voters are being snookered. If Obama becomes president and his bully handlers take over – and they will – it will be because he is an inexperienced figurehead who doesn't know how to make a decision and never had an executive position in his life.

We will lose our country as we know it. And if you don't care, vote for Obama.

New thought – why does Barack Hussein Obama go ballistic and threaten to sue if his middle name, Hussein, is publicly mentioned? So are We the People about to lose our right to free speech also? The Fannie Mae and Freddie Mac fiasco was engineered and continued by Democrats like Barney Frank and Chris Dodd, and they and their Democratic buddies personally made millions for themselves, and now those lying scoundrels are blaming the Bush Republican administration. How do we wake up from this lying nightmare? About Joe Biden – you've got to love that guy's gaffs that are sometimes so true. The other day, he told us all to mark his words, that if Obama wins, the world will test him with some attack to the

U.S. within six months of his Presidency.

We think Biden has been sent back home to Delaware and told to keep his mouth shut until after November 4th.

52

(June 14, 2007) If the Democrats win in 2008, you can kiss good-bye the country which our forefathers created. In the past, the rule of law and the Constitution prevailed. In the past, it was the American citizen who was considered foremost. Now, it's the illegals that the Democrats defer to. Instead of such deference to illegals, why not put effort into deferring to our veterans who are ignored and neglected, whose families struggle desperately financially? These veterans have to beg for the help that they were told they would receive when they entered the military. Recently, when the vote came up to make English the official language, Hillary Clinton – who expects to be president – and Barack Obama – who aspires to be president – both voted against making English the official language. Why? Because they want the votes from the illegals who are possibly going to become legal. How about this – the three most prominent Democratic lawmakers, Hillary Clinton, Barack Obama, and Charles Schumer, all voted to give Social Security to illegals, but these pandering politicians did not bother to consult We The people first, and it is our money they are giving away. I'm not certain that this has become a law yet.

Don't you have the uneasy feeling that we are losing our core beliefs, that our Constitution is being trashed, and that we are in danger of losing our country to greedy scoundrels who will betray our laws for the almighty vote? Isn't this a bad dream that easily could become a reality if we continue in this direction? And don't we see President Bush's conversion before our very eyes? He has the gall to attack those of us who vigorously object to absorbing another 12 million illegals, maybe more. Isn't it true that his presidential predecessors, Bush 41, Clinton 42, and

Bush 43, are totally to blame for this catastrophe? They all deliberately left the borders open and betrayed our forefathers and our nation, and now we will lose our sovereignty unless we demand that they enforce our present laws, and that means no amnesty. Let's stop making a mockery of our laws.

Twelve million illegals can and should go back the same way they came in, through the open borders, taking their American children with them; then they can apply to come back legally. Our laws should be changed so that if illegals have children here, those children are also illegals. Mexico never has any illegal immigrant problems. If someone sneaks in, they are thrown into jail or quickly escorted back to the border. Meanwhile, Mexico continues to unload their criminals onto us. And, saps that we are, we take them in and give them benefits. It's time for us to develop some real backbone and say "Basta! It's enough already." It's time to take back our country.

53

(April 29, 2006) About the Enron fiasco taking over five years, it's finally being dealt with in the courts. President Ken Lay and Jeff Skilling are well coached by their cadre of high-powered attorneys. With a straight face, Ken Lay denies that he knew anything about the dire condition of his corporation.

It's easy to believe that he's lying. By the time he supposedly found out that his corporation was going down the drain, he had already cleaned out the coffers of many millions, maybe billions, so that there wasn't a penny left for the thousands of employees and innocent investors, not a penny left for any retirement pensions.

This scenario is becoming a rotten habit of other American corporations where the leaders walk away with many millions and the workers and investors get nothing – and our government does nothing! Why do We The People put up with this corporate stealing? Laws must be put in place to ensure that all employees, investors, and retirees are paid first, and then if there is anything left over, the leaders of the corporations, whose incompetency made the bankruptcy happen, should get what's left over and possibly go to jail – and not the country club type of jail, which is a joke, but a real jail where real killers are sent, because these corporate leaders are killers – killers of people's hopes for a decent retirement and a peaceful old age. Corporate manipulation and stealing must stop!

54

(June 23, 2006) How long have you known about HR219, the Social Security Preservation Act of 1999, which was meant to insure the integrity of the Social Security Trust Funds? It has yet to be voted upon, seven years later.

While for many years we have been told by our congressional leaders that the Social Security system was in trouble for lack of funds, what they "neglected" to tell us was that the reason the funds were evaporating was that THEY, our "loyal" representatives whom we trust to do the right thing for us, have instead been raiding the Social Security savings trusts for their own projects for their own districts, often unnecessary frivolous projects like bridges that don't go anywhere, just so that they can remain in office. This smells bad.

I learned about this law HR219 recently by chance, when a group of private citizens were soliciting for funds from the public to force our Congress to bring HR219 to a vote.

Evidently politicians were helping themselves to millions and millions of dollars and leaving IOUs in place, which will never be paid back. That's why the Social Security Trust Funds have been diminishing.

Naturally, this shameful information was not publicized by our leaders until some members of Congress with integrity created HR219 to stop this dishonest practice so that Social Security funds would no longer be used for private projects.

EACH one of us must demand that our representatives come clean and vote for HR219, Now, At Once, and stop this financial hemorrhaging. Literally, it's stealing from the public.

When HR219 is law, there will be plenty of funds in the Social Security system for the worried Baby Boomers and for many other generations to come.

Had our politicians been on Social Security like the rest of us, this robbery would never have happened, which opens up another Pandora's Box. I believe that the Congress's own retirement fund is totally illegal and should be challenged in the U.S. Supreme Court.

Nowhere in the Constitution does it say that our elected leaders can make laws for their own personal benefit. We elected them to make laws for All Of Us, but they are getting away with this seizure of the public's money.

The irony is that our elected leaders have dragged their feet on this problem for seven years, continuing to do what they knew was wrong, and now must make a law to make themselves honest. Again, the Congress should be forced to give up their own retirement fund and be part of the Social Security system like the rest of us Americans.

55

(October 18, 2006) Influenced by wishful thinking, political pundits are prematurely calling the outcome of the upcoming November election, saying that it will go to the Democrats in the House and also the Senate.

I say "Not so fast." Shakespeare would have said it even better "There is many a slip between the cup and the lip."

To be sure, both political parties have their share of corruption. So what else is new? About the Foley story, it was timed perfectly, and it was sad and ugly. Likewise, now righteous Democratic spokesman Harry Reed is being exposed for his shady real estate dealings from which he has derived millions. And his own four sons are all lobbyists. Interesting.

The liberal media covers up for Harry while at the same time they crucify Republican Foley.

Neither scandal should influence one's voting, because it's the behavior of a couple of rotten apples.

Despite the bad times now in Iraq, at the end of the day, the American people must ask themselves which party will keep them safe and take Islamic fascism seriously. Which party wants to cut and run and demands a public date for departure? The enemy would love to know.

Which party wants low taxes and a vibrant economy? Which party prefers more taxes and large government? Shouldn't the border between Iran and Iraq be closed finally? Iran funds militias in Iraq, and it is its largest influence. Businesses in Iraq are folding because of the oppressiveness of the insurgents. Reports are also – you won't believe this – that Islamic fascists are killing beauty shop owners for promoting vanity in women. And the beat goes on. What about this? It has been said that Democrats are upset because the president has no plan for losing in Iraq. Why don't they understand that losing is not an option? One could wonder about the pathological hatred so many liberals have had for President Bush these past five years. What kind of leaders could they be in this new world of global terrorism? What real-life decisions will they make? Or will they just want to talk to the enemy? Someone recently made this remark which is, I believe, right on: "I do love my country, but I'm scared to death of my government."

56

(March 23, 2007) In our democratic society, how come the manner in which we elect our most important leader – the president – is not democratic? Whichever politician believes he or she has the wherewithal to be the leader of the greatest and most powerful country on our planet, that person must soon come to the realization that the only requirement is to have a war chest of around $100 million.

This system must have been in place for so long that no one seems to question it. It surely could not have been the norm when our country was new.

True, George Washington was a wealthy and much loved patriot. So was Abraham Lincoln loved and worthy, but he was very poor, and he became president.

At what point in our history did we exclude presidential candidates who may have been wonderful leaders while we looked only to those few who had lots of money, but otherwise would not have been considered as presidential material at all? That's where we are now.

The cost of running for public office went up rapidly once TV became the perfect vehicle to showcase candidates.

Let's take Hillary Clinton – actually, let's not. She has been a presidential wannabe since she moved into the White House.

Remember that foolish campaign wording of "You'll get two for the price of one"? Who ever wanted Hillary in the first place? Her only credential is that she's a woman, and that's not good enough. She has accomplished nothing to make herself a viable candidate for the presidency, except that she has a war chest of over $100 million dollars. And oh yeah, she claims it takes a village to raise a child. That's nonsense.

Some Democrats started the rumor that she is the smartest woman in the world, and that's a crock, too.

No wonder we wind up with mediocre leaders much of the time. Franklin Delano Roosevelt was pretty good, though he was a racist. He couldn't find room in our country for a shipload of Holocaust victims, so he sent them back to Germany to die. Harry Truman the haberdasher was a simple, honest, courageous man who truly meant it when he said "The buck stops here." As vice president, he inherited the presidency when FDR died. He had integrity and respect for the office. He had the courage to make the agonizing decision to end the war in Japan, saving many thousands of lives. His decision heralded in the atomic age.

Back to Hillary – an empty suit, a contrived and staged creature who lives by the polls just like Bill did. Her magnum opus was her government health plan, and it was a disaster discarded by the entire Congress. She was a committed liar who wouldn't remember anything while under oath. She lied about her questionable documents while with the Rose law firm and mysteriously had them brought forth anonymously many months later. She and Bill helped themselves to furniture and other treasures that weren't nailed down when they left the White House, and when ordered to return the furniture and artwork, they did so shamelessly. And now they both want another eight years in the White House? God help us. Their greatest flaw is their arrogance and underestimation of the intelligence of We The People.

While it surely won't happen, the honest way to obtain presidential candidates may be with government rules which state that candidates are not permitted to use their own money to campaign or to be beholden to whomever supplies them with the money. Rather, each candidate should be given the same amount of government funds, and possibly be chosen to run by their own state constituency. That would seem to be a more level playing field. And then may the best one for the job win instead of the one with the most millions.

By the way, when you go to the polls, remember that recently, 34 senators – including Democrats Obama and Hillary and Independent Joe Lieberman – all voted against having English as the official American language. Isn't it time to initiate term limits in Congress?

Also, a whopping 51 senators voted to give illegal aliens Social Security. Most were Democrats, but also included were John McCain, Joe Lieberman and our two California senators, Barbara Boxer and Diane Feinstein. Again, why oh why don't we have term limits? No one should make a lifetime career out of being in political office.

The entire population of the United States must know about this retirement giveaway, unless they don't mind sharing their Social Security with foreign illegal workers who never paid a dime into the system. How disloyal that so many senators are selling out our country. Isn't it definitely time for term limits?

57

(January 17, 2008) Judicial Watch is a 13-year-old organization which identifies and prosecutes lawbreaking by politicians, government officials, and judges.

In fact, 90% of what we Americans know about the Clintons' scandals were exposed by Judicial Watch! One can wonder how the Clintons, who dragged the country through countless embarrassments during their eight-year tenure, now have the chutzpah to believe they should have eight more years of the same or worse. This underscores how people who are basically skunks always underestimate the intelligence of others.

As a member of Judicial Watch, I am about to sign a letter of complaint to the U.S. Senate Committee on Ethics to expose Senator Harry Reed, who serves as the leader of the Democratic Congress, who behaves as if he is above the law. Well, he is not. Here is the letter of complaint:

Dear Senators:

Last year, the Ethics Committee received a letter outlining facts regarding official actions by Senator Reed designed to further the interests of certain Indian tribe clients of convicted felon Jack Abramoff.

These actions violate the Senate Rule that "A member of the Senate should never use the prestige or influence of a position in the Senate for personal gain." And now reports allege that Senator Reed *violated Senate rules by failing to report a Las Vegas land deal that netted him $1.1 million.*

To date, you have not responded to the complaint nor investigated Senator Reed's land deal. This is outrageous. "Dingy" Harry calls this a Republican issue, which he knows is a blatant lie.

The reputation of Congress has sunk to historic lows. The Committee's continued failure to simply undertake an investigation of Reed smacks of exactly the kind of special treatment for fellow members of the club that law abiding Americans find so disgusting. (Like, for example, saying that you will not open an investigation into the Abramoff matter until the Justice Department completes its investigation, which will never happen, and sounds like nothing more than an attempt to avoid doing your duty.)

As a U.S. citizen, taxpayer, and member of Judicial Watch, I urge you to immediately open an investigation into Senator Reed.

Respectfully,

Kay Zwerling

58

(February 29, 2008) Despite eight years of embarrassment and shame from the Clintons, they have the gall to want to be in charge for another eight years. It would be a nightmare to have Hillary and Bill in the White House again. A few following reasons – with the help of one Roy Lovitt to jolt my memory, and my own strong opinions, let's call it "Hillary hopes you have forgotten. Have you?" Hillary Clinton has been telling America that she is the most qualified candidate for president based on her record which she says includes her eight years in the White House as first lady or co-president. Whoever voted her in as co-president? And her seven years in the Senate, also. Here is a reminder of what that record includes: as first lady, she made herself in charge of health care reform. That cost the taxpayers over $13 million. But it was opposed. She could not even get it to a vote in Congress controlled by her own party, and in the next election, her party lost control of both the House and the Senate.

Hillary assumed authority over selecting a female attorney general, and whom did she choose? Janet Reno, who has since been described by Bill himself as "my worst mistake."

Hillary recommended her former law partners – Web Hummell, Vince Foster, and William Kennedy – for positions in the Justice Department, on the White House staff, and in the Treasury, respectively. Hummell was later imprisoned, Foster committed suicide, and Kennedy was forced to resign.

She also urged her husband not to settle the Paula Jones lawsuit.

Countless women accused Bill Clinton of rape, and it was Hillary who threatened these same women to shut up or else. You want her to be president? And where is her self- respect? She refused to release the Whitewater documents which led to the appointment of Ken Starr as prosecutor. After $80 million of taxpayer money was spent, Starr's investigation led to Monica Lewinsky, which led to Bill lying about, and later admitting, his affair. Then they had to settle with Paula Jones after all. And Bill lost his law license for lying to the grand jury and was impeached by the House.

And Hillary almost got herself indicted for perjury and obstruction of justice when she repeated under oath "I do not recall," "I have no recollection," and "I don't know" 56 times.

And you really want that disgusting person as your president? Hillary wrote "It Takes A Village," demonstrating her socialist viewpoint. When Hillary left the White House, she later had to return White House furniture, china, and artwork which she had stolen. No remorse, no apology, no shame, and you want this role model to lead our country?

As president, Bill further protected her by asking the National Archives to withhold from the public until 2012 records of their time in the White House. There are ongoing lawsuits to force the release of those records. And the withholding of public information should be outlawed.

As the junior senator of New York, where she never was a resident, Hillary has passed no major legislation. Her one notable vote was supporting the plan to invade Iraq. She has since disavowed it.

Quite a resume, don't you think? Sounds more like an organized crime family instead of two pathetic wannabes who yearn for another eight years to rule our country. Talk about raw arrogance. With my apologies to the many good people living in mobile homes, Hillary and Bill are "trailer trash."

Last evening, I saw a rerun of a movie called "Man of the Hour" – or was it "Man of the Year?" It concluded with a very timely remark: "Diapers and politicians should be changed often.. and for the same reason."

59

(April 11, 2008) When We the People go to the polls in November or fill in our absentee ballots, many of us would want to check "none of the above." But voting is the greatest privilege that each of us has, and we certainly must use it always.

I do not recall when the three choices given for president were so.. shall we say.. anemic. Hillary would be a lying disaster. John McCain clearly is not a real conservative. And Barack Obama is full of hope and a skilled orator. What else? Obama is also an extremist who expects to pull out of Iraq immediately. He will also raise taxes and create big government to take care of everyone from the cradle to the grave. And, as a typical liberal, he believes that if he talks nice to Ahminajad, everything will be great, and Iran will be our friend. How simplistic. If you believe that, I still have that bridge in Brooklyn I'd like to sell you.

Basically what is wrong with this picture is first, our method of picking leaders is faulty and artificial.

Now one must have millions of dollars to even think of becoming a candidate, so the pickings are very very limited. Do you really believe that George W. Bush, a good man, would have had a chance in a million to become president if he didn't have the big money and the big contacts from his dad? With so many brilliant individuals in our society to represent us as a world leader, is this current triad the best we can come up with? Ideally, to keep it honest, no candidate should use his own money, and the government should give each candidate chosen by his own political party the same amount of a modest sum of money (certainly not $100 million), a shorter campaign, say several months, then maybe more worthy and logical candidates would have a chance to run. But that won't happen easily.

Now, about the hundreds of sanctuary cities free to protect illegals and give our federal laws the middle finger. I believe the Congress should eliminate those sanctuaries at once or before long, we won't have a country at all. Right now, it's an impotent mess, and greed and apathy prevail. Please, let's wake up. Let's demand logic and strength of character from our Congress.

60

(May 15, 2009) Recently, our president showed a touch of real class. He changed his mind about exposing our troops to difficulties if he had allowed certain pictures to be publicized – despite pressure from the despicable ACLU to do so.

Kudos to Obama. If he can continue to see the reasonable way, we might make him conservative – hence, more logical – and the next four years might be not so bad after all.

Also, our president just made it known that he wants to deal with the national health care issue at once and hopes to have it in place shortly.

Since many of my listeners enjoy senior citizen status, or will some time soon, you might be interested in the following health insurance information.

Most of you know that the Senate version of the recent stimulus bill includes provisions for extensive rationing for senior citizens. The author of this part of the bill, former Senator and tax evader Tom Daschle, was credited recently with the following statement. Daschle said, "..health care reform will not be pain free. Seniors should be accepting of the conditions that come with age instead of treating them." Put another way, "Don't expect the government to let you have certain expensive procedures or drugs since you are too old and you won't be around much longer anyway."

I heard somewhere, some unknown heartless lawmaker state that for those over 75, it is our duty to quietly leave willingly since the world is getting too crowded.

About Daschle and his cavalier attitude – remember that he and his congresspeople did not like our Medicare benefits, so some time ago they quietly chose something much fancier and superior which covers them and their spouses for life – and I suspect that We the People pay their premiums – and they do not fall under the same rule of being denied treatment like the rest of us oldies. And when they are no longer in Congress, they and their spouses each receive hefty lifetime pensions. Hopefully those of us who can afford private insurance will be able to do so. However, it bugs me how our leaders take outrageous perks for themselves that We the People pay for and will never know exist or be able to change.

So, let's change the subject, and let's wind this up with a little joke that is floating around:

A U.S. congressman was seated next to a little girl on the airplane. The congressman said, "Let's talk. I heard that flights go quicker if we strike up a conversation with a fellow passenger." The little girl, who had just opened her book, closed it slowly, and said to the congressman "What would you like to talk about?" "Oh, I don't know," he said. "How about the banking crisis?" and smiled. "OK," she said "That could be an interesting and timely topic. But, let me ask you a question first. A horse, a cow, and a deer all eat the same stuff – grass. Yet a deer excretes little pellets, while a cow turns out a flat patty, and a horse produces clumps of dried grass. Why do you suppose that is?" The congressman, visibly surprised by the little girl's intelligence, thinks about it and says "Hmm, I have no idea," to which the little girl replies, "Do you really feel qualified to discuss banking when you don't even know sh-[bleep]?"

61

(May 22, 2009) In the year 1907, President Theodore Roosevelt expressed his ideas on immigrants and being an American. Please listen carefully.

"In the first place, we should insist that if an immigrant who comes here in good faith becomes an American and assimilates himself to us, he should be treated on an exact equality with everyone else, for it is an outrage to discriminate against any such person because of creed or birthplace or origin. But this is predicated upon the person's becoming in every facet an American, and nothing but an American... There can be no divided allegiance here. Any man who says he is an American, but something else also, is not an American at all. We have room for but one flag, the American flag. We have room for but one language here, and that is the English language... And we have room for but one sole loyalty, and that is the loyalty to the American people. Every American citizen needs to know this."

Theodore Roosevelt would be appalled if he were to revisit his beloved America today and see how, in the name of political correctness and displaced compassion, our last four or five presidents stopped putting Americans first and deliberately kept our borders open.

Now we find ourselves almost totally supporting, housing, educating, providing jobs for, and hospitalizing countless millions of uninvited – who now even demand free college tuition, and most lately – the American flag was taken down by these people and replaced by a foreign flag on top, and the American flag underneath.

Our financial burdens are collapsing us. Many hospitals are closing for lack of funds because of these extra freebies to those uninvited.

And, to top it off, in the past 100 days, we have learned that President Obama's vision of change means change toward socialism, which We the People do not want and will not tolerate.

No president can continue to bypass the Constitution and the people and survive to serve a second term. With regard to tolerance, I am continually haunted by the wise saying "Tolerance is the last virtue of a dying society."

People, we must wake up and say "No" to many of these new happenings, like dozens of bailouts. We are about to lose our beloved capitalist way of life.

Our leaders must not make these arbitrary decisions without abiding by our Constitution and without the approval of We the People.

62

For starters, kudos to President Bush for standing firm against the liberal members of Congress who insist upon announcing the precise day of our departure from Iraq. The enemy would really appreciate that information.

This is so crazy, it feels like a bad movie. And those lawmakers who only won by a few votes last November are making crazy decisions. They are almost saying to President Bush, "Move over. We'll run the war now."

The bill for our troops' funds should be a separate bill without congressional conditions. Clearly, the liberal left Congress is blackmailing the president. Let the departure condition be a separate bill, also, for which the lawmakers in Congress take full responsibility when we fail in Iraq. However, the president would veto that one, also.

And finally, the disgusting habit of sneaking in billions of pork dollars (billions with a B) into the funding for the troops bill is merely to coax the indecisive Democrats to go along with Pelosi and Harry Reed against the wishes of the military generals who advise the president. It's feeling like the inmates are running the asylum. Thank God for the veto.

And now, the Clintons. After 16 years of being in Washington (eight as president and world Romeo, and eight as Hillary representing New York in Congress as Bill's mouthpiece) both of them liars who remember nothing when under oath, who consider the American people real stupid, now these Clintons want another eight years in the White House. How do we wake up from this nightmare?

63

Several weeks ago, KSCO devoted the two-hour Saturday Special to discuss Ron Paul. I called his honest appraisal a breath of fresh air, but alas the powers that be in our country refuse to take his message seriously. But I suspect that Ron Paul opened a door which will not close — it may take four years or longer, but finally he will be taken seriously as a contender for the presidency.

In one place, I must part company with Ron Paul. Those who created our Constitution may have been justified to think of our nation being isolationists then. It's no longer that simple in this age of nuclearism and world Islamic terrorists determined to destroy all who do not embrace the Muslim religion, some of which is many evil beliefs.

The following compelling arguments, from the Internet, say it better than I could:

Well now, Republicans say "We have a nominee." That may very well be, but there was only one clear winner in the confusing GOP nominating contest, and it was not John McCain.

The winner was Ron Paul. And the effects of his win will be felt for years to come.

Ron Paul made a classic political mistake. He told the truth. In debate after debate, he pointed at his party, his president, his fellow contenders for the GOP nomination, shouting aloud like the little boy in the proverbial story, "They have no clothes," and lo and behold we looked and they didn't. They were all naked.

He showed that the conservative movement has lost its way, its moral authority, and its logic. He showed us that we have become a Red team vs. a Blue team. But since we have decided that this is a political war and all normal rules are suspended, conservatives can do liberal things to win it. Conservatives can run up big deficits if it helps their side win. They can dole out needless pork known as earmarks if it elects another conservative to Congress. They can go to war if it makes their president look like a leader and wins him another term.

But in the process, Ron Paul showed us that we have lost our way. We are no longer conservatives. We are fighting for power, not for principles. We have become corrupted by the process, and the only way back is to retrace our steps and find all the things we discarded along the way.

Barry Goldwater lit a similar fire with his "Conscience of a Conservative." Its truth and arguments were so obvious and so honest that one laughed aloud while reading it.

But Goldwater himself was doomed to political defeat. And Ron Paul has no chance to win this election either. One could see that when he first opened his mouth. And yet the words and arguments of Ron Paul are still resonating. They still hang over the election. They are haunting and troubling. They are producing blogs, papers and books – and like Goldwater's revolution, they will one day be very likely to produce their own Ronald Reagan. And when those heady days happen, a small but hardy band of pioneers, who first had the nerve to join him and start shouting from the street "They aren't wearing any clothes" will be able to say that they could see what the country missed. They were there when history was made.

John McCain and his poorly chosen words, of staying in Iraq 100 years, have almost guaranteed that he will be the answer to the trivia question, "Who was the Republican candidate who lost on the ticket but claimed the first woman and black for the presidency?" Another question may very well be: "What other candidate ran that year and launched the movement that has dominated national politics for the last generation?" And that answer will be Ron Paul.

64

(2008) About Obama, we know at least that during his first 18 years, he was very much exposed to Islamic beliefs, mostly while living in Indonesia with his mother. Most important, however, are his core beliefs, and to what extent he has internalized those teachings.

Early on during his campaign for the presidency, he said he supports homosexual marriage, racial prejudices, gun control, socialized medicine, and the absolute right to abortion, including partial birth abortion, which to me is barbaric. A baby about to come out of his mother's womb could have a gun put to his head legally by the attending physician because his mother gets cold feet at the last moment – and this has happened.

Obama is anti-war, voted against the Patriot Act, and opposes the death penalty and school vouchers. How could anybody oppose school vouchers?

He says he loves Jimmy Carter and he, Obama, was one of the most liberal members of the Senate during his short tenure. He voted to give Social Security to illegals, along with Hillary, and they both voted against making English the official language of the U.S.

So, there we are.

Of course, he may have adjusted those core beliefs, especially since his trip to Iraq, Europe, and Afghanistan, where he tasted the power of becoming president. Too bad that it was more important for him to show the world what a great basketball player he was while he dissed the soldiers standing in line for a long time to shake his hand.

Most of us know about McCain's background, which is an open book. But do we know enough about Obama? If he wins and burdens our fragile economy with taxes and more taxes, we may go into a deep depression.

There is a new kind of terror invading the U.S. in the form of Sharia law, and because our national media will not expose it, it could be dangerous for our country. In the name of Islamic honor, some Muslim fathers have killed their daughters who merely wanted to be able to choose their own husbands. We are hearing more and more about this oppressive, cruel religion.

Middle East Muslims are coming to America in record numbers and are building hate-filled churches, buying our corporations, and suing us over our traditions.

Please think very carefully before you put your trust in this unknown, inexperienced, elitist young man, who for 20 years was very comfortable listening to anti-American sermons. What we do this time will determine our direction in the world. Will we remain a world leader or perhaps become a mediocre third-world country?

65

(September 5, 2008) Politically speaking, the next ten weeks will be very interesting. To their credit, Obama and Biden say that criticizing a candidate's family is off limits.

I am really happy about Sarah Palin for VP. She is my kind of person: clear thinking, direct, and fearless. She takes on anyone whom she believes is wrong, especially those in her own political party. And about experience – she has infinitely more executive experience than Obama ever had.

McCain, The Maverick, sure threw the cocky liberals a curve. It is delightful to see how they are falling apart.

So now we learn that Sarah's 17-year-old daughter is pregnant and will keep the baby, and that she and her boyfriend will get married.

The liberal media chose to gleefully announce the pregnancy, but deliberately neglected to mention the forthcoming marriage. It is a fact that honest American media reporting is dead.

Years ago, the liberals insisted that condoms should be readily available in high schools because parents cannot change young peoples' behavior. I believe it is weak and idiotic to think that way. Isn't it better to convince your own children to abstain from reckless, irresponsible behavior instead of giving them encouragement with condoms? It is a credit to Sarah's daughter, who chose to keep her baby rather than have an abortion. Since she and her boyfriend will marry, that should be the end of the gossip. But it's not.

If a girl has the courage and conviction to endure the pregnancy to term — and finances are a problem — our same government, which provides condoms to schools, should also finance the pregnancy until an adoption can occur.

About Roe v. Wade — for many years, I was pro-choice, believing that no law could rule my body. Then, I saw a while ago on TV (and I have mentioned this before) how it is commonplace at the end of the third trimester for a physician to legally shoot the baby's head with a gun as it is coming out of the womb. All because the mother panicked. There is more than just a woman's body involved. At the moment of conception, there is another body growing, and morally, the woman should not discard it, because that is murder. It should be allowed to grow to completion, and then if the mother still does not want the baby, there are so many couples who would gladly want to adopt it. The only valid justification for abortion is the mother's health, or a rape, or incest.

This is an emotional topic, but it is timely and should be confronted, though there are no easy answers that would please everyone. However, many women who opted for abortion are regretful, filled with guilt, and scarred for life. Sadly, I know a few of them.

66

It's a colossal wonder to me to understand how our government, which I'm sure, no matter who is in office, sincerely cares about fair play; however, it's becoming more frequent that large corporations put on a good face and continue to urge people to buy their stock at the same time that their president and the leaders of the corporation are selling their own stocks, stashing away millions for themselves, then declaring bankruptcy. Then they deny knowing that anything was wrong. Like Ken Lay — he walks away with millions, or billions, and the employees and stockholders are left destitute with no pension, no jobs, no retirement. This is wrong. The president of the company should relinquish all his absconded millions, which should be spread among those underlings and investors who trusted in his good judgment. Then and only then, if there's any money left, can he keep it. More and more corporations are finding it easy to go bankrupt, even if they're forced to go to jail (of the kind that's more of a hotel). They tough it out for a few years, but they still keep the stolen money. Our government is very remiss on this issue, and We The People must force stringent laws to protect the workers and the helpless retirees. Anything less is corporate stealing.

67

President Ken Lay and his sidekick, Jeff Skilling, are both appearing very well coached by their group of high-powered attorneys. Lay is charming, but he denies that he knew anything about the financial condition of his Enron Corporation. I say that's bull pucky. If you believe one word of his protest, I have a bridge in Brooklyn I'd love to sell you. He is lying. By the time he supposedly learned that his corporation was going down the drain, he had already cleaned out the coffers of many millions, in fact, so many that there wasn't a penny left for the thousands of loyal employees, retirees, and pensioners.

This situation has become a righteous habit of large corporations; the leaders walk away with many millions, and the workers get nothing. Why does the government put up with that? It's way past time for the U.S. government to step in and demand that the employees, investors, and retirement pensioners should all be paid off first, and then if there's anything left over, the owners, president, or the leaders of the corporation whose incompetence made the bankruptcy happen should get what's left over, and possibly go to jail.

If those types of laws were in place to protect the retirement and pension rights of investors and employees, then leaders wouldn't decide on bankruptcy so easily. It's a no brainer. The director of the business must take responsibility for the failures. Will our government do the right thing? Not unless We The People make a big, big stink about this issue and about this gross injustice. This corruption is being allowed without any accountability or punishment.

68

As Yogi Berra might say, "It's deja vu all over again." Shades of Peter Werbe, the fanatic lefty, who spewed his political bile at the conservatives daily on KOMY even after 9/11, when our country was trying to recover from the shock of the horrible terrorist assault which killed 3,000 innocent Americans and changed our carefree lives forever.

After 9/11, my family and I felt uncomfortable subsidizing the lefty Werbe agenda. No other business or person would pay for his hate program, which his followers— in this supposedly Hate-Free Zone— just loved. We finally pulled the plug. For months thereafter, the ingrate Werbe spread his hate about us owners via email all over the world, for "stifling his free speech". He never bothered to mention that ours was a privately owned, for-profit radio station.

For months now, there have been peace marchers protesting the possible war with Iraq to stop leader Saddam Hussein from developing, and possibly using, nuclear bombs against neighboring countries, and especially against the United States and Israel. The marches are well organized and fine — that is the American way.

For the past several months, we at KSCO have given the local left a daily noon free forum in which to voice their concerns. It has been, for the most part, a good experience. We have many new listeners and callers who say that they appreciate our letting them express their thoughts also. But now, once again, we owners are feeling conflicted. Our country is now at war. Our fighting forces are putting their own lives on the line to eliminate the cancer and unbelievable cruelty by Saddam Hussein to the Iraqi people before he tries to control the world.

So now, it is really time to close ranks and be a united country. It looks, however, like that will not happen, at least not here on the left coast. The war protesters refuse to give up gracefully. Organized by Sam Farr, they are making plans for a town hall meeting. Today, Sam Farr said on KSCO that he is against the war, but he will support our service people. Is that being on the fence or what? Shame on you, Sam, always thinking of the next election and keeping your cushy job, which you have had too long already. You are not talking to idiots. If you support the service people, you must do it unconditionally because they are fighting the war for you and the rest of us. Other protesters are calling for more peace marches, and some even for incidents of civil disobedience. Some are calling President Bush disgusting, derogatory names and insisting it is all about oil. How misguided and how simplistic.

About hating Bush— it is the electoral college which decides who wins the presidency, not the popular vote. Instead of bitching, change the law. Bush won the electoral college vote, so get over it. He won legally. Do you want to talk about Gore signing up all the thousands of illegals who got to vote for him? Or maybe we shouldn't go there. What do you protesters hope to accomplish now? Where were your voices when President Clinton was busy having oral sex with a White House intern under the desk in the Oval Office of the White House? He disgraced the office of the presidency and made the United States the laughing stock of the world. Where were your loud mouths then? Can't you people stop being so selective in your indignation, so politically transparent, so always partisan? Can't we all just be Americans now? Can't we all give our fighting men and women our unconditional support?

So I say to the divisive sore-heads, "Give it up. Take it like a man. Stop the bitching. Let us be a united country at war. Please, stop with the protests. You are only helping the enemy."

69

(October 11, 2004) So now Kerry puts his daughter in the public to talk about the environment and score President Bush for neglecting to deal with this issue. One must remind John Kerry and his followers that while the environmental situation is certainly serious, it pales against the need to finally take seriously the priority of dealing with terrorism. The truth is, John Kerry thinks and acts with a pre-9/11 mindset. For this reason alone, it would be a disaster for him to become president and leader of the free world. He is not a leader, and his priorities are muddled. If terrorism is not made issue #1, we citizens will not have to be concerned with the environment — there might not be any.

70

(Spring 2009) Last week I received an urgent letter for funds to support Sheriff Joe Arpaio of Arizona. It appears that the powers that be do not like the fact that Arpaio is being too successful in his job.

Arpaio is being punished for being "tough on crime".

He continues to fight to stop illegal immigration, and he forces prisoners to wear pink jumpsuits, and he cracks down on the criminal wave coming across our southern border with Mexico.

According to the Wall Street Journal, "Since February 2007, Sheriff Arpaio has arrested about 30,000 illegal immigrants, and the administration is now attempting to curb the powers of this true American". Now, Obama wants to discredit Arpaio and silence him, and remove him from his job.

Why, you might wonder, would our leader who promised change, honesty, and transparency want to discard the Sheriff who is doing such a good job for our Country?

Well, here is the simple answer: Liberals led by the ACLU have filed 2700 lawsuits against Sheriff Joe – accusing him of illegally profiling Latinos. But, they are indeed illegal, and they are Latinos from Mexico. And, that is not profiling.

Also, President Obama has been doing a dismal job as President and he knows that if he has any chance of remaining in office for more than one term – clearly he must do everything in his power to convince the Country to give amnesty to the illegal immigrants who are here. If that happens, of course, those new Americans will keep him in office for two terms.

Along with amnesty the following will happen: The illegals will expect Welfare benefits, free healthcare, free hospitalization for childbirths, and free schooling in Spanish. And, who will pay for those perks? You and me!

Most Americans do not get these taxpayer-funded handouts. Why should those who come here illegally get them?

The Left likes to think there are 11 million illegals here. That was the estimate eight years ago. The amount could now be closer to 29 million.

To make this wonderful tough honest American Sheriff Joe Arpaio the fall guy for Obama's agenda, I say, it stinks.

Sheriff Joe should remain where he is, and remind convicts they are not serving time in a hotel, and continue to expose illegals. And, We the People should support Arizona – and remain alert and not allow amnesty for illegals and the U.S. government should close the borders.

71

This is a compelling story about foreign subsidies in our Country. It caught my interest in a recent Readers Digest short story written by Michael Crowley, who titled it "Phony Farmers" and lamented how our federal government for many years has foolishly spent billion in tax dollars to frauds who never plowed a field. How did this system get so corrupt?

Some of you may have read it, but if more of us become aware of it even briefly, in these financially difficult times maybe some of these loopholes can be discarded if we make noise to our government.

This astonishing issue came to light a year ago in November when a Miami television station analyzed records of federal farm subsidies paid to South Florida residents.

By cross-referencing payments against death notices, the reporter found that at least 234 people listed as deceased were still getting checks from Washington – and some had been dead for over eight years.

Clearly those checks are being endorsed by certain entities, of them companies.

The most maddening federal programs evidently are farm subsidies.

According to the Heritage Foundation, farm subsidies are America's largest corporate welfare program.

Also, the agricultural industry has 1200 registered lobbyists in Washington, and they spend $133 million a year to make sure the money keeps flowing.

These shenanigans are astonishing. So, how can our government ever balance the budget?

If you are enraged enough, tell Michael Crowley about it at readersdigest.com/crowley.

For KSCO, this is Kay Zwerling.

72

So, I just finished reading the political reality of the story of the two Joe's in America – Joe Legal and Jose Illegal.

Most of you will anticipate what I am about to say, but I will say it anyhow.

Because we Americans are a compassionate people, for the past several decades during which our Presidents chose to leave our borders open, of course people came in illegally.

Most of them were searching for a better life. OK.

But, many, also, are criminals.

Consequently, we turned ourselves inside out to help the good illegals, so much so that Jose Illegal and his family began to receive and continue to receive many perks and opportunities that are not available to Joe Legal and his family.

This irony must stop because it has become overkill.

One example – Jose Illegal's children are admitted to our universities often free of charge or with very low tuition while Joe Legal must pay full tuition for his children. He is being punished for being legal, and how fair is that?

When I say our compassion has become overkill – witness the marches and protests springing up from among many illegals, one march with a sign demanding free housing, free food, free education, free everything.

We Americans have spoiled the illegals. They now feel entitled to all the freebies, and are beginning to demand it like it is their right.

During the recent campaign for President, our First Lady Michele Obama called ours a mean country, despite the fact that she received a superb education, no doubt gratis, as probably did our President. No doubt that is also why he spends our money so easily. He does not know how hard it is to accumulate it, because according to his own resume he never had a real job.

Now, as we speak, the courageous Governor of Arizona wants to stop the enormous financial drain on her State from illegals pouring in and she is asking for proof of citizenship from people coming from the border to Arizona – a perfectly normal request.

So, now our President and federal government are appalled. They don't want to hurt peoples' feelings by having them being asked a logical question, and Obama has been threatening to sue Arizona for enforcing the same law which the federal government refuses to enforce.

This reaction from our President is irrational and crazy.

Also, only a reckless incompetent leader would continue to harp on new laws like Cap & Trade and want to further indebt us with another useless stimulus bill.

Mr. President, many of us are rapidly losing confidence in your ability to lead us.

For KSCO, this is Kay Zwerling.

73

(Summer 2010) Only an entrenched irresponsible Congress urged by an irresponsible President would vote into law an irresponsible healthcare reform Bill of over 2000 pages, which nobody in Congress read before voting for it, and which will bankrupt and destroy our Country.

We the People must finally demand term limits.

Last week, local resident Bob Lessley, offered creative sensible ideas about changes in our government focusing on term limits and States' rights.

Now, another concerned citizen who believes States' rights and term limits are a must, came up with other creative ideas, calling it "The Congressional Reform Act of 2009".

So, let's examine the ideas in this Reform Act, and maybe a groundswell of citizens will get started on Congressional changes from both of these Americans' ideas.

Senators could introduce the Bill in the U.S. Senate, and Representatives could introduce a similar Bill in the U.S. House. These people could become American heroes.

These ideas are from a modest fellow who calls himself merely "A fellow American".

And, here are his eight concise reforms:

#1. Term limits: 12 years only for each person in office. I would limit it to six years per person for the Senate, and six years per person for the House, because serving in Congress is an honor, not a career. The Founding Fathers envisioned citizen legislators, serve your term, then go home and back to work.

#2. No tenure – no pension.

Congress will collect a salary while in office, and none when out of office.

#3. Congress past, present, and future participate in Social Security.

All funds in the Congressional retirement fund moves to the Social Security system where Congress participates equally with the American people.

#4. Congress can purchase their own retirement plan, just as we all do.

#5. Congress will no longer vote themselves a pay raise. Congressional pay will rise by the lower of CPI or 3%.

#6. Congress loses their current healthcare system (poor babies), and participates in the same healthcare system as they created for We the People.

#7. Congress must equally abide in and by all laws they impose on the rest of us.

Remember: Serving in Congress is an honor, not a career. The Founding Fathers envisioned citizen legislators, serve your term, then go home and back to work.

And, finally –

#8. All contracts with past and present Congresspersons are void effective 1-01-2010 because the American people did not make contracts with Congressmen. Congressmen made all these contracts and deals among themselves.

P.S. – Let's limit lawyers to no more than 15-20% of the Congressional membership.

To conclude, I say – kudos to this modest American who proclaims "It is my sole intent not to make anyone mad with this email, but instead to make people THINK! We need to get our freedoms back before it is too late."

And, I say, "Let's go for it. Let's take portions of Bob Lessley's proposals and combine them with this one, and together we can take back our Country. It can be done.

For KSCO, this is Kay Zwerling.

75

(Summer 2010) For a long time, our Congress has not been performing well. It is stale, tired, disinterested, predictable, and as we have emphatically observed this past year – very corruptible.

For too many years, we have tolerated people serving who have made a lifetime career of being in Congress, and being comfortable making illegal deals – i.e., promising one State perks in the millions at the expense of all other states, with the blessing of our leaders.

I further believe what our Forefathers intended was citizens to represent each State for a year or two, then leave. We have needed term limits. We desperately now need term limits.

But, Congress likes the status quo, and they make the laws. Once voted into office, they try to make the job a lifetime career. They vote themselves hefty salaries, hefty pensions, and for many years they have had the gall to vote pensions even for their spouses. They don't consult the People when they take money for themselves. That must change!

That is outrageous.

What is also outrageous, is – they have voted that even if a person remains in Congress for only one term, he or she shall still receive a pension for life. Maybe they have had the grace and fairness to change that rule, but I doubt it.

The latest outrage: We are in a bad Depression, but that has not stopped Congress from giving itself a 12% Cost of Living raise.

Congress has been forbidden to use the special fund that was set up many years ago to be used solely for a Social Security fund, and nothing else, and for many years, Congress disregarded that ruling, and helped themselves to large sums of money from that fund for their other projects and left in place IOU's.

Those IOU's were never repaid, and now those of us on Social Security, and those becoming of age for Social Security, are being told that those stolen funds are no longer there, and Social Security is in danger going broke before too long.

This past year, we recipients were not given our yearly Cost of Living increase for the very first time.

Congress is getting away with much dishonesty and stealing. Only an irresponsible Congress urged by an irresponsible incompetent President would vote into law an irresponsible corrupt healthcare reform Bill which nobody read, and will bankrupt and destroy our Country.

So, clearly, we must demand term limits.

One concerned citizen who knows term limits are a must came up with some wonderful ideas calling it "The Congressional Reform Act of 2009".

Thus far, I believe nothing has come of it, but let's share the ideas in this possible Congressional Reform Act during next week's Commentary, and maybe a groundswell of citizens will get it started and help make it happen.

For KSCO, this is Kay Zwerling.

77

(Summer 2010) This is in honor of Memorial Day. At a time when our current President and other politicians tend to apologize for our Country's prior actions, here is a refresher on how some of our former patriots handled negative comments about our Country. JFK'S Secretary of State, Dean Rusk, was in France in the early 1960s when DeGaule decided to pull out of NATO. DeGaule said he wanted all U.S. military out of France ASAP. Rusk responded, "Does that include those who are buried here?" DeGaule didn't respond. You could have heard a pin drop. When in England, at a fairly large conference, Colin Powell was asked by the Archbishop of Canterbury if our plans for Iraq were just an example of "empire building" by George W.Bush. He answered by saying, "Over the years, the U.S. has sent many of its fine young men and women into great peril to fight for freedom beyond our borders. The only amount of land we have ever asked for in return is enough to bury those that didn't return." You could have heard a pin drop. A U.S. Navy Admiral was attending a naval conference that included Admirals from the U.S., English, Canadian, Australian, and French Navies at a cocktail reception. He found himself standing with a large group of officers that included personnel from most of those countries. Everyone was chatting away in English as they sipped their drinks, but a French admiral suddenly complained that, whereas Europeans learn many languages, Americans learn only English. He then asked, "Why is it that we always have to speak English in these conferences rather than speak French?" Without hesitating, the American Admiral replied, "Maybe it is because the Brits, Canadians, Aussies, and Americans arranged it so you wouldn't have to speak German." You could have heard a pin drop.

And finally this story fits right in with the above – Robert Whiting, an elderly gentleman of 83, arrived in Paris by plane. At French Customs, he took a few minutes to locate his passport in his carry on. "You have been to France before, monsieur?" the customs officer asked sarcastically. Mr. Whiting admitted that he had been to France before. "Then you should know enough to have your passport ready." The American said, "The last time I was here, I didn't have to show it." "Impossible. Americans always have to show their passports on arrival in France!" The American senior gave the Frenchman a long hard look. Then he quietly explained, "Well, when I came ashore at Omaha Beach on D-Day in 1944 to help liberate this Country, I couldn't find a single Frenchmen to show a passport to." You could have heard a pin drop. Finally, this has been floating around for a while, but it is timely and really worth repeating.

Some people have the vocabulary to sum up things in a way you can understand them. This quote was translated into English from an article appearing in the Czech Republic as published in the Plager Zeitung of April 28, 2010.

"The danger to America is not Barak Obama, but a citizenry capable of entrusting a man like him with the Presidency. It will be far easier to limit and undo the follies of an Obama Presidency than to restore the necessary common sense and good judgment to a depraved electorate willing to have such a man for their President."

The problem is much deeper and far more serious than Mr. Obama, who is a mere symptom of what ails America. Blaming the prince of the fools should not blind anyone to the vast confederacy of fools that made him their prince.

The republic can survive a Barak Obama, who is after all merely a fool. It is less likely to survive a multitude of fools such as those who made him their President.

For KSCO, this is Kay Zwerling.

78

(2010) This is about just one hospital, and you would see that it is unbelievable. Parkland Memorial Hospital in Dallas, Texas, is a famous institution for a variety of reasons. JFK died there in 1962, Lee Harvey Oswald died there shortly thereafter, and Jack Ruby, who killed Oswald, died there a few years later. Parkland has the second busiest maternity wards in the Country, with almost 16,000 new babies arriving each year. That is almost 44 per day every day.

A recent patient survey indicated that 70% of the women who gave birth at Parkland in the first three months of 2006 were illegal immigrants. That is 11,200 babies born every year just in Dallas.

Records show the hospital spent over $70 million delivering 15,938 babies in 2004, but they managed to end up with almost $8 million in surplus. Medicaid kicked in over $34 million. Dallas County taxpayers kicked in more than $31 million, and the feds tossed in another $9.5 million.

The average patient in Parkland maternity wards is 25 years old, married, and giving birth to a second child. She is also an illegal immigrant. By law, pregnant women cannot be denied medical care based on their immigration status or ability to pay.

OK – fine – that does not mean they should receive better care than everyday middle class American citizens. But, at Parkland Hospital they do. Parkland Hospital has nine prenatal clinics – NINE!

These illegal women receive free prenatal care including medication, nutrition, birthing classes, and child care classes. They also get freebies such as car seats, bottles, diapers, and formulas.

Most of these things are available to American citizens as well, but only for low income applicants, and even then the red tape involved is almost insurmountable.

Because these women are illegal immigrants, they do not have to provide any sort of identification – no proof of income. An

American citizen would have to provide a Social Security number, which would reveal their annual income – an illegal immigrant need only claim to be poor, and the hospital must take them at their word.

Presently, there are about 140 U.S. patients who receive roughly $4 million for medical care. As it turned out, they did not qualify for free treatment because they resided outside of Dallas County. So, the hospital is going to sue them. Illegals get it all free, but U.S. citizens who live outside the Dallas County get sued. How stupid is this?

How much longer will Dallas and Parkland Hospital pander to illegals, and punish legal residents? When will Congress step in and send illegals back to Mexico? This kind of preferential treatment to illegals at the expense of Americans is sheer insanity! It is financial stupidity. Let's send them back and close the borders.

If you question these figures and costs, you may call Parkland Hospital for verification.

And, kudos to you Marilyn of Capitola.

For KSCO, this is Kay Zwerling.

79

(2010) Because their existence in our Country remains incongruous, let's examine sanctuary cities in the U.S. How long have they been allowed to flourish, and more importantly – why? Surely there were none when the 13 states were born in 1776.

For those of you who don't know, sanctuary cities are places that welcome and protect known illegals in our Country.

Also, for your information, there are 31 sanctuary cities in our Country. Los Angeles was the first, that was in 1979. San Francisco is one of the very active ones. It protects various illegal incidents that would otherwise not be tolerated by any other cities in our Country. New York City is another. These 31 American cities have ordinances banning city employees and police from asking about immigration status. Some States forbid sanctuary cities because they know it undermines the laws of the State.

Why should there be places in the U.S. which encourage and condone illegal behavior, and are protected and coddled for breaking our laws?

Those leaders of sanctuary cities could agree that because we are a free nation people should have the right to change the laws if they can get away with it. That sounds crazy to me, but that is exactly what sanctuary cities do.

Very interesting, though. Right now, and what the Governor of Arizona did a while ago to protect her State which is overrun with illegals and their problems, all sanctuary cities are crying out and accusing Arizona of committing the shameful act of possibly inquiring that people who look Mexican or Spanish should show proof of citizenship. The federal government refuses to keep the border closed so those numerous problems with illegals must be dealt with by the Arizona Governor.

Our bleeding-heart liberals think it is unforgivable to embarrass any Spanish-looking person if he or she is here illegally. Why are we concerned about their tender feelings if they cross the border and broke our laws? If they break into your home, would you still be polite and gentle with their feelings?

If I try to enter Mexico illegally, I would either be shot or incarcerated, or maybe even both.

U.S. federal and state leaders should develop some backbone and close and protect our borders now – right now – and eliminate sanctuary cities or our federal and State laws will soon become meaningless. The world should be laughing at us for tolerating sanctuary cities.

For KSCO, this is Kay Zwerling.

80

(2010) What's occurring in Arizona as we speak is a grotesque situation where it appears that right is wrong and wrong is right. That is to say, the illegals are screaming like they belong here, like they were welcomed here, because they were. Because of our leaders' delinquencies, illegals in our Country for the past 20-25 years were given the wrong message. They figured if the borders from Mexico were open, they were welcome to come here. Many came for a better life, and who can blame them? Now, we want them to go home.

The blame for this probable five-decade disaster, which is now coming to haunt us, can be laid to our past four to five Presidents, namely: President Bush Sr., President Reagan, President Clinton, President Bush Jr., and now currently for the last 1-1/2 years President Obama.

They all left the borders open knowingly. They broke our laws. Why? Possibly for cheap labor, which could have been obtained from the able-bodied Americans allowed to remain on Welfare indefinitely, which is sad, because those who do no work, and are able to, have no self-respect and dignity. The irony is now illegals are getting the few jobs that are available, and the American citizens are not.

Our President has been telling us lies about the amount of illegals living and working here – he says "maybe 11 million", when it is possibly more like 30 million. We will never really know. And, those immigrants who waited, and became citizens legally, are also very angry that illegals are being given extra perks for breaking our laws. Example: Some free college educations. And, the new legal citizens did the right thing, and they're not rewarded.

Obama made sure everyone is included in the new universal healthcare debacle, which hopefully will be repealed. That amount of illegals has been soft-pedaled, and not mentioned specifically – because the government will probably be paying the bill for them. They cannot be excluded, and they are accustomed to excellent healthcare here in all U.S. hospital Emergency Rooms.

We the People must demand loud and clear that our borders must be kept closed now! Our jails are already overcrowded with unsavory characters, many from Mexican gangs here illegally, and it is all at our expense, and Mexico may be laughing at us and our stupidity.

The future for America looks bleak. Either we could lose our beloved U.S. by overcrowding illegals, which Obama needs to win another four-year term – or by Obama socialism. Please – let's wake up before it is too late. Let's demand our laws be enforced.

For KSCO, this is Kay Zwerling.

81

(2010) Here is some very interesting information about Sarah Palin, sent by an unknown Alaskan. He says "The last 45 of my 66 years I have spent in a commercial fishing town in Alaska. I understand Alaska politics, but never understood national politics well until this last year. Here is what I know about Governor Sarah Palin":

#1. Democrats forget when Palin was the darling of the Democrats because as soon as she took the Governor's office away from the fellow Republican and tough SOB, Frank Murkowski, she tore into the Republicans' "Corrupt Bastards Club" (CBC), and sent them packing. Many of them are now residing in State housing and wearing orange jumpsuits.

#2. Now, with the CBC gone, there were fewer Alaskan politicians to protect the huge giant oil companies here, so she constructed a new system of splitting the oil profits called ACES. Exxon, the biggest corporation in the world, protested and Sarah told them "Don't let the door hit you in the stern on your way out." They stayed, and Alaska residents went from being nearly wealthy to being filthy rich. Of course, the other huge international oil companies meekly fell in line. Which other Governor in the Country that has done anything similar?

#3. She also walked into Governor's office with a list of State requests for federal funding for projects, known as Pork. She went through the list, took 85% of them and placed them in the "When Hell Freezes Over" stack. She let locals know that if we needed something built, we would pay for it ourselves. She also sold the previous Governor's jet because it was extravagant.

I'm still waiting to hear the names of those other Governors.

#4. Also, she managed to put together a totally new approach to getting a natural gas pipeline, which would be the biggest private construction project in the history of North America. No one else could do it, although they tried.

#5. For 30 years, Exxon held a lease to do exploratory drilling at a place called Point Thompson. They made excuses the entire time why they couldn't start drilling. In truth, they were holding it like an investment. No Governor for 30 years could make them get started, and she told them she was revoking their lease and kicking them out. They protested and threatened Court action. She shrugged and reminded them that she knew the way to the Courthouse. Alaska won again.

#6. After the recent national election, she was content to return to Alaska and go to work, but the haters wouldn't let her. They kept tormenting her with frivolous lawsuits, and they always lost. No one ever told them what happens when you continually jab and pester a barracuda. Without warning, it will spin around and tear your face off. They should have known better.

Now, you have just heard the truth about Sarah Palin which sends the media along with the Democratic party into a wild frenzy to discredit her. So, I say "You go girl". I only wish the men in Washington had your guts, determination, honesty, and morals. Kudos to the unknown Alaskan for this information. No wonder the pathetic Democrats are terrified. What's the best thing they could come up with? A leader busy dismantling our free Country and changing it into a socialistic one. Is that the change he promised us?

For KSCO, this is Kay Zwerling.

82

(2010) This story was written by an anonymous author, and in addition to other reasons for this repetition, I think it bodes well for those of us who are older to remember this when we go to the polls in November.

Also, if we are to save our Country from the Obama abomination in November, we must change the Congress. It will be our only chance to save this free Country we love so much.

Here is this story:

Wednesday, I was at the doctor, to whom I have been going since we moved down here to Palm Desert, California. He is the one who discovered my cancer. I have to get a very expensive shot every three months. Each time it costs $3,000. That is designed to keep the PSA down, and help to prevent a recurrence of the cancer. It has some uncomfortable side effects, and I was questioning the need to continue with it when the doctor assured me that it was necessary. He then asked how old I was, and when I replied 70, he said that if this new legislation does go through as intended by the powers that be, that I probably would not be able to get it next year anyhow, as that would be money better spent on someone else with greater longevity. I would be referred to someone to counsel me. That is barbaric! I asked him why the AMA had endorsed the plan, and he replied that only about 15% of the nation's doctors were members of the AMA, and most of them were not really on the front lines of doctorhood, but in some other areas of medicine, like teaching.

This man got part of his training in London, and practiced in Canada for 16 years before coming to the U.S., and he has no use whatsoever for socialized medicine regardless of how you wrap it or what kind of bow you put on it. He said that we have a shortfall of around 400,000 doctors at the present time, and many of today's doctors are of the Baby Boomer generation who are nearing retirement, and will decide to hang it up rather than be forced to decide who will live and who will die.

This is scary, my friends. The picture of our over 69 age group is not pretty in Obama land.

In fact, "Nobody over 59 can receive heart repairs, stents, or bypass because it is not covered, because it is too expensive and not needed," he said.

Obama wants to have a healthcare system just like Canada and England's. And, he wants to discard the one we have, which is the best in the world.

If this does not sufficiently raise your fear level, just remember that our esteemed Senators and Congress people have voted themselves, at the cost of the taxpayers, their own healthcare plan that is very low co-pay. They and their families are guaranteed this plan for the remainder of their lives. They are not subject to this new law. They specifically wrote into the Bill a section exempting themselves. I say, if it is so good for us, why did they exempt themselves? Their behavior is despicable.

Please, use the power of the internet, and any other method, to get this message out. Talk it up at the grassroots level. We have an election coming up in about seven months, and we have the ability to stop and possibly reverse this dangerous direction Obama and Congress have begun, and in the interim let's make their lives miserable!

You know, I am old, and wonder how dare those miserable skunks in charge of our government now play God with We the People while they embrace their own special exclusive health-care program.

For KSCO, this is Kay Zwerling.

83

(2010) This may be the most critical week our Country has ever experienced – if Congress finally votes on the future of government-controlled universal healthcare. Obama is fully aware that most Americans reject this Bill – but he wants it so he can usher in socialism and discard free enterprise. The weekly conservative Human Events condenses his agenda this way:

Is this our last chance to take back America?

Dear fellow conservatives,

I am not a person given to dire predictions, but when I say the next several months leading up to 2010 elections may be our last chance to save America from socialism, I am not exaggerating.

You see, right now Barack Obama is desperate, and that makes him dangerous. Sensing that his window of opportunity for "fundamentally transforming" America will slam shut in November, he is rushing to ram through the most radical parts of his agenda by any means necessary.

First on his list is the government takeover of our healthcare system that the American people have made clear that they Do Not Want.

Next is Cap & Trade climate legislation that would drive up the cost of energy use for businesses and homes costing millions of jobs, crippling our economy, and ceding American competitiveness to other nations like China for decades to come. I say, Obama is deliberately trying to destroy our beloved Country as we know it.

Then, there is the amnesty and open borders immigration "reform" Bill that Obama has just signaled he wants to put back on the fast track because he knows it will be unpassable after the midterm elections. I say, it is not enough that we now have over 30 million illegals and Obama does not admit that we will be covering them in this healthcare monstrosity, which will surely bankrupt us.

Indeed, because of the unpopularity of these Bills – and of other radical initiatives such as closing Gitmo – that Obama is pushing to enact them now before he loses political power.

And, if he succeeds, this Country will never ever be the same.

That is why it is so important that we conservatives seize the momentum that we have gained in recent months and act now to take back America from those who would destroy us... before it is too late.

I say – P.S. – Last summer, our local Representative Sam Farr on this topic of universal healthcare, during his local hearings announced numerous times that he plans to vote in favor of this despicable Bill whether we the people like it or not. If he continues and votes for it, we must vote him out of office because he will be voting against free enterprise and for socialism.

Friends, please listen – our Country is in grave danger now. If this Bill passes, Obama will not stop until Washington governs every major business in America, sets all our salaries, and controls every aspect of our lives.

For KSCO, this is Kay Zwerling.

84

(2010) Congressional Republicans may resurrect Obamacare from the dead. You heard that right. Republicans in Congress may actually fall for a political trap being set by Barack Obama designed to breathe new life into Obamacare. That is why it is imperative that we take decisive and immediate action to stop them. Many conservatives are sending messages and emails to their representatives to make sure to be aware and not fall for Obama's traps.

President Obama said recently that he would convene a half day bipartisan healthcare session at the White House to be televised live this month. The day is already set for next Thursday, February 25. Obamacare is dead, but he will trick the Republican leaders to help him revive it.

Radio talk show host Rush Limbaugh read the handwriting on the wall perfectly. He also called Obama's invitation a trap, an attempt by the President to portray Republicans as the party of No, and that is the characterization that many Republican legislators do not like.

I feel differently about that. I have no problem with remaining the party of No as long as our President spends money recklessly, and makes immature and destructive decisions, and refuses to listen to the wishes of The People. I think it is important to say No to an Administration that by its actions this past year has lost the confidence of both conservatives and many liberals, also.

Too bad Obama's enormous ego always gets in the way of sensible logic.

Make no mistake – Obama is not calling this televised meeting to listen to opposing ideas or to make a real effort to reform healthcare. When asked by Katie Couric if he would agree to discard the current Bill rejected by most citizens, and start over, the President said No he would not.

I say the Republicans should not attend the White House meeting unless a totally new bipartisan realistic Bill could be discussed.

The Washington Post reported that Obama does not plan to scrap months of legislative effort on the issue, and he plans to come to the Summit armed with the same old Democratic Bill.

So, it is nothing more than an underhanded attempt to play to the weakness that Republicans have exhibited time and again, a tactic that could turn his Obamacare defeat into a victory.

Indeed, Republicans should stay far away from this bogus Summit.

For KSCO, this is Kay Zwerling.

85

(2010) We in California are about to confirm whether we have Statesmen for Senators or just lowbrow politicians.

Kudos to my very intelligent friend Andy Anderson who asked that this timely topic be discussed, and contributed significantly to this commentary.

Let's take a moment and look back at what our Founding Fathers said about U.S. Senators. Our Founders stated clearly that the States were to remain sovereign, and that the Federal Government was to play a smaller role in the States' affairs. They knew what a big central government would do with the power. They established that the Senators from each State will be appointed by the legislature of each State, thus assume their loyalty to the State. The Senators' proper role was to go to Washington D.C. and protect their States' security and sovereignty foremost from the abuses of federal authority. They were not to be seduced or threatened by influences originating out of Washington. If they failed in this rule, they were replaced.

In 1913, a federal onslaught took place in our Country. Federal Reserve banking was established, the Internal Revenue Service was created, and our Senators were voted into office by popular vote. Just ask yourself – what have our Senators done lately to protect California's sovereignty and security from an overreaching federal government, which has become paramount and the States have become subservient, and our Forefathers opposed and predicted that situation?

Now come Senators Feinstein and Boxer. Senators – are you going to ignore our government's appeal to vote no on this universal healthcare Bill because it would add billions more to our State's debt? If you vote yes, it will be clear that you are not the least bit interested in the sovereignty, security, and wellbeing of the citizens of California. So, we shall soon see whether or not you are just two more lowbrow politicians we sent back to Washington at our expense.

My afterthoughts: It is time for Feinstein and Boxer to be voted out! They have served too long, are too entrenched, and it is time for two fresh new Senators who will listen to The People of California. The same goes for Representative Sam Farr, who during local hearings on this healthcare last summer did let We the People speak, but prefaced every speaker with his own remark by stating "I'm voting for it." He doesn't get it either. He is supposed to represent us, The People, not himself. So much for term limits, a topic most Senators would rather never discuss. They like to make a lifetime career out of serving as Senators. They give themselves excellent salaries plus superior healthcare, much better than what they are planning for the rest of us, they have probably a car, an office, and no doubt other perks, and they voted themselves several years ago pensions for themselves and pensions for their spouses, which was totally unacceptable and inappropriate, and no doubt those pensions still exist. With such an interesting and lucrative job, why would any Congressperson want term limits? And why do We the People allow our Congress to set their own salaries. We should have a citizens committee for that chore.

For KSCO, this is Kay Zwerling.

86

(2010) Let us call this "We may have an American Judge who will not be bullied. Pray for him."

In the recent past, numerous Americans have attempted to file lawsuits to determine whether Barack Obama is a citizen of our Country. He has repeatedly refused to expose his birth certificate, and claims he was born in Hawaii.

The media, which protects the President, rarely prints anything derogatory or negative about him.

Evidently no Court agreed to hear this case until now.

Judge David Carter, of Federal Court in Santa Ana, just agreed to hear this case and expedited the date to this coming Monday, January 26, 2010.

Many concerned Veterans and citizens attended the hearing in Federal Court in Santa Ana in the lawsuit against Barack Obama to determine his eligibility to be President and Commander in Chief. About 150 people showed up, almost all in support of the lawsuit, to demand that Obama release his birth certificate and other records that he has hidden from the American people.

Judge David Carter refused to hear Obama's Request for Dismissal. He indicated there was almost no chance this case would be dismissed. Obama is arguing this lawsuit was filed in the wrong Court. He would prefer a "kangaroo court" instead of a Federal Court.

The Judge, who is a former U.S. Marine, repeated several times that this is a very serious case, which must be resolved quickly so that the troops know that their Commander in Chief is eligible to hold that position and issue lawful rules, or lawful orders, to our military in this time of war. He basically said, "Obama must prove his eligibility to the Court. Americans deserve to know the truth about their President."

The two U.S. attorneys representing Barack Obama tried everything they could to sway the Judge that this case was frivolous, but Carter would have none of it, and cut them off several times. Obama's attorneys left the Courtroom after a 90-minute hearing looking defeated and nervous.

This is a great day in America for the U.S. Constitution. The truth about Obama's eligibility may be known fairly soon – Judge Carter practically guaranteed it.

Congratulations to Plaintiff's attorney, Dr. Orly Taitz. She did a great job, and won some huge victories. She was fearless.

P.S. – There are some rumors floating around that this hearing is canceled, but we cannot find any proof of that. It is confusing, therefore, we will go on with the assumption that the Court case will still be heard this Monday, January 26, in Santa Ana, California, Federal Court, with Judge David Carter presiding.

For KSCO, this is Kay Zwerling.

87

(2010) The title of this is "Israelis Baffled By News Of Defenseless U.S. Soldiers".

It would be remiss to let this story go away without exposing the one simple reason why that tragedy had to happen.

Like a broken record, for many years – since Political Correctness was created by the foolish American Left, and spread quickly all over Europe – in the early 1960s – I lamented the many wrong episodes that P.C. promoted.

Along comes my good friend, former Santa Cruz resident and KSCO talk host, Andy Anderson, who exposed for us what our own media either did not know or was too embarrassed to tell, and that is the following:

Many Israelis, and the rest of us, want to know, why didn't the soldiers at Fort Hood attacked by the U.S. Army Major – turned terrorist – return fire?

When a Muslim goes Muslim in Israel, he is typically shot to death within seconds by someone for screaming "Allah Ahkbar" and shooting.

In contrast with the Israeli experience, it took ten minutes before a civilian police officer at Fort Hood was able to shoot and stop Muslim fanatic, Nidal Malik Hasan.

During those minutes, Hasan killed 13 soldiers, and shot and injured 30 others.

How could that happen? How could so many people trained in the strategies and tactics of modern warfare be so defenseless?

The answer – and this may astonish many Americans – is that the victims were unarmed. U.S. soldiers are not allowed to carry guns for personal protection, even on a 340-acre base quartering more than 50,000 troops. Is this believable?

So it goes in brain-dead liberal America. And, our current liberal President vigorously promotes that philosophy.

It is also liberal brain-dead to Mirandize enemies known to want to annihilate Americans.

Fort Hood is a gun-free zone, thanks to regulations adopted in one of the very first acts signed into law by anti-gun President Bill Clinton in March 1993. Evidently that foolish barbaric law still exists.

Contrary to President Obama's crocodile tears, his Administration is bent on further disarming the U.S. military and all Americans. Obama and his people will not rest until every American is a sitting duck.

The upcoming trial turned circus in New York re the Guantanamo Bay criminals will further diminish our respect in our government's judgment by the world who sees our leaders as unrealistic, weak, and impractical. God help us!

For your information – Israeli teachers, from kindergarten on up, are also armed; so a Fort Hood type slaughter is highly unlikely at an Israeli school or university.

Israelis who have had to combat terrorism all their lives are not afraid of guns. They are an armed people, ready, willing, and able to defend themselves and their Country.

Unlike indoctrinated Americans, paralyzed by fear and Political Correctness, Israelis understand that people, not guns, kill people. Put another way – guns never kill people – people kill people.

Again, kudos to you Andy Anderson for this urgent clarification.

For KSCO, this is Kay Zwerling.

3

Part Three: The World

1

(February 21, 2003) About 60 years ago, the winds of World War II began. Adolph Hitler planned to control all of Europe first and then the world. To avert war, Britain's prime minister, Neville Chamberlain, had Hitler agree to settle for taking over just one country, Czechoslovakia. Chamberlain returned to England and proclaimed to the world that now-famous quote, "There will be peace in our time." He was wrong. Hitler, soon after, took over Poland. The allies ordered the German army to get out of Poland or face war. That was the beginning of World War II. Chamberlain and the allies learned a bitter lesson: Appeasement does not work; it only allows the enemy more time to become stronger. It only delays the inevitable.

Who in his civilized mind could ever have imagined Hitler's final solution, the total annihilation of the Jews in Europe? Today, history revisionists claim that the unthinkable never could have happened, and they leave that world event out of the history books. The Holocaust happened. It was a tribute to man's inhumanity to man. Six million Jews were burned in the ovens of concentration camps. A part of my family was wiped out. My own horrified German sister-inlaw tells how many Germans at that time wondered about the strange smell that permeated the atmosphere around Munich.

It was not our finest hour either. Our own President Franklin Roosevelt denied refuge to a shipload of Jews in New York Harbor and forced them to turn back to Germany to be incinerated. I was a child of about 12, and I remember all that well.

One may wonder why the Jews went to the concentration camps so passively. The answer is that Hitler's first edict, once in power, was to confiscate all firearms so that the people were powerless.

So now I say to all those marching for peace now, "Change your placard messages. You're not marching for peace. Your marching for appeasement, and appeasement is deadly." By the way, everyone wants peace, not just the protesters. However, the realists understand that the stockpiling of weapons of mass destruction by the proven monster Saddam Hussein can no longer be tolerated. Saddam Hussein must be removed now, before he obtains and uses nuclear power. He has gassed his own people, and for minor offences, cuts out their tongues and ears and chops off their hands. It is way past time to liberate the people of Iraq who pray everyday to be free of Saddam's hell.

2

(April 20, 2004) About the International Court of Justice, because it is blatantly biased, it surely is not a court of justice. More to the point, it is a court of injustice. The following letter received in the local Sentinel and written by Gil Stein of Aptos, confirms the above, and I quote:

"The International Court of Justice has spoken. Israel has no right to self-defense. With more than 20,000 attacks on its people in less than four years with nearly 1,000 deaths by suicide bombers, the court has declared Open Season on Jews. Only hours after the decree, a bomb exploded in Tel Aviv, killing a teenager and wounding many others. The message is clear from the Court of Justice, no matter how much blood is on Arafat's hands, we will support him and his murderers. Will the Decree stop the building of the fence? No way. If the Palestinian authority won't stop the bombers, the Israeli people will. By attacking them before they get to Israel, and by keeping them out. This is how you fight terrorism."

Kudos to you, Gil Stein, for always telling it like it is. Now, here are some facts about the Middle Eastern conflict:

Israel became a nation in 1312 BCE, 2000 years before the rise of Islam.

Arab refugees began identifying themselves as part of the Palestinian people in 1967, two decades after the establishment of the modern state of Israel.

The Arabs are represented by eight separate nations, not including the so-called Palestinians. There is only one Jewish nation. The eight Arab nations initiated all five wars and lost. Israel defended itself each time and won.

The PLO's charter still calls for the destruction of the state of Israel. Israel has given the Palestinians most of the West Bank land and autonomy under the Palestinian authority. Big mistake.

In 1948, advised by their Arab brethren, the Israeli Arabs left Israel expecting to return after the eight nations won their initiated wars. All that never happened. One might expect that over all these many years, the Arab countries would have had the compassion to embrace and assimilate the very refugees they urged to leave their homes in Israel. That never happened, and never will, because the Arab nations prefer to use the refugees as political pawns. So much for helping your own. As long as Arafat is permitted to call the shots, literally, there will never be peace in the Middle East, and Arafat's agenda is for the total destruction of the State of Israel.

So, for me, an American Jewess, it is a sad fact that anti-Semitism, or more specifically anti-Buddhism, is an incurable social disease, and for the most part, Israel stands very much alone in the world of public opinion, except for the support of our United States, world Jewry, and perhaps some fair-minded world citizens.

To paraphrase Golda Meir, one of the earlier prime ministers of the modern state of Israel, I can forgive many things; however, forced to defend ourselves for our own survival, I can never forgive that in order to defend ourselves, our sons were forced to become killers."

3

(December 14, 2004) Human relationships are always complicated. There is one area; however, where human interaction is predictable, yet that aspect is often avoided, or overlooked. If one is asked by a good friend to lend him some money, if able, one would say "Of course". Initially, the borrower's reaction is gratitude, followed a sense of discomfort and indebtedness. After a while, he may feel irritation, disdain, and finally avoidance. At this point, the lender thinks maybe it would have been wiser for him to have said no to the friend's request, in which case their friendship may not have gone sour. Wasn't it in one of Shakespeare's plays when someone was advised to "Neither a lender nor a borrower be"? These wise observations fit snugly into the interaction between the U.S. and the U.N.

In 1945, after the last World War, 51 countries called the United Nations joined forces to again try to avoid further wars and other global issues. Everyone involved was full of hope and eager to find common ground. The U.S. built a beautiful high-rise in New York City for the U.N. The membership has now grown to over 100. Each country has one vote. While the U.S. continues to be the largest benefactor, paying 22% of all the U.N. expenses, countries with a fraction of our size and population have the same voting power. Inequitable? Yes. But we the U.S. allowed that to exist. Do our fellow members like us? Absolutely not. At first, 60 years ago, there was gratitude and respect for our generosity and hospitality. But before long, those feelings began to turn into entitlement, disrespect, arrogance, and finally overt contempt. Most U.S. proposals are vetoed.

The U.N. has become corrupt and impotent, and the U.S. continues to pay most of the expenses. It is like throwing money down a rat hole. Like the League of Nations, the U.N. is another failed experiment. It has been the enabler for the horrendous Oil-For-Food scandal. About Kofi Annan, regardless of the outcome of this foolish investigation where the corrupt U.N. is investigating itself, Kofi should smell the coffee and peacefully resign, because he allowed the scandal to happen on his watch. World opinion likes to position the U.S. as a bully and aggressor. The exact opposite is true. Blessed with abundant resources and abundant compassion, we have always tried to help the needy and oppressed. After World War II, we actually rebuilt the conquered lands of Germany and Japan, the enemies who initiated the wars against us. Now, they are both democracies. Are they appreciative? Japan maybe, Germany no.

The United Nations, at long last, has worn out its welcome here in the United States. It is time for it to leave, and instead go leach on France, Germany, or Russia. And maybe we should seriously consider resigning from the U.N., and instead help create a League of Democracies, because democracies and dictatorships together cannot seem to agree on anything.

Finally, kudos to those fed-up Americans working to evict the United Nations from our country. They may be reached at MoveAmericaForward.org.

4

It was General John Abizaid, in charge of the entire Middle East conflict, who said that to understand the Osama Bin Laden mentality, one should understand that the enemy is using 20th century technology to spread their vision of a 7th century paradise. He also added that a war of transformation will take decades. Our democratic, Geneva-Conventions-respecting leaders had better change their own military mindset if they hope that our vision of a democratic world will finally prevail. We are dealing with a suicidal Islamic fascist fanatic enemy who laughs at fair fighting and the Geneva Conventions. They fight dirty and figure that the end justifies the means. Saddam Hussein taught them well, that to win and control, anything goes. Chopping off hands, feet, and heads of innocents, and cutting out tongues and ears— that has been the modus operandi for decades in Iraq. And we still agonize about treatment of prisoners and enemy combatants detained at Abu Ghraib, and we hesitate to use loud music and tough interrogations to obtain information to protect our own soldiers. It is like Nero. We continue to fiddle while Rome burns.

About a year ago, our military captured Saddam Hussein hiding underground. They dug him out of a rat hole looking like a cornered dog, filthy with long straggly hair, beard and tattered rags. They bathed him, put him into a comfortable cage with probable amenities like radio, television, and three warm meals a day. That was proper treatment, by our way of thinking. So what is the deal about sending him to a beauty shop to style his hair and beard? And, what is with the designer suit? Are we nuts? He should have been showered and cleaned but left looking like the animal he is, wearing his own cleaned tattered rags. We made him look like a movie star, and he still believes he is the leader of Iraq. And now, after a year of letting him languish comfortably, plans are for a long, drawn-out civil trial led by the Iraqis, to let him explain his innocence? This is a civil farce and trivializes his horrendous guilt. Wouldn't a quick Iraqi military tribunal have been more appropriate, where he could have been disposed of his style, chopping off his hands, his feet, his ears, and cutting out his tongue, and finally gassing him like he did to thousands of his own people?

Most Iraqis, contrary to what those opposed to the war think, are very grateful to have our military there to help them create a democratic society. The Old Testament says, "an eye for an eye and a tooth for a tooth". The New Testament teaches "turn the other cheek" and "love thy neighbor". The choices we make now will decide if our civilization will survive or will be doomed.

Time is of the essence, and our leaders should seek divine guidance on this call. And the rest of us ... PRAY.

5

(March 21, 2005) This is about forgiveness and irony. In 2004's last issue of U.S. News and World Report, editor Mortimer Zuckerman devoted his weekly commentary to forgiveness and the merits derived therefrom. I learned long ago that to forgive feels good. If you can forgive unconditionally, it is like God is patting you on the head saying "That's good." Also, remember the timeless proverb "To err is human, but to forgive is divine."

And now, about irony. For years, China was called The Sleeping Giant. In 1979, The Sleeping Giant was awakened when Richard Nixon, representing the United States, went to China to complete arrangements to initiate economic relations. My husband Bernard and I happened to be visiting there at that exact time. We were part of an initial group of Americans permitted to visit that communist country, and it was memorable. As a result of the Nixon visit, we saw the Chinese people rejoicing and dancing in the streets of the city then called Peking, now known as Beijing. Led by English-speaking government tour guides, we observed that because cars were scarce, people had bicycles. All wore the same government-issue black cotton uniforms, and they withstood the winter cold by wearing layers and layers of cotton. Wherever we were taken, people gathered, intrigued by our white skin and especially by our few Polaroid cameras. They laughed with astonishment when given an instant photo of themselves. The tour guides were very curious about us and asked many questions. For example, why are there so many divorces in America, and how come people are permitted to have so many children? Chinese couples were allowed only one child, preferably a boy. That was 1979.

Fast forward now to 2005, 26 years later. China is a booming economy with Big Mac burgers and all the other trappings of capitalism and many budding entrepreneurs. Now comes the irony. From China, the U.S. imports enormous quantities of manufactured goods, including millions of artificial Christmas trees. These trees are made to look more authentic with real wood trunks made from unclean Chinese wood which houses Chinese brown fir beetles.

And now Chinese mercury is polluting our environment. The very pollution that our country sought to eliminate by sending most of our own manufacturing industry to China and other countries because we wanted to focus more on clean service industries and electronic industries, has now made us globally dependent and is polluting our own land in ways we never dreamed of. In other words, in order to meet our manufacturing needs, China now has 2000 factories using coal burning furnaces, and that is about to become 4000 factories with coal burning furnaces. With her newfound prosperity, China is learning ways to obtain electronic information from us to compete with us in the world markets. Also, I hear that China is now exporting Chinese cars. Have we helped to create a clever, maybe unbeatable monster?

The final irony – President Bush, the perennial whipping boy, blamed for everything possible, was ostracized by the world community and the liberal American press for declining U.S. participation in the Kyoto agreements to clean up world pollution. His reason for declining? China, the world's worst polluter, was exempt from participation in the agreements. Some joke, huh? Did the world press and the American media even bother to mention that fact?

6

(June 4, 2005) Many have asked me: "Was it really worth it for us to go to fight in Iraq when we have lost over 2,000 soldiers?" This is my answer:

9/11 was a wake-up call to the realization that Islamic world terrorism will not go away and is committed to destroying our way of life. Suicide bombers are a new phenomenon. Our world has changed forever. One philosophy will prevail. It will be the Islamic terrorist, 16th century way or ours — not both. Like President Bush, I would rather fight them in Iraq than here in America. As a mother, I would be torn up if my sons were soldiers fighting in Iraq and were injured or lost their lives. However, remember that those who joined the voluntary military did so willingly and knew the possible risks of combat. It is so much worse this time—the fanatic enemy cuts off heads of innocents, they blend into the regular society and do not wear uniforms. They are barbaric. Saddam Hussein is a monster, proven to have gassed and murdered hundreds of thousands of his own people. Witness the many mass graves our soldiers have uncovered. Are we not better off without him?

I believe the WMDs are still around, deep in the earth of Syria, Iran, or Saudi Arabia, or maybe in all of those places. Even if they aren't, the fact remains that Saddam Hussein broke every treaty he signed to get off the hook after the 1991 war. He gave the U.S. and the

U.N. the middle finger and got away with it for ten years. The U.N., France, Germany, and Russia refused to participate in bringing Iraq to justice, and now we know why – they were too busy themselves being on the take along with Saddam Hussein and Kofi Annan in the Food for Oil scandal, so they left us to do the dirty work for the world.

About the corrupt U.N., I am in favor of leaving that impotent organization and forming a group with other world democracies. The

U.N. should be evicted or disbanded. In any case, they should leave our country because I think that we are sick of subsidizing them for the past 50 years.

Thanks to the U.S., Britain, and other allied countries, Iraq is becoming a democratic society – and wonder of wonders, the surrounding oppressively ruled countries might also see the joy and benefits of freedom, and gradually follow suit. This fact is painful to our own liberal extremists and our liberal media, who would rather see us fail in Iraq.

I do vigorously object to our military being forced to do multiple sessions of combat in Iraq. We should now resort to the draft if we must in order to help preserve our democratic way of life. All who enjoy those benefits of freedom should participate as we all did willingly in World War II.

My hope is this, and I suppose it is unrealistic: once Iraq becomes a successful and prosperous society, they might show their appreciation for our liberating them by deciding to pay back the US and the other countries who laid out billions for them. They could pay us back with oil. That would be a wonderful possibility. But, even if that does not happen, I still believe we did the right thing to liberate Iraq.

7

If our planet does not blow itself up first, history will record that the Islamic terrorists' gift to the world has been the suicide bomber, an evil phenomenon which, like the atomic bomb, has the power to destroy the world. When else has a human being made a conscious decision to die first in order to win? The Kamikazes? They needed planes.

Like an uncontrollable plague, this exercise in self-extinction is spreading to all countries on the globe. What evil minds were capable of inventing this kind of warfare that crosses all boundaries of fair play? The same diabolical religious fanatic leaders who, for almost six decades of fighting with the state of Israel, have shown, by placing their own wives and children in the line of fire, by making them expendable, that they believe like all extremists that the end justifies the means, no matter how barbaric.

The world is bewildered about how to deal with suicide bombers. Despite our superior equipment and enormous assets, with the intrusion of political correctness, our country has a difficult time settling wartime differences, because since the Vietnam war, our military has been forced to fight with one hand behind its back. They were taught above all to be humane, and that is an oxymoron in wartime. The enemy always fights to win. This failed U.S. modus operandi had better change if we are to survive.

Will suicide bombers come to our land? Yes, decidedly yes, and anytime soon, so long as our physical parameters remain porous. Surely many Mexican Americans deserve the right to a better life, but entering legally will keep Americans safer, and terrorists will be kept out.

What is our president thinking? And, what is he waiting for? The decision about keeping the borders open, inviting suicide bombers, is deadly. The safety of all Americans must be the president's first priority. How can we continue to keep our freedom and way of life faced with a vicious enemy who recruits gullible young men brainwashed into being willing, even eager, to die for God and the promise of umpteen virgins waiting for them? Perhaps I am naive and unrealistic, but I hope that those Islamic/fascist religious leaders, the creators of the human bomb, will reverse their orders and say to the bombers "Do not do this any longer, or you will go to hell, and there will be no virgins waiting." Those terrorists may listen to their leaders, and that may be the only way to stop the global human carnage.

8

(December 20, 2005) The Democrats are really self-destructing. And, many constituents are losing confidence in their judgment. George Murtha wants the troops to leave Iraq at once. Nancy Pelosi agrees with him. And Howard Dean says we can't win the war in Iraq. Liberals protect the rights of criminals, but they ignore the rights of victims. Now they believe that our military is cruel to capture terrorists. Islamic terrorists slice off the heads of their captive victims. Where's the outrage about that?

Congress just crafted into law gentle parameters for our troops to abide by while interrogating the captive enemy. This is crazy. It is also demeaning and insulting to our troops. Unlike the fanatic insurgents, our troops are not barbarians. They are civilized, trained soldiers who love our country. They must have the freedom to use their judgment in fighting this war while confronted every day with the new phenomenon of the suicide bomber. There is no level playing field, so they must not be forced to succumb to the boundaries of the politically correct. The elimination of terror in interrogation sounds noble, but it doesn't work unless both sides agree. The enemy is laughing at us.

About Abu Ghraib — as a result of the foolish and reckless judgment of a few soldiers, the American and European media have had a field day dissecting this unfortunate episode, and they kept it alive for months, much to the detriment of the morale of our troops. It should not have happened. What was done to the captive detainees was shameful, but the embarrassment endured by those detainees pales against what the terrorists do to our captive soldiers, like slice off their heads. Again, where is the outrage?

Why are we so concerned about how the world, especially Europe, views us? These countries always dislike us. And now they judge and set moral standards for our behavior and that of our military while at the same time they decline to get involved. This is war. It is ludicrous for us to be obsessed with not offending countries like France, Germany, and Russia, who all join forces with the scoundrels Saddam Hussein and Kofi Annan to steal billions of dollars earmarked for the hungry of the world in the Oil for Food scandal. Where is the outrage there?

Now, the Congress is involved in the execution of the war. What a bummer that is. By making laws against the use of terror to obtain valuable knowledge from the enemy—knowledge which could and does save many lives and could possibly bring an end to the combat sooner—Congress ties the hands of our military leaders, and that is idiotic. And, it demeans our Generals.

To the Democrats who are shamelessly politicizing this war by their endless negativity, I say "Back off. Let the troops do their job. Stop with the gloom and doom which continue to delight and energize the enemy." And to those who stoop to call our president a liar and a fool and other derogatory names, I say "You will never regain political majority and power with those tactics. And that's why I think you are self-destructing. When you demean the presidency, you demean yourselves and you demean our country. Shape up. Get a grip."

9

(February 16, 2006) Can one ever forget the pictures of Saddam Hussein flashed on TV screens, being pulled out of the earthen hole looking like a cornered, scared rat? The once-leader of Iraq reduced to filthy tattered clothes and dirty long stringy hair and beard. Our humane military pulled him out, gave him a bath and shampoo, and a warm cell. They should have washed his tattered clothes and put them back on, and not touched his long hairdo. Instead, he was given a stylish haircut, trimmed beard, and a designer suit to wear. Big, big mistake, because Saddam looked in the mirror, and then he lost his fear and humility. He decided that he is still the leader of Iraq and started throwing his weight around. If he received special privileges also while languishing in jail, like a TV, that was another big big mistake.

When will we ever learn that animals like Saddam Hussein do not respond well to kindness, which they see as weakness? They respond to chopped off hands and tongues. What a shame that we are too civilized to have Saddam experience what he did to so many of his people for minor infractions.

Now, both Saddam Hussein and Zaccharias Moussowi, terrorists, are making mockeries out of their trials. Both should be put into solitary confinement and then put to death for their crimes. But that won't happen easily, because our side is calling the shots. Their trials will go on and on just so the world will see how fair and foolish we are. It is all an exercise in futility, because our country is too worried about our world image, and that won't change. By generously helping and defending needy countries, we have made those recipients feel indebted so they dislike us. That is another ironic flaw of human nature. No one likes to feel indebted, so it is easier to find reasons to criticize and dislike.

So what's the answer? I don't know if there is any answer. Nevertheless, the U.S. will still continue to help those in need and hope for goodness and fairness to prevail in the world, and that is very good.

And I am glad to be American.

10

(June 16, 2006) This is about the elephant in the room, which is a stylish synonym for the existence of a very obvious unpleasant issue, which sooner or later must be dealt with. This time, the elephant is the relationship between our nation and the United Nations, the latter of which was created over 60 years ago in San Francisco right after World War II. Many nations joined together in high hopes of preventing any future wars. That did not happen.

One must wonder now, since the world learned some time ago that Kofi Annan, elected head of the U.N., was in bed with the Iraqi scoundrel Saddam Hussein. Kofi personally received millions of dollars earmarked for the Food for Oil program, and he secured a very cushy job for his own son, among other shady deals. He is not fit to be leader of a world organization. He is a bad role model. Yet he is still there, running the U.N. His credibility is gone. So, why is he allowed to keep his lucrative and important job? It's a known fact that when a fish stinks, it stinks from the head down. Kofi Annan refuses to resign, and he is the head that stinks.

Our country is appearing embarrassingly impotent. We are the main contributor, giving billions of our dollars to support the U.N., whose members have been our guests for a long time. More often than not, most U.S. proposals are routinely vetoed because many member nations of the U.N. vigorously dislike us. But they love our free hospitality, and they live in New York City like royalty, with many privileges the rest of us Americans do not have. For example, they are immune from receiving tickets for traffic violations, and that's insane. We're hated not only because of the Iraqi war, but because we allow ourselves to be used by the U.N., which long ago wore out its welcome here.

Let's have the strength of character to say, "It's time to leave and find another place to live." Maybe France, Russia, Germany, or another country should host the irrelevant U.N. We should stop being rich chumps who continue to subsidize a useless and corrupt organization.

We should resign and instead help create an honest and credible league of democracies, because dictatorships and democracies don't mix and will never agree.

Most recently, Kofi Annan, emboldened by his continued power, actually suggested that the next U.S. president should be an internationalist and not an American. So much for globalization, which our wise forefathers warned us against many years ago, because it will be our undoing. We no longer have a manufacturing industry, and we're slowly becoming more and more dependent. It's really time for us to say good-bye to the U.N. and take back our own national self-respect.

11

(July 1, 2006) In the early 1930s, when Hitler became leader of Germany, his first law was to take the guns away from the people, so the Jews went quietly to the ovens, six million of them, including my maternal uncle and his family.

I am a vigorous opponent of gun control because it's naive and stupid to believe that taking guns away from citizens will eliminate or lessen crimes. That's nuts.

Listen to the following news from Australia, which underscores the folly of taking guns away from the people. This is dated March 5, 2006, and it's from Ed Chenel, a Police officer in Australia:

"Hi Yanks, I thought you all would like to see the real figures from Down Under. It has now been 12 months since gun owners in Australia were forced by a new law to surrender 640,381 personal firearms to be destroyed by our own government, a program costing Australian tax payers more than $500 million. The first year's results are in now. Australia-wide, homicides are up 8.2%. Australia-wide, assaults are up 9.6%. Armed robberies are up 44% – yes, 44% in the State of Victoria alone. Homicides with firearms are now up 300%, and that while the law-abiding citizens turned them in, the criminals did not, and criminals still possess their guns.

While figures over the previous 25 years showed a steady decrease in armed robbery with firearms, this has changed drastically upward in the past 12 months since the criminals now are guaranteed that their victims are unarmed. There have also been dramatic increases in break-ins and assaults of the elderly while the resident is in the home.

Australian politicians are at a loss to explain how public safety was decreased after such monumental efforts, and expenses are expended in successfully ridding Australian society of guns. You won't see this on the American evening news, or hear your governor or members of the State Assembly disseminating this information, because they have an idiotic mental block.

The Australian experience speaks for itself. Guns in the hands of honest citizens save lives and property, and gun control laws affect only the law-abiding citizens. It's a no brainer. Take note, Americans, before it's too late. Remember, guns do not kill people; people kill people. Put another way.. when guns are outlawed, only outlaws will have guns.

Please, forward this information to everyone you know. Don't be a member of the silent majority. Be one of the vocal minority who won't let this happen in the USA."

12

(2006) I recently saw the documentary "An Inconvenient Truth", a really excellent title for a worldwide issue all of us must sooner or later confront. Go see it.

Kudos to Al Gore for continuing to bring this problem into the open where it belongs. I have not been a fan of Al Gore's, always having viewed him as somewhat silly or foolish for claiming that the novel and movie Love Story was all about him and his wife, plus his claim that he invented the Internet. Like other politicians, Gore often makes the fatal mistake of underestimating the intelligence of the people. On the other hand, putting politics aside, global warming is a universal issue which transcends politics or partisanship.

That having been said, I believe in Gore's sincerity and passion about global warming, and he deserves kudos for researching and keeping this concern alive. Not the least of it being his mention of the electric car introduced about ten years ago and heralded as a very successful alternative to our gasoline-guzzling, pollution-producing automobiles. How come the electric car disappeared very quietly, and why? Was it the powerful automobile and energy corporations who squelched this reasonable alternative? Those economic giants making enormous profits NOW care very little about problems of the future.

Another issue discussed in the movie was the Kyoto Agreements in which most of the world's countries are willing to jointly reduce the pollution in the global atmosphere. After careful consideration, President Bush declined to have the U.S. participate, and he has been ridiculed by the American media because of it. What the media does not mention is that the United States will not participate so long as the world's two worst polluters, China and India, are exempt from participation. That makes the treaties a farce and an exercise in futility.

Many credible scientists agree that the warming process may have existed for many years; however, the movie explains that lately there is evidence that the damaging effects of global warming are accelerating very rapidly.

Other credible scientists ridicule the immediate concerns, saying that the Earth has had, for centuries, cycles of warming and then cooling, and then warming. Meanwhile, nothing is being done. Suppose the opinion of poo-pooing is wrong. Without the bickering back and forth, wouldn't it be wise and expedient to go on the assumption that global warming is a fact, even if it isn't urgent? Shouldn't all of us help clean up our atmosphere NOW?

Expecting everyone to switch to bicycles or walking is out of the question, but surely the electric car for every driver in the world— including India and China—would go a long way toward cleaning up the atmosphere. At least it's a start.

One dubious friend became a believer in global warming when he saw the monster glacier in Yellowstone not too long ago, now almost melted away.

13

(July 17, 2006) I wrote the following thoughts several days ago. Since then, the world situation has rapidly changed. Israel is at war with Hamas and Hezbollah in Lebanon, both terrorist organizations funded by Syria and Iran, the latter whose leader more than once has told the world that Israel must be destroyed. Despite my forthcoming remarks, I hope that the U.N. finally comes up with some solutions and advice to justify its existence for the U.S. and other democracies. This is a moment of truth for the U.N.

Not unlike the predictable reaction of Pavlov's dogs, who learned to salivate happily every time a bell rang, I experience a similar, though negative, reaction when I think about the U.N. It was created in 1945 in San Francisco after World War II, and all the nations who participated were filled with hope that together they could solve the world's problems peacefully. It was deja vu all over again like the League of Nations created after World War I, which turned out to be a dismal failure.

The U.N. is also a dismal failure. Countries with different basic principles and moral standards can never homogenize. Add to that the inevitable human fact that those endowed with less will hate those endowed with more, and like it or not, most in the U.N. hate the U.S.

Also, an organization which knowingly stands by its dishonest leader, Kofi Annan, who was a party to stealing millions of dollars from Saddam Hussein's Food for Oil program and who continues to lead the U.N., is doomed to failure because it operates without integrity. So, why do we remain host to this dirty group, and also donate – I believe it is about three billion dollars a year to keep it alive and provide each nation member a place for its representatives to live and be immune from any accountability whatsoever? Are we not crazy? And where is our national self-respect?

Haven't we seen throughout the years that when we turn to the U.N. for wisdom and counsel, nobody is home? Recently, we have urged the U.N. to come up with solutions for the North Korea problem – which could blow up the planet – and Iran – which surely could do likewise – yet no decision is forthcoming, because the U.N. is filled with intrigue, corruption, and prejudice. Let's face it, most members hate us with a passion because we are their foolish, generous benefactors.

I sound like a broken record, but let's invite the U.N. to leave the U.S., resign from it, and let's make an alliance with other democracies whose philosophies match ours, of decency, fairness, and accountability, and move ahead to make the world safer. Maybe then the rogue nations will fall in line.

As an addendum, here's another possible, less-extreme, solution. The U.N. has been the only kid on the block for 61 years and has shamelessly vetoed most U.S. suggestions. Thus far, it has cost our country possibly 61 times three billion dollars. Before separating irrevocably, why not create a separate United Democracies now, and add another perspective and dimension to global solutions? Hopefully then, the U.N., faced with competition, will become energized instead of weak and disengaged, all of which may become a useful tool for true world peace. What do you think?

Also, for those naive souls who believe Kofi Annan is clean, I have a bridge in Brooklyn I'd love to sell you.

14

It's easy for many Americans to feel wistful and envious after learning how the Australian government is now dealing with their immigration problems. If we had felt the same way 30 years ago when political correctness clouded our viewpoint and inhibited us from speaking out about how we run our country, and if we had had more backbone instead of blind approval for diversity, we would be in better national shape now. We were so eager to make the newcomers feel welcome that we didn't see that we were diluting our own unique beliefs. We relinquished our precious standards to accommodate those with different beliefs, and now we are a discontented mess, and nobody is truly happy.

Listen to the following, and wonder: Is it too late for us to assert our own American identity? This is called "Immigration

Common Sense" and it was spoken by Prime Minister John Howard of Australia.

"Muslims who want to live under Islamic law were told recently to get out of Australia as the government targeted radicals in a bid to head off potential terror attacks. Immigrants, not Australians, must adapt, take it or leave it. We're tired of this nation worrying about whether we're offending some individual or their culture. Since the terrorists' attack on Bali, we've experienced a surge of patriotism by the majority of Australians.

However, the dust from the attacks had hardly settled when the politically correct crowd again complained about the possibility that our patriotism was offending others. We're not against immigration, nor do I hold a grudge against anyone who's seeking a better life by coming to Australia; however, there are a few things that those who have recently come to our country need to understand. This idea of Australia being a multicultural community has served only to dilute our sovereignty and our national identity. As Australians, we have our own culture, our own society, our own language, and our own lifestyle.

We speak mainly English, not Spanish, Lebanese, Arabic, Chinese, Japanese, Russian, or any other language. Therefore, if you wish to become part of our society, then learn the language. Most Australians believe in God. If God offends you, then I suggest you consider another part of the world as your new home because God is part of our culture. We're happy with our culture, and have no desire to change, and we really don't care how you did things where you came from. By all means, keep your culture, but do not force it on others.

This is our country, our land, and our life-style, and we will allow you every opportunity to enjoy all of this, however, once you are done complaining, whining, and griping about our flag, our pledge, our beliefs, or our way of life, I highly encourage you to take advantage of one other great Australian freedom – the right to leave.

We didn't force you to come here. You asked to be here."

So, KSCO listeners, this gem speaks volumes for the fervent wishes of many, many Americans. I believe maybe it's not too late to take back our country and our own national language and our own civil and religious beliefs. And only those willing to abide by them should stay, and the others should leave and go elsewhere. I know this is wishful thinking. Let's take back Christmas and the Ten Commandments, and all our other national beliefs, and best of all let's embrace Almighty God.

[This part spoken by MZ.] Except that we're not allowed to play that on KOMY because we don't want to offend its audience. True, true, we're not. We switched KOMY to Air America Radio a little more than a year ago, and for the first ten months, we made it a point to keep Kay's commentaries off KOMY. After about ten months, we decided "Hey, no one is supporting the radio station, there are certainly no advertisers, so to hell with them — Let's put Kay's commentaries on!" and then the bleep hit the fan. The people got so upset they had nervous breakdowns. The comment lines just melted down. We were called horrible names. What's going on with this world?

At least you found out the listeners were alive.

We knew that there were a good amount of listeners, and are, they are just no advertisers.

15

It's no secret that I have no use whatsoever for the United Nations. It's corrupt, self-serving, and ineffective, and we should remove ourselves from its membership and send the U.N. to live elsewhere, like Venezuela.

But it's even worse than I thought. Recently, I received information from a Tom DeWeese, president of the American Policy Center and editor of the DeWeese Report, who released a copy of his reactions to the debate he had with the United Nations representative in October before the Cambridge Union Society.

A political activist, DeWeese was surprised to have been invited, but he attended, and the subject was "How Far Gone Property Rights Are at the U.N." What you are about to hear is very scary. Here are some of DeWeese's observations:

The U.N. is a dead loss. Initially it was meant to be the place for governments to come together to discuss and air their differences. That was the image of the U.N. sold to the world since its inception. A second mission was for countries to pool resources to provide charitable aid to those who are starving or are victims of natural disaster. That is not the reality. The world is in chaos, and it's the U.N.'s fault. It gives validity to zealots and petty bigots. It helps to keep tyrannical dictators in power. It gives a voice to international terrorists. Delay. Negotiate. Recommend. Study. Reconsider. Then, do nothing. This is the game that the U.N. has played in nearly every international crisis. This is the reason North Korea remains a threat after 50 years. It's the reason why the Chinese government is able to ignore U.N. rules that it dislikes – while growing as an international military and economic threat. And it is the reason why a terrorist nation like

Syria can be given a seat on the United Nations Human Rights Council. What a joke.

The U.N. internally is a mess. It's buried under scandals. Peacekeeping missions actually bring fear to the local citizens they are supposed to protect. Rob, rape, and pillage seems to be the U.N.'s modus operandi. How can we be surprised by such revelations? Who has the power to oversee and control its actions? The media has little access behind the scenes. Who audits the accounting books? According to Kofi Annan, and many others, reform means global governance. Since its inception, the U.N. has advocated the desire to eradicate sovereign nations while imposing what it calls "world mindedness". A 1949 Unesco document said, nationalism is the major obstacle to the development of world mindedness. In the 1990s, a U.N. leader said, it's not feasible for sovereignty to be exercised unilaterally by individual nations. Therein lies the true goal of the United Nations. The U.N. is openly working to gain power for itself in order to become independent and supreme over its member nations.

On September 19, this year, plans were approved to begin the creation of a global tax, mostly through airline tickets ostensibly to help pay for the treatment of AIDS. There are several other tax schemes on the U.N. wish list including a carbon tax on CO2 emissions, a currency tax on transactions of foreign currency exchanges, and taxes on the Internet, to name a few. If the U.N. gains the power to tax and the enforcement power necessary to collect them, the U.N. will become an unstoppable force in the world.

Three things – the ability to collect taxes to provide unlimited funds from independent sources, the ability to enforce its will with a military force, and a court system to impose its own brand of justice, are all that is required to create a world government. Clearly the United Nations wants to be much more than a place where nations can come together to air their differences.

Again, the truth is today, 50 years after the inception of the U.N., the world is a dangerous place. The world has more wars, more poverty, and more suffering than any time in human history. Obviously the U.N. is irrelevant as a body to deliver world peace. It is more interested in meddling in the sovereign affairs of nations, seeking to impose its own agenda and what it calls social equity in a drive to set itself up as a world government. The U.N. was wrong from the beginning, and wrong now because it has always sought to interfere with national sovereignty rather than to promote a unique forum to help keep the peace. It should be tossed on the trash heap of history so that we may start over and create an honest enterprise that seeks to help nations, not eradicate them. It's a criminal enterprise in which no moral nation should ever participate let alone perpetuate.

These were the honest observations of Mr. Tom DeWeese. Thank you Tom. You are right on.

And I add, we must never, never subordinate our sovereignty to any world government. The sooner we pull out of the U.N., the better. We are in quicksand. Please, let's wake up before it's too late. If President Bush is in favor of a world government to supersede our own sovereign nation, then I am totally against him or any other president who would advocate such an atrocity and betrayal.

16

(January 18, 2007) It was the late 1970s. My husband and I were part of a small group visiting China. We were there the day that Richard Nixon signed the treaty with China to have joint economic relations. That day, the Chinese people were dancing in the streets. There were no cars then, only millions of bicycles, and everyone wore black outfits, and it being bitter cold, bitter winter, they wore layers and layers of cotton clothing.

I had mixed feelings for the people in their celebration. Despite their forthcoming Americanization and prosperity, the Chinese would lose a certain simplicity and peaceful existence and trade that in for capitalism and its companion, stress.

Let's fast-forward to 2007. U.S. manufacturing is almost non-existent. Most of it went to China and other countries. International corporations convinced our leaders that trade with China would benefit our country.

I have never understood how we benefit when China inundates us with enormous amounts of stuff, much of it inferior, and takes only a fraction of our products in return. Our leaders allowed and condoned that practice, and now China owns us.

The following, floating around the Internet, author unknown, underscores my dismay and disgust with trade imbalances allowed by our government. This will scare and anger you.

"December 26, 2006. When one day a year either makes or breaks the bank, how fragile indeed has our economy become? Decades ago, when we manufactured almost everything here in America, the Christmas holiday was just that – a holiday. Retail businesses made money, but the money spent on gifts stayed in American pockets. Now, almost everything is made in China,

India, Mexico, and many other countries. Once the money is sent out of the country, it will never return.

If you do not believe this, check the trade imbalance between the U.S. and China. We buy everything from them, while they buy pitifully little from us. It is a lucrative one-sided deal for China and the corporations who engineered this scheme, with the American worker coming out the loser. And if you think that this stuff on a grand scale is not hurting America – well, listen to this – America's finances are in such bad shape that China, our so-called most favored trading partner, is taking the billions of American dollars which it has accumulated in this one-sided trade deal and is now wisely trading them in for Euros and precious metals.

The Chinese are well aware of America's deepening financial morass, and they are not going to get stuck with billions of worthless American dollars if the bottom falls out. And my friends, unless our do-nothing Congress acts soon to reverse this looming economic disaster, the once mighty dollar will wind up like the post World War I German Mark, worthless.

As we speak, the dollar is losing value. What is worse, however, is the mindset of the average American, who seems to be more concerned about his neighbor's dog pooing on his lawn than about the impending collapse of the dollar. I say our government is really worse – nobody's home.

Once the bottom begins to drop out, Americans will eventually get their heads out of the sand, and demand an end to the so-called free-trade schemes and a return to fiscal responsibility. However, by that time it will be too late, and a depression equal to, or worse than, that of the 1930s will be upon us. I lived through that one, and it was not good.

17

What I am about to relate to you is almost unthinkable. It's deja vu all over again. I was a child in the 1930s and remember that this is exactly how it started, and it's starting again. A friend living in France asked me to distribute this information Once again, the real news in France is conveniently not being recorded as it should be". To give you an idea of what's going on in France with between 5 and 6 million Muslims, and about 600,000 Jews, here is a message from a Jew living in France.

"Will the world say nothing again, as it did in Hitler's time? I am a Jew, therefore, I am forwarding this to everyone I know. I will not sit back and do nothing. Nowhere have the flames of anti-Semitism burned more furiously than here in France. In Leone, a car was rammed into a synagogue and set on fire. In another French city, the Jewish religious sector was fired on – so were synagogues in Strasbourg and Marseilles. So were the Jewish schools in another French city, all recently. And the list goes on and on.

So I call on you – whether you are a fellow Jew, a friend, or merely a person with the capacity and desire to distinguish decency from depravity, to do at least these three simple things: First, care enough to stay informed. Don't ever let yourself become deluded into thinking that this is not your fight. I remind you of what Pastor Neimoller said in World War 2, "First they came for the communists and I didn't speak up because I wasn't a communist. Then they came for the Jews and I didn't speak up because I wasn't a Jew. Then they came for the Catholics and I didn't speak up because I was a Protestant. Then they came for me, but by that time, there was no one left to speak up for me."

Second, boycott France and French products. Boycott their wines and their perfumes. Boycott their clothes and their food stuffs. Boycott their movies. Definitely boycott their shores.

3. Send this along to your friends and your family. Think of all the people of good conscience that you know, and let them know that you and the people that you care about need their help.

Also, you should know that the number one best selling book in France right now is "September 11th, the Frightening Fraud" which argues that no plane ever hit the Pentagon. The French press is deliberately suppressing all this evil information.

18

(July 12, 2007) What I am about to disclose to you is unbelievable and disappointing.

Having always looked upon the British government and its people as closest to Americans in our thoughts of respect for human rights and acceptance of different religions, it is with sadness and shock that I learned what the British Union of Colleges and Universities, a labor organization representing 125,000 British academics, has chosen to opine to the world on human rights, democracy, and peace in the Middle East.

This organization will not denounce Iran, which is developing nuclear weapons and has declared its intent to obliterate Israel. Neither will it denounce Saudi Arabia, which executes prisoners in public by stoning and beheading, and which is widely known to finance terrorism around the region. Nor does it care about Syria, which holds sham elections and tolerates Hamas, or Egypt, where opponents of the government are tried by secret military tribunal.

You will not find any of these countries on the black list considered by the British Union of Colleges and Universities. Instead, this organization claiming concern for human rights is considering a boycott against the only democracy in the Middle East: Israel.

Under the terms of the boycott, Israeli academics will not be permitted to publish in British journals or attend academic conferences in the United Kingdom. Joint research between British and Israeli scholars – whether about strategies for peace or cures for disease – would be barred, and student exchange programs would immediately come to a halt.

The purpose is clear – to punish Israeli scholars and isolate Israeli universities – and these foolish British scholars will shoot themselves in the foot in the name of hate and bigotry. Don't these so-called educated academics understand that academic boycotts are a loss for everyone, that boycotts of this nature – besides being unethical and biased – are counterproductive to human progress and world peace?

Many pioneering innovations beneficial to the global community evolved from collaboration between colleagues in different parts of the world. And some of the most significant discoveries made in Israel are shared gladly with the scientific world community. Some of these recent discoveries are:

A revolutionary drug developed in Israel that holds hope for tens of millions who suffer from schizophrenia.

A biological control for mosquitoes and black flies that spread malaria and blindness, saving the sight and lives of millions of people in Africa and China.

Velcade, an effective new cancer drug, based on research that won two Israeli professors the 2004 Nobel prize.

These are but a few of the Israeli scientific contributions to the world for the betterment of humanity. And this is what the British scientists want to throw away in the name of hoping to destroy the Jewish state of Israel? They want to boycott a cure for cancer? They want to stop drip irrigation – invented by Israeli scientists? And they want to prevent scientific cooperation between nations? These actions by some British academics, who do not speak for the people of Britain, who want to boycott Israelis, have lost all their colleagues their credibility.

The only explanation for their strange actions could be that some British-born Muslim scientists have infiltrated the British organization and brainwashed the membership to hate Israel. The Israeli response is to educate the world community of these strange actions of the British scientists.

19

So, you want to boycott Israel? I'll be sorry to miss you, but if you really are doing it, think about it carefully. Let me help you. How about telling your pals to boycott the following.

An Israeli company has developed a simple blood test that distinguishes between cancer and severe cases of Multiple Sclerosis.

An Israeli-made device helps restore the use of paralyzed hands. This device electrically stimulates the hand muscles, providing hope to millions of stroke sufferers and victims of spinal injuries. If you wish to remove this hope of a better quality of life for these people, go ahead and boycott Israel.

Children with breathing problems will soon be sleeping more soundly thanks to a new Israeli device called The Child Hood. This innovation replaces the inhalation mask with an improved drug delivery system that provides relief for child and parent. Please tell anxious mothers that they shouldn't use this device because of your passionate cause.

These are just a few more examples of how people have benefitted medically from the Israeli know-how that you wish to block.

The movement disorder surgery program in Israel's Hidasa Medical Center has successfully eliminated the physical manifestations of Parkinson's disease in a select group of patients with a deep brain stimulation technique.

Israel is developing a nose drop that will provide a five-year flu vaccine.

These are just a few of the projects that you can help stop with your Israeli boycott.

Most of the latest Windows operating system was developed by Microsoft-Israel. So set a personal example, and throw away your computer.

Voice mail technology was developed in Israel.

The technology of the AOL Instant Messenger ICQ was developed in 1996 in Israel by four young Israeli whiz kids.

Both Microsoft and Cisco built their only RND facilities outside the U.S. in Israel.

So, due to your complete boycott of anything Israeli, you can now have poor health and no computer.

But your bad news does not end there. Get rid of your cellular phone. Cell phone technology was also developed in Israel, by Motorola A, which has its biggest development center in Israel. Most of the latest technology in your mobile phone was developed by Israeli scientists.

A phone can remotely activate a bomb, or be used for tactical communications by terrorists, bank robbers, or hostages takers. It's vital that official security and law enforcement authorities have access to cellular jamming and detection solutions. Enter Israel's net line communications technologies with their security expertise to help the fight against terror.

SO ALL THE NOISE ABOUT THE USA LISTENING TO OUR PRIVATE PHONE CALLS, YOU SHOULD KNOW THAT IT IS ISRAEL THAT IS DOING THE LISTENING FOR US.

I also want you to know that Israel has the highest ratio of university degrees to total population in the world.

Israel produces more scientific papers per capita (109 per 10,000) than any other nation.

Israel has the highest number of startup companies pro rata. In absolute terms, the highest number besides the U.S., Israel has the highest number of patents filed.

Israel has the highest concentration of high-tech companies outside of Silicon Valley. Israel is ranked #2 in the world for venture capital funds behind the USA.

Israel has more museums per capita.

Relative to population, Israel is the largest immigrant absorbing nation on earth.

These immigrants come in search of democracy, religious freedom or expression, economic opportunity, and quality of life.

Even Warren Buffett of Berkshire Hathaway fame has just invested millions with Israeli companies.

So you can vilify and demonize the state of Israel. You can continue your silly boycott, if you wish. But, I wish you would consider the consequences and the truth.

Think of the massive contributions that Israel is giving to the world – including the Palestinians – and to you, in science, medicine, communications, security. Pro rata for population, Israel is making a greater contribution than any other nation on earth.

Pass this on to everyone you know, whether pro Israel or not. Thanks

20

(March 28, 2008) Much of the following was suggested by my bright and concerned friend Zolton Egerizi who left his native Hungary and family at the age of 18, feeling he could no longer live in an oppressive communist community. This commentary is called Nobel Prize for Fraud.

For many years, the Nobel Prize has been bestowed upon the best and brightest. Some of these prizes were given for the right reasons to the right individuals, say for medicine, economics, inventions, or whatever makes human life better.

In recent years, the Nobel Prize for peace has become more often a political joke for promoting international socialism, the U.N., and the new European Union's public political agenda.

Yasser Arafat, the inventor of airline highjacking, received a Nobel Peace Prize for promoting peace in the Middle East, which has been a total failure. Arafat, the Middle East's biggest corrupt leader, stashed away over $10 million in Swiss accounts, so the useful idiots in Palestine could keep on rioting on the issue of property and especially about the existence of the state of Israel.

Along came Kofi Annan, the U.N.'s General Secretary, who received a Peace Prize for organizing the U.N. to be a more efficient, accountable organization. Oh sure – this was nothing more than the biggest bold-face lie. During the reign of this Nobel Prize international mafia don of the U.N., he managed to swindle more than $24 billion (with a B) from the Iraqi people using the Food for Oil scam to move money into the coffers of the U.N.'s socialist lawyers.

The moral of this story is, if you steal, steal big, then nobody will put you in jail. You get more jail time for stealing a car than for a multi-billion-dollar fraud. Some of Kofi Annan's people did receive some jail time, others hid behind diplomatic immunity, but nothing happened to Kofi Annan.

The U.N. must have a more transparent and clear accounting system and be accountable to all member countries. If not, the U.S. should just get out of that socialist cesspool.

For years, I have wanted our country to remove itself from that corrupt self-serving group whose only agenda is to rule the globe and subordinate all the countries under its rule.

Along comes the latest fraud – Al Gore, the new high priest of the global warming scam, trying to scare the uninformed. He was given a Peace Prize for what? It should have been called Nobel Prize For The Biggest Lie. This global warming garbage is nothing more than a fake for the U.N. to come up with an international tax system collected on energy, energy use, and the ability to control other nations through the U.N.'s dictatorship.

The U.N. received 51 prostituted votes from liberal climate scientists on the left, and on government payroll, during the Paris Climate Conference. Yet it ignored 400+ other scientists who dispute that CO2, or man, is the cause of global warming. That is nonsense.

The U.N. is after taxes again. They blame the USA and people who could be taxed and leached upon while their communist friends in China, India, or South Korea can pollute the air all day and all night. Well, the capitalist smoke really bothers them, but not the marijuana smoke – first or second hand.

15,000 global warming jihadists, the environmental activists with their chief alarmist Al Gore, met in Bali a while ago to urge all nations to hurry up and sign the new treaty. It is like a band of bank robbers – hurry up before they find out that we have looted them.

The media continues to neglect to mention that President Bush will not sign the Kyoto Agreements because the world's worst polluters, China and India, are exempt from cleaning up their filth.

Who do you think paid for this nice winter vacation for most of the delegates? The U.N. – from money they collected for the Indonesian tsunami victims. They collected over $1 billion and gave out less than $100 million, so they are having a good time on your donations.

The U.N. also wants to highjack the internet domain registration control from the U.S. so countries like Russia, China, Iran, Venezuela, and others could block internet traffic not approved by their dictators.

The U.N., under the L.O.S.T. Treaty, wants to control the seas all around the world, and the minerals and oil in the sea beds, tax the resources and distribute it among third-world countries. The Robin Hoods of New York, the U.N., will get a very handsome commission, plus the control of where our Navy can sail or not sail. We are totally sick of this U.N. mafia.

Kudos to you, Zolton, for shining a light on much of this important information.

Isn't it time for We the People to direct our government to resign from the U.N., which we have tolerated and subsidized for more than 60 years? They routinely veto whatever our representatives recommend and have leached upon us long enough. Clearly, their agenda is to rule the world. America, please wake up before it's too late.

21

(May 19, 2008) In the late 1920s when I was a child, I remember relatives and friends who yearned to go live in the Holy Land. They went to the Middle East and purchased small plots of land from various Arabs who were happy to dispose of their arid property.

Only after they saw that the Jews, by creating drip irrigation, made their arid land blossom, those Arabs became envious, and tensions arose. Those tensions still exist, and will never go away.

I was a young mother in my mid 20s when Israel became a state in 1948, and suddenly the surrounding Arab countries were joining together to annihilate Israel for becoming a recognized state.

Israel urged those Arabs living peacefully among them to remain in their homes and be protected by the new state. But their Arab brethren urged them to leave, assuring them that the Israeli Jews would easily be crushed, and the Arabs could then return to their homes victorious and safe.

That never happened. Since they chose to leave Israel, Israel no longer wanted them back.

So, what happened? Those displaced Arabs were not taken in by their Arab brethren who lived in large, wealthy oil countries and could easily have absorbed them. Instead, those Arab countries chose to keep the Israeli Arabs in camps.. indefinitely.

Why? Specifically, to keep the displaced Arabs as political pawns, to make the world feel sorry for them and hate Israel. Then they admonished their displaced brethren to never accept the Palestinian state offered to them until Israel is destroyed.

That was 60 years ago.

They could have had their own country for the last 60 years. But the stubborn Arabs still hope to throw Israel into the sea. That has not happened yet, but who knows? Surrounded by enemies, Israel is doomed to remain in a constant state of war. It is a shame. Israel is a tiny country which can be traversed from north to south in eight hours, and east to west in three hours.

Ideally, the Arabs should accept their Palestine now, next to Israel, and both should live in peace and mutual respect. The world would be much happier for it.

P.S. - A few listeners called to remind me that I attributed last week's commentary to the wrong Miller. It was a Larry Miller, not Dennis Miller. I Googled Larry Miller, and found a number of them, and learned that the original Larry Miller in 2002 never got credit for that Palestinian piece nor others of his writings. I'm sorry for that error. But the message was interesting, though the right Larry Miller should have received the credit, and the kudos for it.

22

(May 27, 2008) After watching 60 Minutes recently, I think that we Americans should be deeply ashamed for the lack of proper action from our government. Are our leaders losing their marbles, or are they so wrapped up in their own earmarks that nothing else matters?

Briefly, over 100,000 Iraqi citizens, who agreed to help our military with valuable information when they were asked, now find themselves marked for death by other Iraqis who deeply resent our military intrusion in their country.

Our government should move rapidly to bring those Iraqis and their families who are in danger here to the U.S. But that's not happening easily. Our Congress claims that the process to bring these Iraqis to the U.S. must be slow and deliberate because some of them could be terrorists. I say, "Bullpucky."

There is something wrong with this picture. As I've mentioned many times, President Bush, and the three or four presidents for the past 30 years, clearly have not shown any concern about our open borders, so that now there are thousands of possible terrorists, criminals, and other unsavory people entering our country without any inspection whatsoever. Now they are suddenly careful about those Iraqis who helped our military in Iraq.

After five years, and over the billions we taxpayers are spending in Iraq, one becomes weary about our situation. Whatever our good intentions, we are in a very difficult mess, and leaving now may also be disastrous. However, there is another dimension to this dilemma.

Amazing and wonderful things are happening in Iraq, things which our occupation made possible. Now there is the possibility of another democracy like Israel in the Middle East. Thanks to our fighting men and women, we are achieving success in Iraq. (Did you know? Probably not. How could you? The media won't share the current good news.) Did you know that 47 countries have reestablished their embassies? Did you know that the Iraq government currently employs 1.2 million people? Did you know that 3,464 schools have been renovated and that 265 schools are under construction? You didn't know that. And, that in higher education, there are 20 universities, 46 colleges, and four research centers currently operating? Of course you didn't, because our media won't let us know that.

Did you know that the Iraqi Navy and Air Force are operational? And the Iraqi police service has over 55,000 fully trained officers? And there are five police academies in Iraq that produce over 4,500 new officers every eight weeks? Did you know that there are more than 1,100 building projects going on in Iraq, including schools, hospitals, and railroad stations? No – nobody told us.

Did you know that 4.3 million Iraqi children are enrolled in primary schools? And there are 1,192,000 cell phone subscribers in Iraq? Did you know that Iraq has 75 radio stations, 180 newspapers, and ten television stations? Bet you didn't know that. Did you know that two candidates in the Iraqi presidential election had a televised debate? Of course you didn't know.

Why didn't we know? Because our media won't tell us. Tragically, the left accentuating the negative in Iraq serves two purposes. It's intended to undermine the world's perception of the U.S., thus minimizing consequent support, and it's intended to discourage American citizens. The media is despicable to withhold this honest information.

Despite the disloyal American media who want us to fail in Iraq, another democracy may be borne in the Middle East, which will benefit all democracies and, indeed, the world.

These facts are verifiable on the Department of Defense website. And kudos to you, Paul Trigg of Santa Cruz, for sharing this information with us.

23

(June 15, 2008) As we think about China, and how she has so rapidly become a world presence, we may remember Napoleon's famous description: "Let China sleep, for when she awakens, she will shake the world".

Today, China is not only awake, but because of her enormous population, she is —or will become— arguably the greatest force in the world. So, despite what our sophisticated Wall Street types have to say, China is getting richer and stronger, and we are becoming weaker. Ironically, China's funds are so invested in America that if she removes those possible billions and trades them into Euros, our economy may collapse. But the Pandora's box is now open, and it will never close.

Why did we allow this inequity to happen? Wouldn't fair trade have been better than free trade? Fair trade means that I give you 50%, and you give me 50%.

Recently, I read a most intriguing article with regard to China, who is much more aware and aggressive than we are about acquiring the world's dwindling raw materials. China is now engaged in Africa, specifically the sub-Saharan countries like Mozambique, which supplies lumber, and Zambia, which supplies copper. The Congo has a wide range of minerals, and equatorial Guinea has oil. China, at a frantic pace, is swooping up the copper, timber, natural gas, zinc, cobalt, and you name it.

Because China can see that in the foreseeable future – factoring in the recent luxury needs of China and India, plus all of Europe, Asia, and the United States – there will be a shortage of these raw materials. The awakened giant is now buying up everything that the poor sub-Saharan countries will willingly sell her.

Evidently we are either too timid, not looking ahead, asleep at the wheel, or maybe too obsessed with corrupt American politics. In fact, our country is involved in the sub-Saharan countries, but not in the aggressive way that China is.

We should wisely remember the forgotten work of Thomas Malthus, who said some two centuries ago, "The power of population is infinitely greater than the power in the earth to produce subsistence for all mankind." In other words, eventually there may not be enough of the raw materials to serve all mankind. Like China, shouldn't we be more aggressive about obtaining the raw materials while they are still available?

24

(July 11, 2008) In 1979, my husband and I were in China, just when our two governments agreed to trade with each other. The Chinese people were dancing in the streets. I wondered how all this would play out. The agrarian country was now becoming a world trader. Fast forward to 2008.

In our eagerness to trade with China, it became—and still is — lopsided. It's called free trade, where one side only benefits. Along the way, somehow we seduced ourselves into giving up our own industries which had kept us independent. We thought being a serviceoriented society would be okay. The U.S. has really been living in a fool's paradise on a phony economy. Now we are world dependent. We have helped China to become so wealthy that she owns us, because most of her profits are in billions and are invested in our nation.

A recent interview in Barron's, the financial periodical, is very compelling. Listen... "We haven't been through anything like what we're going through now, probably for more than 20 years. We have been able to convince the world to lend us, and to provide us with, goods that we don't produce anymore and that we can't afford to pay for. And now the problem is big, especially since the real estate bubble.

We borrowed so much money from abroad that our trade deficits are now enormous, and our industrial base has been allowed to decay for so long that we can only survive in this economy thanks to the charity of the rest of the world.

The U.S. is now an empire that is sustained by borrowing from friends and anyone else who will give us credit. Our creditors hold hundreds of billions of dollars, but the dollar continues to weaken, and our foreign creditors could take a huge loss in their dollar holdings.

To compensate, some of our foreign friends have formed sovereign wealth funds made up largely of dollars. These sovereign wealth funds seek to unload some of their dollars by buying up tangible assets. A recent example was Abu Dhabi's sovereign wealth fund buying New York's Empire State Building for $900 billion.

Neither McCain nor Obama will ever mention the problem of the U.S. empire living on borrowed money. This is the biggest problem facing the U.S. today."

Are we now a global mess?

Can it be the slow drifting to globalization whereby countries try to work together and delegate so there is no duplication – a sort of global dependence? Did our national leaders err by encouraging us to give up our own industries? If all this is true, our leaders are withholding this information at least until after the election.

Perhaps we must resurrect what worked for us before – that is, our own industries, and reject our dependency on other nations. That is the path our forefathers vigorously admonished us to take when our nation was created. We must, however, factor in that the world has changed. Once the world had workers in the millions. Now, with China and India in the world market, the global workforce is in the billions. So the inflation of workers creates resentment and competition. The stage is set for the inevitable confrontation of China and India vs. the U.S. and Europe. And how that situation will play out remains to be seen.

25

(January 24, 2009) The United States is struggling with an inferiority complex. Our country is probably the best nation that has ever existed, because it is generous, honest, brave, and because it was blessed with men of wisdom at its creation centuries ago. They made laws to promote freedom for the citizens to define themselves. We are the envy of other countries on this globe, and now we are being verbally assaulted – very unfairly – by those countries who have been, and still are, recipients of our financial generosity and help whenever it is needed. Rarely, if ever, do those countries send troops to help when freedom is in danger.

We are being taken advantage of by those who have regularly been helped and elevated by us.

Most of the countries which make up the United Nations dislike us. In 1945, at our expense, we built the beautiful building in New York City for all nations to come together to help each other get along. They do not get along very well, and we pay all or most of the expenses, while representatives of many countries, even third world countries, are treated like visiting royalty.

Somewhere along the way, many of the leaders of the U.N. became corrupt. They have stolen millions of dollars for themselves, money which was meant to help world poverty. Now they have another agenda.

The U.N. wants to rule the world and is quietly taking over different nations' properties. Outrageous? Research it yourself. Is it possible that the U.N. has already taken possession of our own U.S. National Parks? Check it out.

But, I am diverting from the original thought of this topic, which is that many of the countries in the world do not approve of the U.S., and the liberal extremist wimps in the U.S. are anxious for us to change our image so that the world will like us more. That is bullpucky. We have done nothing wrong or immoral. On the contrary, we must let our military fight to win and not let our image be the priority.

When in war with an enemy who slices off the heads of our soldiers, we must use waterboarding, which never kills, which creates fear for a few minutes, but gets valuable information to save our soldiers' lives. A little torture is ok, competing with slicing off heads.

Please, let us not buy into this politically correct guilt.

While we are grateful for allies like Britain, Australia, Turkey, and several other countries, our existence is not dependent upon those judgmental and jealous countries who love to criticize but will always find excuses to not help their fellow humans.

26

(February 20, 2009) If President Obama is able to pull off this quiet, outrageous executive order without being challenged or stopped by the Immigration Department, then it will also be possible for him to ignore Congress totally and rule by executive order only.

Kudos to you Zoltan for alerting us.

Also, by breaking his promise to let the people scrutinize the enormous stimulus bill for five days before signing it himself, he has destroyed his credibility.

The following is Obama's executive order – subject: Hamas is coming to the USA on your money. This information compiled by Dr. Paul L. Williams and was posted on Saturday, February 7, 2009, at 11:40 a.m., by New Media Journal.

By Executive Order, President Barack Obama has ordered the expenditure of $20 million (plus) in immigration assistance to the Palestinian refugees and conflict victims in Gaza. The "presidential determination" which allows hundreds of thousands of Palestinians with ties to Hamas to resettle in the United States, was signed on January 27, and appeared in the Federal Register on February 4.

President Obama's decision, according to the Federal Register, was necessitated by "the urgent refugee and migration needs of the victims". I say, what about the urgent need of our poor and our veterans in our country? A few on Capital Hill took note that the order provides a free ticket, replete with housing and food allowances, to individuals who have displayed their overwhelming support of the Islamic Resistance Movement – that is, Hamas – in the parliamentary election of January 2006. The Charter for Hamas called for the replacement of the nation of Israel with a Palestinian Islamic state. That means kill all of the Israelis and let the Palestinians move in.

Since its formation in 1994, Hamas has been responsible for initiating hundreds of terrorist attacks in Israel, including the 2002 Passover suicide bombing. The leaders of the movement signed the World Islamic Statement of 1998 – a document penned by Osama Bin Laden – which declared war on America and Israel.

President Obama's executive order is expected to bring hundreds of thousands of Palestinians – many with ties to radical Islam – to our shores, furthering a process that was inaugurated in 1995 by Senator Ted Kennedy – is this bad karma? – and the Sedar-Hart Bill.

Where is our president's head? Do we need those enemies in our midst?

Those of you who voted for change, and Barack Obama – look what you have done to inadvertently betray your country. Surely you did not expect this kind of change.

27

(February 27, 2009) Mea Culpa. I am so sorry. Hereafter, I will search carefully the authenticity of material sent to me.

President Obama did not arrange for thousands of displaced Palestinians to come to the U.S. Thank goodness! The $20 million (plus) requested by the U.N. was sent to help the displaced Palestinians to build homes lost during the recent Israeli-Palestinian war.

The world media chooses to ignore the fact that Hamas, since ruling Gaza for the last two years, has daily sent exploding bombs into southern Israel. The recent cease fire lasted only days, and now Hamas has already broken the agreement and is sending bombs again and again into Israel.

The reason for so many Arab casualties during war is because Hamas, Hezbollah, and all other Arab terrorists routinely use Palestinian women and children as human shields, especially at schools and hospitals, to run up their casualties and receive world pity. These cowardly, despicable skunks consider their own people irrelevant, and they fight dirty.

For the past 60 years, the Arabs have refused to have a state of their own – they only want Israel dead. So the stalemate goes on, and the world chooses to blame Israel, who merely wants to exist in peace.

Did you know that when Palestinian leaders become ill, they always ask to be admitted into Israeli hospitals? And they are always accepted.

Because we are all bummed out and depressed for various reasons, not the least of which is the fact that we are quickly sliding into socialism, let's end this on a happier note with the following funny observations written by a black man with a great sense of humor and a lot of creativity. Here goes.

When I was born, I was black. When I grew up, I was black. When I went in the sun, I stayed black. When I got cold, I was black. When I was scared, I was black. When I was sick, I was black. And when I die, I will still be black.

Now, you white folks – when you are born, you are pink. When you grow up, you are white. When you go in the sun, you get red. When you are cold, you turn blue. When you get scared, you are yellow. When you get sick, you are green. When you bruise, you turn purple. When you die, you look grey. So, who are you all calling colored folks?

28

(March 25, 2006) Many Americans are confused and would like to understand what led up to the bitterness that has existed in the Middle East between Arabs and Jews for more than half a century. One must go back to the early 1930s to learn that because of repeated references in the Old Testament, many older American Jews and other Jews from Eastern Europe had a lifelong yearning to go to the Holy Land called Yarooshliem, which we call Jerusalem. Most stayed and purchased little parcels of land from the local Arabs. In time, many other Jews from Russia and other counties migrated to Jerusalem and also purchased parcels of land from local Arabs, land which at that time was ruled by the British. Arabs and Jews got along well, and as society grew, there were Arab and Jewish lawmakers who were equal citizens with equal rights, who lived together peacefully side by side.

The Arabs who still live in Israel have equal rights, and some are in the Knesset and help make the laws of the country.

When the British decided to relinquish the area in 1948 for a Jewish state and an Arab state, the Jews accepted the British offer and declared their portion a state of Israel.

By the way, the word Palestinian was not invented until after the 1967 war.

The young Jewish state was instantly challenged by the surrounding Arab countries, who declared war on Israel. Those governments urged all Arabs living in Israel to leave their homes and join their brethren to defeat Israel, saying that they could return to their Israeli homes after Israel was defeated. Well, that victory never happened, not in 1948, and not in the Arab initiated war of 1967.

Tiny Israel is only, from south to north in a car, 12 hours long and from east to west, about four hours wide. Astonishingly, Israel won both wars. I believe God intervened.

Strangely, in the entire world, when the victor wins, the victor keeps the conquered land, but the law changes for Israelis and Jews. They are expected to return what they conquered. The world likes to call that land the occupied land when it really is the conquered land. Wouldn't one think that the wealthy, oil-rich Arab countries, like Saudi Arabia and Syria, could easily absorb their displaced brethren who left Israel at their urging? Of course not. Instead, those displaced Palestinians have been forced for five decades to live in camps and poverty while their own Arab brethren live in oil-rich luxury. Not one Arab country has been willing to absorb their displaced brethren who left their homes in 1948 when Israel urged them to stay. For those decades, the defeated Arab countries had been using their displaced brethren as political pawns to try to blame and embarrass Israel. Israel would surely not take them back now, not after they became Israel's enemies. These displaced Arabs are victims created by their own brethren.

Enter Arafat, the lying scoundrel who many times was offered a Palestinian state but refused. His only agenda was to annihilate Israelis. He invented the suicide bomber, a new kind of vicious warfare which has killed thousands of innocent Israelis and many gullible young Arabs.

One strange irony – if the Arabs living in Israel before the 1948 war had remained loyal to Israel and stayed, they would be the dominant political party now, because through over five decades, they have reproduced many fold more than the Israelis.

The truth is that Israeli citizens are largely homeless survivors of the Holocaust who yearned for a peaceful homeland, but that wish has never been fulfilled.

One must admire the tiny democracy which turned centuries-old arid land into the beautiful oasis supplying the world with oranges and human cures, the country which introduced drip irrigation to the world and many other improvements for society, who wants more than anything to live in peace. Israel is also on the cutting edge of stem cell research. Stem cells are more abundant there because in Judaism it is believed that the embryo becomes alive only after 40 days when the soul enters the fetus.

To conclude, Golda Meir, one of the early prime ministers of Israel, said, "We can forgive the Arabs many things, but we cannot forgive that our sons have been forced to become killers."

29

(April 22, 2006) The American dominant media, namely ABC, NBC and CBS, have been shamelessly lying to us, and it is called The Sin of Omission. They have become networks of political manipulation instead of deliverers of honest news. They still remain very powerful since one of them just hired a mediocre morning commentator for $13 million per year, proving they have more money than good judgment.

Since President Bush became president, over five years ago, these liberal networks – along with most, but not all, liberals – have never gotten over the fact that the Democrats lost the last two elections. In the first election, Al Gore used his clout as then vice president to create drive-by voting for thousands of illegals to vote for him as president, with no questions asked.

He still lost and never became president, thank God.

The members of the Left do not lose gracefully, and when they lose, they fuss and moan and attack the opposition personally. In short, they have tantrums.

The liberal media report every bad incident occurring in Iraq and omit all of the U.S. and Iraqi armies' victories. Along with the endless bashing of President Bush, their dishonest, reckless actions delight and embolden the enemy terrorists and prolong the bombings of our troops and innocent Iraqi citizens. The American media want us to fail in Iraq, and that is treason.

After Afghanistan, world intelligence did believe that there were WMDs in Iraq and that Saddam Hussein was cruel and unstable enough to possibly use them. Except for France, Russia and Germany, who were busy receiving billions of bribe dollars from the scoundrel Hussein, from the Oil for Food scandal, the entire United Nations unanimously voted that we must disarm Iraq. Our entire Congress voted and agreed.

Now, they all have amnesia. When things are rough, all the Monday morning quarterbacks – who never would have predicted that all the world's Islamic terrorists would converge in Baghdad to try to prevent democracy from taking hold – are complaining and blaming Bush for everything constantly. How cowardly. Weaklings always search for scapegoats instead of having the cajones to say, "Perhaps we all made some mistakes."

Nonetheless, returning soldiers and visitor to Iraq continue to report that wonderful things are happening there. The conniving media refuse to report anything positive.

Eventually, the troops will leave. The jury is still out about the direction in Iraq. More time will tell if the Iraqi people have the will and fortitude to create and maintain a democracy. It won't be easy.

Kudos to our own troops, the best and brightest, going there willingly and courageously to fight the Islamic terrorists, thereby ensuring that they do not come to our shores. Kudos also to the Bush administration for keeping us safe from terrorist attacks since 9/11. About the media, shame on their dishonesty. May they self destruct.

30

(July 28, 2006) About the recent commentary on global warming – there were no definitive answers, only my pragmatic suggestion that we should clean up our world environment no matter what. There are three very knowledgeable gentleman listeners, all scientists, who all responded and who, based on their extensive research, agreed that global warming does not exist. At least one believes it is a political myth fostered by the Democrats. His following letter is fascinating for its comprehensive coverage on the issue. So, having the author's permission to read it on KSCO, here it is.

"Hi Kay,

Glad I had a chance to meet you at the Veterans' meeting on Flag Day. I am a Hungarian plumber, electrician, international tour guide, I speak six languages, and I am an inventor, etc., and a solid listener to Rush and Michael Savage.

About global warming, the pro-Kyoto Agreement supported by the Euro commies and international liberals was never ratified by the Congress during Clinton's time. It was voted down 100 to nothing, yet the liberal media keeps on bugging Bush for not signing it. He had nothing to do with it. But the massive liberal brainwashing machine never mentions this vital information. Clinton and Gore had a major defeat on this potential economic suicide. The European Union commies wanted to reduce our economy using this insane Kyoto Agreement to close down hundreds of factories so their EU economy could be more competitive with ours. They are using the global warming scare tactic as a disguised economic attack against the U.S.A.

Remember, the Chinese, Indian or Mexican smoke is okay for them, only the capitalist smoke bothers them. They just cannot stand the fact that we can live better than the socialist masses. My old friend for over 25 years, from Belgium, doesn't talk to me anymore since he found out that I voted for Mr. Bush. I'm sad that the basic liberal hateful poisons lost me my friend.

What really affects our climate is the sun, volcanoes, and all natural forces. The ozone hole has disappeared by itself. There are periods of sunspot activities, and we had several ice ages, and all the snow and ice had melted away before the first Ford assembly line got into operation or before the tree huggers got their worthless diplomas from Berkeley.

Your A.M. shows, Rush and Savage, have more valuable information than I can get elsewhere.

Stay in good health, Kay, and I'll keep on listening.

Signed: Zoltan Egeresi"

Well said, and thank you, Zoltan.

This commentary was aired again in 2007 with the following preface:

Because global warming is a myth, and Al Gore is making political points to influence the forthcoming national election. I believe it is timely to do an encore of my commentary broadcast last July 28, 2006. The liberals and other gullibles all are accepting this nonsense, and isn't it fascinating how a non-truth, repeated often enough, becomes believable. Shades of World War II, when Hitter floated outrageous lies repeated so often that most people came to believe them. And here it is ... .

31

(August 17, 2006) FYI – four weeks ago, on July 19th, retired Captain Dave Wilson of the U.S. Navy wrote a unique clarification of the war initiated by Hezbollah against Israel. No, Captain Dave Wilson is not Jewish.

It was Hezbollah's ultimate behavior to create this war by killing so that Israel took the bait and went to war, intending to destroy Hezbollah once and for all.

Captain Wilson's title was "Why the world should stand back and let Israel do what it has to do." Here is the plan. See how Israel fell into the trap.

President Lahoud of Lebanon, a big supporter and close ally of Syria, has been shrieking non-stop to the United Nations Security Council for the past several days to force Israel into a cease fire. Clearly, he has been reading his autographed copy of "Military Success for Dummies: Arab Despots" by the late Gamel Nasser, leader of Egypt. Ever since Nasser accidentally discovered the trick in 1956, every subsequent Arab leader has stuck to his tried and true formula for military success. It's called 'Instigate a War.' Once the war is well underway, and you are in the process of having your ass handed to you, get a few world powers to force your Western opponent into a cease fire. Whatever you do, don't surrender or submit to any terms dictated by your enemy. That would ruin everything. All you have to do is wait it out and eventually the world will become sickened by what is being done by your soldiers and civilian population, and it will force a truce.

Once a truce has been called, you can resume your intransigence (which probably caused the conflict in the first place) and even declare victory as your opponent leaves the field of battle. This tactic has never failed – not once. In fact, it worked so well for the Egyptians in 1973 that to this day they celebrate the Yom Kippur War, a crushing defeat at the hands of Israel, as military victory. No kidding. Its' a national holiday in Egypt.

President Lahoud of Lebanon, keeps shrieking like a schoolgirl to the U.N. Security Council, "Stop the violence, and arrange a cease fire. And then after that we'll be ready to discuss all the matters."

Uh-huh. Forgive me if I find that hard to swallow. He allowed Hezbollah to take over his country. He has turned a blind eye while Iranian and Syrian weapons, advisers and money have poured into his country. And now that his country is in ruins, he wants to call it a draw. As much as it may sicken the world to stand by and watch it happen, strong hands need to hold back the weak-hearted and let the fight continue until one side finally admits absolute defeat. That did not happen this time.

Thank you, Captain Dave Wilson, for telling it accurately. Now it's after the fact. We'll probably never know for sure why Israel capitulated to whatever pressure was put upon her to agree to the ceasefire before the job was done.

Maybe the realization that, in fact, Israel was fighting four enemies at once – Hezbollah, the phony Lebanon president, Syria, and Iran – the latter two who supplied all the thousands of katyushas and other weapons pointed at Israel non-stop.

And now comes the phony ceasefire. After one day, Hezbollah reneged on the peace agreement and refuses to give up its arms and an important U.N. peace force now will not be in place for months, and the Lebanon Army, inflated with Hezbollah, will keep the peace. What a sick joke.

Before Islamic fascism takes over the world, Israel, the U.S., and other peace loving countries, must wake up now and eliminate both the Iranian and Syrian power before Hezbollah can surely be destroyed.

Put bluntly, we are presently living in a twilight zone where goodness is perceived as evil and evil as goodness. If goodness does not band together and deal once and for all with the Iran, Syria and North Koreas of the world, our civilization will be on its way out.

32

(November 7, 2005) The following is a very compelling and thoughtful article written by a Spanish journalist, Sebastian Villar Rodriguez. Written in the first person and seen on the internet by many, it is really worth repeating. It is called, "Europe Died in Auschwitz."

"I was walking along Raval (in Barcelona) when all of a sudden I understood that Europe died with Auschwitz. We assassinated six million Jews in order to end up bringing in 20 million Muslims. We burnt in Auschwitz the culture, intelligence and power to create. We burned the people of the world, the ones who were proclaimed the chosen people of God, because it is the people who gave to humanity the symbolic figures who were capable of changing history – Christ, Marx, Einstein, Freud, and who were the people of progress and well-being.

We must admit that Europe, by relaxing its borders and giving in under the pretext of tolerance to the values of a fallacious cultural relativism, opened its doors to 20 million Muslims, often illiterates and fanatics, that we could meet at best in places such as Raval – the poorest of the nations and of the ghettos, and who are preparing the worst such as 9/11 and the Madrid bombing, and who are lodged in apartment blocks provided by the social welfare.

We also have exchanged culture with fanaticism, the capacity to create with the will to destroy, the wisdom with the superstition. We have exchanged the transcendental instinct of the Jews, who even under the worst possible conditions have always looked for a better, peaceful world. We have exchanged that for the suicide bomber. We have exchanged the pride of life for the fanatic obsession with death. Our death and that of our children.

Because we stood by and allowed the Holocaust, what a grave mistake we have made."

33

(May 18, 2006) It started with NAFTA, the North American Free Trade Agreement, which many Americans were emphatically against, but it became President Clinton's first big agenda besides the failed health benefits project of Hillary Clinton. NAFTA was great for Central America and certain American corporations, but a dismal failure for the United States. We learn now that Mexico spent billions of dollars to help make NAFTA a reality. Who received that money, and where is it? It's been a downfall for us ever since.

We're losing our power and sovereignty, making other countries stronger and ourselves weaker (i.e., outsourcing z .h / * . , jobs to India, and totally giving our manufacturing away to China). All our trade with China and other countries is stupidly lopsided. They send us many times more than we are allowed to export to them. Is that fair trade? We sit still for years while Vicente Fox dumps his criminals over our southern border and his poor and sick Mexicans for us to support. He views us as stupid and incompetent, because that's how we've behaved, and he's tough with immigrants that want to enter Mexico. Fox has become so emboldened that he's dictating how we should protect (I really mean obstruct) plans to close the border.

President Clinton ignored the problem for eight years, President Bush ignored the problem for over five years, and now his proposal to close the border may be too little too late. We can't spare 6,000 troops, maybe until 2008? Isn't it true that American troops have been stationed in Japan and Germany since 1945 after World War II? Are they still there? If so, isn't it time for Germany and Japan to use their own troops to take care of themselves? Why can't our troops be released to go protect our borders NOW – not in 2008?

Let's end on at least one good note. I believe that the wall will work for us. It has worked very well for Israel.

34

(September 23, 2006) Added to the countless criticisms about everything our president attempts to do for democracy in Iraq, now there is an uproar in Congress about our military's so-called inhumane treatment of captured enemy combatants.

Most recently our military used the persuasion of keeping a high-level captured combatant in a very cold room, sleep-deprived for some time, and forced to listen to loud music. Valuable information was obtained.

President Bush has asked our Congress to interpret Common Article #3 of the Geneva Conventions, which loosely defines proper treatment of captured enemy combatants. Not for one second do the Islamic fascists concern themselves with the Geneva Conventions. They laugh at those rules, and more often than not, our captured soldiers are either tortured or annihilated on the spot.

Some in Congress are more concerned about our world image than they are about the welfare of our fighting military, who deal with these barbaric animals on a daily basis. Is a good world image more important than protecting our soldiers? As long as half of our Congress (mostly the Democrats) and the media keep putting politics above winning in Iraq, our side will continue to lose soldiers.

In retrospect, nobody could have predicted that every terrorist in the world would converge in Iraq to prevent democracy from taking hold there.

We have one elected Commander in Chief, and that is President George Bush. We do not need the entire Congress running the war. So complainers, back off. Let the president do his job. Stop with your political whining. You're hurting your country and helping the enemy, and that's called treason.

As a response addendum to a few passionate listeners who believe in free speech at any cost — Does one not agree that when one's country is in a war to preserve one's free way of life, some restraint is in order if one's free speech gives information to the enemy that could hurt the country? Isn't it possible that unconditional free speech could be the dark side of freedom?

35

(July 2007) For the past 3 and a half years, the Democrats brainwashed themselves into believing that Bush stole the election. Nevermind that candidate Gore had stuffed the ballot boxes with votes from instant sworn-in people. These were illegals who were asked no questions whatsoever, and then on-the-spot voted in a drive-through polling place. Many thousands became citizens with that slimy Gore move. So the popular vote, which Gore to this day claims he won, was a corrupt sham.

Finally, we're experiencing an economic recovery, a jobless one. Millions of U.S. jobs no longer exist, and the Democrats are using this fact as a campaign issue to blame Bush, and they demand that he create new jobs. So let's go back to about halfway through the first Clinton term. Clinton, convinced by corporate advisers and lobbyists, urged Congress to create the North American Free Trade Agreement, known as NAFTA. That plan was to make world trade a level playing field for all nations, even the poor ones. NAFTA did become law, but over the vigorous protests of many Americans and labor unions, who saw that our country would not benefit from these agreements.

One year later, GAT (the global form of NAFTA) also became law. That low swishing sound at first was thousands of U.S.

companies sending pink slips to millions of longtime employees, after which those companies set up operations in other countries where labor was much cheaper. It took time before the full impact of NAFTA and GAT was felt. Foreign trading partners and American companies in foreign countries have benefited at the expense of the

U.S. economy. To add to the NAFTA and GAT fiascos, shortly after our government gave China "Most Favored Nation" status, certain well-placed politicians stood to gain big time by the China move.

The results of those two trade treaties are now obvious. A large part of the U.S. manufacturing industry died. Untold amounts of U.S. jobs are gone – forever. Now, China and other countries produce most of our clothing and much of everything else. Many high tech companies have left our shores for greener and cheaper pastures, as did other industries. Furthermore, our trade agreements are lopsided. We buy much more from China and elsewhere than they choose to buy from us, and that's crazy. Trade only makes sense if it's balanced. Otherwise, it's a joke.

This brings to mind another short-sighted disaster created by that one-time Democratic president, Jimmy Carter, a prime example of the disconnected left. He gave away the Panama Canal, which we built and completed in 1914. Guess who controls that now – China does. And that liberal move will haunt us for a long time to come. In 1992, Bill Clinton won the election with a frequent use of a quote, "It's the economy, stupid." And now, in 2004, George Bush will win if he remembers to remind the electorate again and again what really happened to the evaporation of U.S. jobs. "It's NAFTA and GAT, stupid."

36

(July 2010) This is called "If Israel is not evil, the world is in big trouble."

Kudos to Tammy Benjamin for sharing this current information, and I will add my thoughts, also. As an American Jewess, I am pained by the unfair twisting of the truth about Israel because of media omission.

Dear Friends,

As usual, Dennis Prager is the beacon of moral clarity in a sea of moral confusion. The last few sentences of his column of Tuesday, June 8, 2010, are the best and the most frightening, but you must wait for about three minutes to hear them.

With the exception of the United States, nearly all the world's nation, newspapers, radio, and TV news stations, the United Nations and the world's Leftists academics and organizations have condemned Israel over the Gaza flotilla incident. The characterizations of the Jewish State range from a society so evil that it should not be allowed to exist.

Well, let's hope the world is right.

Israel is almost totally isolated. A visitor from another planet would have every reason to report back home that the greatest problem on planet Earth was the planet's Jewish State. Though Israel is the size of the State of New Jersey, and smaller than El Salvador, and though its population is smaller than that of Sweden and Bolivia, it is the most censured country in United Nations' history. I must add, Israel can be traversed in a car from south to north in eight hours, and east to west in three hours. And, that is how small Israel is.

Let's hope the world is right.

Though Israel is a thriving liberal democracy for all its citizens, including the one out of five that is Arab (83% of whom are Muslim) with an independent judiciary and press, though it signed an agreement establishing an independent Palestinian State, at the same time Israel became a State, though it returned to Egypt every inch of the Sinai Peninsula, a land mass larger than Israel itself, with major oil reserves – the world deems Israel a villain.

Let's hope the world is right.

Though Hamas runs a theocratic police state in Gaza based on torture and terror with no freedom of speech, no freedom of any religious expression outside of radical Islam, seeks to annihilate the Jewish State and its State-controlled media depict Israelis and Jews as worthy of death, the world sees Israel, not Hamas, as the villain.

And, let's hope the world is right.

I say – the world media omits the vital information. Israel's only concern when regularly entering the ships, which go to Gaza with supplies, is to examine the ships so that bombs and explosives are not also sent to Gaza, which daily sends them to explode in Israel. The world media refuses to print that information.

It was routine for Israel's soldiers to enter the ships never expecting to be attacked and ambushed with metal pipes. They shot the nine attackers only in self-defense. But, the world media will not report that.

To conclude, the reason mankind has to hope that the world, its leaders, the newspapers, the so-called human rights organizations, and the United Nations are right about Israel is quite simple, if Israel is the decent party in its war with the Palestinian authority and Hamas and nearly all the world's countries, nearly all the world's media and the United Nations are morally wrong – what hope is there for humanity? If the world's moral compass is that broken, are we not sailing into a dark age?

For KSCO, this is Kay Zwerling.

37

(Spring 2010) This got by me while on vacation recently, but it is a true logical gem. Kudos to Rae Williams for sharing this. It bears repeating. Maybe Obama will put to sleep his agenda to change our free Country into socialism. But, it is unlikely.

As the late Adrian Rogers said, "You can't multiply wealth by dividing it." An economics professor at a local college, made a statement that he had never failed a single student before, but recently he failed an entire class. That class had insisted that Obama's socialism worked, and that no one would be poor and no one would be rich, and that is a great equalizer.

The professor then said "OK, why don't we have an experiment in this class on Obama's plan." All grades will be averaged and everyone would receive the same grade, so no one would fail and no one would receive an A. After the first test, the grades were averaged and everyone got a B. The students who studied hard were upset, and the students who studied little were happy. As the second test rolled around, the students who studied little had studied even less, and the ones who studied hard decided they wanted a free ride, too, so they studied little.

The second test average was a D (like in dove). No one was happy.

When the third test rolled around, the average was an F (like in fail).

As the tests proceeded, the scores never increased as bickering, blame, and name calling all resulted in hard feelings and no one would study for the benefit of anyone else.

All failed, to their great surprise, and the professor told them that socialism would also ultimately fail because when the reward is great the effort to succeed is great, but when government takes all the reward away no one will try or want to succeed.

It could not be any simpler than that.

Remember, there is a test coming up within the next five months – the midterm election in 2010. Don't forget to vote.

For KSCO, this is Kay Zwerling.

38

Philosophically, we humans grasp at inventing illogical expressions when we are uncomfortable with our own prejudices.

Case in point – let us examine the expression "occupied territory", which came into vogue only after the State of Israel was legally created in 1948.

The British who owned the territory offered land also to the Palestinians. They declined and continue to decline. They want Israel annihilated.

Immediately after Israel became a State, five Arab countries in the Middle East declared war on the new Jewish State – they were all defeated in a matter of days by the little new Country. That is when the expression "occupied territory" or "occupied land" came into being.

Israel the victor was and is the true owner of the conquered land – but the U.S. government called that land "occupied". Is that supposed to mean that the aggressors still owned that land?

Another opposite case in point – during the Mexican-American War in 1846 through 1848, the U.S. invaded a part of Mexico known as Texas, which Mexico had received from Spain along with other land in the Southwest. The U.S. won the war, took Texas and the other States in the Southwest, and California. It is said that Mexico was given a token $500 million for all that land. The Mexicans have been resentful and angry since then. They want their land back, but that will never happen. Shouldn't that conquered Mexican land also be considered occupied land?

Fast forward to the present situation.

Jordan, a country which owned East Jerusalem in 1948, wanted all of Jerusalem shortly thereafter, so she declared war on Israel. She lost, so now Israel owns that territory. The U.S. maintains it is occupied land, and Obama forbids Israel to build houses there – even high-rise apartments for its burgeoning citizenship.

Prime Minister Netanyahu of Israel has told Obama he cannot dictate to Israel about Israeli land – and therein lies the stalemate between the two democracies. I say kudos to Netanyahu for not allowing the U.S. to bully Israel.

Meanwhile, the despicable U.S. media picks and chooses what it wants to expose, and never mentions that Israel won all that land.

It is all unfair, unjust, untrue, and Israel stands totally on its own.

Please – someone – explain the nonsensical expression "occupied land" or "occupied territory", which is only used for territory won fair and square by the Jewish State of Israel after it is attacked. It is an honest issue our government refuses to recognize.

For KSCO, this is Kay Zwerling.

39

(Fall 2010) Breaking news: Suicide bombers in Britain are set to begin a three-day strike shortly.

They are in dispute over the number of virgins they are entitled to in the Afterlife. Emergency talks with Al Quaida management have so far failed to produce any agreement.

The unrest began last week when Al Quaida announced that the number of virgins a suicide bomber would receive after his death would be cut by 25% this month, from 72 to only 60. The rationale for the cut was the increase in recent years of the number of suicide bombings and a subsequent shortage of virgins in the Afterlife.

The Suicide Bombers Union, the British Organization of Occupational Martyrs (B.O.O.M.) responded with a statement that this was unacceptable to its members and immediately balloted for strike action.

General Secretary Abdul Amir told the press, "Our members are literally working themselves to death in the cause of Jihad. We do not ask for much in return but to be treated like this by management is a kick in the teeth."

Mr. Amir accepted the limited availability of virgins, but pointed out that the cutback was expected to be borne entirely by the workforce and not by the management.

Last Christmas Abu Hanza alone was awarded an annual bonus of 250,000 virgins complained Amir, and you can be sure they will all be pretty ones, too. How can Al Quaida afford that for members of the management, but not 72 for the people who do the real work?

Al Quaida Chief Executive Osama Bin Laden explained "We sympathize with our workers' concerns, but Al Quaida is simply not in the position to meet their demands. Thanks to western depravity, there is now a chronic shortage of virgins in the Afterlife. I do not like cutting wages, but I would hate to have to tell 3000 of my staff that they will not be able to blow themselves up."

Bin Laden defended management bonuses by claiming these were necessary to attract good fanatical clerics. "How am I supposed to attract the best people if I cannot compete with the private sector?"

Talks broke down this morning after management's last ditch proposal of a virgin-sharing scheme which was rejected outright after a failure to agree on allocation quotas. Certain virgins sign up to be available in the Afterlife to accommodate the honored suicide bombers. One virgin who refused to be named was quoted as saying "I will be compromised if I am agreeing to anything like that.... It is just too much to swallow." Unless some sort of agreement is reached, suicide bombers will stop the explosives shortly.

The entire Australian continent stated that this situation would not affect their operations because there are no virgins in that area anyway.

Late news: Apparently the drop in the number of suicide bombings has been put down to the emergence of Susan Boyle – and now that bombers know what a virgin looks like, they are not so keen to go to Paradise.

For KSCO, this is Kay Zwerling.

40

(Fall 2009) Thank you Gene Sanden for this timely prayer from the heart. I changed the end to acknowledge Almighty God. Because I am Jewish, I believe there is only one God; however, I still love Jesus, a very special human, because he taught the world about love, to love one another. Such wisdom, and if we listened, the world would be a better place. And now the prayer.

Lord, I just want to say thank you because this morning I woke up and knew where my children were; because this morning my home was still standing; because this morning I am not crying because my child, my brother or sister needs to be removed from underneath a pile of concrete; because this morning I was able to drink a glass of water; because this morning I was able to turn on the lights; because this morning I was able to take a shower; because this morning I was not planning a funeral, but most of all I thank you this morning because I still have life and a voice to cry out for the people of Haiti.

Lord, I cry out to You, the One who makes the impossible possible; the One who turns darkness into light; I cry out that You give those mothers strength; that You give them peace that surpasses all understanding; that You may open the streets so that help can come quickly; that You may provide doctors, nurses, food, water, and all that they need in the blink of an eye. For all those who have lost family members, give them peace, give them hope, and give them courage, and continue to go on. Protect the children and shield them with Your power. I pray all this Almighty God in Your name.

And now, also from Gene, this interesting suggestion:

It is an idea for Haiti's government. I heard on the news that Haiti is without a government. To help them out, let us donate to them Obama, one Pelosi, one Reid, one Frank, one Coakley, and two Clintons. They can keep them permanently. We can give them a Constitution, but we cannot find it easily right now. Now, isn't that a great idea?

P.S. – About my recent mention of another Court case, re the Obama birth certificate, it was dismissed. It was an old story. Sorry. My mistake. Mia Culpa.

However, along with many other Americans, why do I have this lingering feeling that this story is not yet finished?

For KSCO, this is Kay Zwerling.

4

Part Four: Potpourri

1

The other evening ushered in the ten most important days of the year for Judaism, beginning with Rosh Hashanah, the Jewish New Year, and concluding with Yom Kippur, the day of atonement. On that day, Jews examine their past behavior toward their fellow humans and attempt to make amends to those they may have wronged. This ten-day period is known as The Days of Awe because that is when God judges our past actions toward one another. Because Judaism is a religion mainly of ethics, and because it does not proselytize or seek converts, its philosophy rather respect however or not one chooses to believe in a higher being. In this spirit, I would like to share one psalm and one prayer from the High Holy Days prayer book, which people of various faiths and convictions may relate to because our world today is very troubled and everywhere can be found negativity. Hopefully, many may find comfort in the following. This is called Psalm 15:

"Do we deserve to enter God's sanctuary? How can we merit a place in His presence? Like this: live with integrity, do what is right, speak the truth without deceit, have no slander upon your tongue, do no evil to your fellow man, do not mistreat your neighbor, spurn a contemptible person but honor those who revere the Lord. Never retract a promise once made even though it may bring you harm. Lend no money at usurious interest. Accept no bribes against the innocent. Make these deeds your own, then shall you stand firm forever."

And now a prayer for our country:

"Our God, and God of our Fathers, we ask Your blessing for our country, for our government, for its leaders and advisors, and for all who exercise just and rightful authority. Teach them insights, that they may administer all affairs of state fairly, that peace and security, happiness and prosperity, justice and freedom, may abide in our midst. Creator of all flesh, bless all the inhabitants of our country with Your Spirit, then citizens of all creeds will forge a common bond in true brotherhood to banish all hatred and bigotry to safeguard the ideals and free institutions which are our country's pride and glory. May this land be an influence for good throughout the world, uniting all people in peace and freedom, and thus we say, Amen."

2

(January 20, 2006) On the philosophical discussion of what's it all about, Alfie, evolutionists who have had easy access to public classrooms now vigorously oppose that same access to believers of intelligent design, a newly coined phrase to describe and explain human existence conferred by a higher being, who many of us call God. These are two separate valid theories, so why shouldn't they both be discussed openly in classrooms? Evolutionists contend that humans evolved first as a cluster of cells which, through millions of years, became apes, then Neanderthals, and finally, homo sapiens – or human beings – with highly developed brains.

One can wonder: at what point did the original cells separate and become male and female? Evolution is a neat scientific theory which leaves important issues not addressed, and many of us reject it as incomplete. How was the world itself created?

Proponents of intelligent design contend that God first created the world, then a man, and then the man's companion, a woman, both exquisitely formed human creatures, who together learned how to reproduce themselves in their offspring. Every single organ is so perfectly functional with brains like high-powered computers protected in bone skulls, eyes to see, ears to hear, thumbs to grasp. Every other organ which makes up a human being is so complex and equipped with deep emotions and sensitivity and the ability to reason.

All in all, the person is such a complex creature that it's too simplistic to believe that it all came together by way of evolution.

Back to the here and now. Evolutionists believe that there is no place in the classroom for intelligent design because the Constitution states that there must be a separation of church and state. That is, in fact, a red herring. No place in the Constitution does it mention the separation of church and state. Our country was founded on Judeo Christian principles. Our forefathers borrowed from the Ten Commandments and the Golden Rule and incorporated them with the Bill of Rights and the Constitution to create the greatest and most enduring democracy in the world, despite complaints from secularists, who are always offended and want to eradicate every public mention of God and religion. Many of us are becoming weary of pandering to the delicate sensibilities of the secularists at the expense of our own beliefs, so I trust that will not be happening much longer.

Recently we made sure that "Merry Christmas" remains and "In God We Trust" will not be removed from our coins and currency. So to those complainants, I say, "Get over it". If it's too painful, check out Canada.

About our young people, I believe both evolution and intelligent design should be taught in classrooms, preferably at the college level in a comparative religion class – definitely not in a science class, as some listeners assumed. Intelligent design is faith-based, not science-based. Let students decide for themselves what they choose to believe.

I saved the best for last. Think about it. God has endowed every human being with a soul that will endure through eternity. Does evolution believe in the existence of a soul?

3

I wrote this story about my mother in 1981, two years after her death. I was studying clinical philosophy at that time, a new discipline, which was deep, personal, and analytical, and while I was still missing my mom, I thought about her a great deal then.

Parents and children have powerful and intimate relationships and perspectives about each other – sometimes positive, sometimes negative, and sometimes neutral. Here I reveal my mother through my own appreciation of being a child, a parent, and a grandparent. I address a philosophical problem, that of finding a sense of groundedness in response to the universal human problem of the abyss – that is, the lack of meaning and aloneness – or nothingness. My mother found her ground in God, and in so many ways, now I do, too. This is called "My Mother's Ground".

She came to America from Greece in 1912, or thereabouts, at the age of 16. The fourth in a family of six children, quite poor, she had been a young schoolteacher in her village. Her sister and brotherin-law living in New York sent her the fare to join them in the land of hope and opportunity.

She met and married my father, had three children, became a widow at 42. With the three of us married, or gone soon after, she remained alone in the big house, and somehow managed to make the money last.

I worried and wondered at her aloneness every night. She would say to me "God will take care of me; I'm not afraid." God was my mother's ground.

An invalid for six years, and in need of continual custodial care, my 82-year-old mother spent her final years in a local convalescent home. At times, she was amazingly alert – other times, forgetful. Most often, strangely peaceful and content. In the early days of her confinement, she would often ask in bewilderment, "Por que el Dios me hizo esto?" (Why did God do this to me?)

Interestingly, after her second stroke, she communicated almost exclusively in Spanish, her native tongue, despite the fact that she had been quite articulate in English.

What made it possible for my mother to face each day with valor, even a smile? Her philosophy, which she affirmed each day when we were together: "Todo lo que hace Dios es para bien" (Everything that God does is for good.) God was my mother's ground. In a way, I envied her very much, for I don't believe she ever allowed herself to see the abyss. She chose very early in her life to insulate herself from the anxiety of nihilism by a total and daily commitment to the will of God.

What a fascinating and incongruous polarity of personality was my mother: A most gentle, benign imposition of an iron will in areas concerning her children, and a personal complete and total surrender to the will of God. Indeed, God was my mother's ground.

4

(November 19, 2005) To those listeners who do not believe in the existence of God, I respectfully suggest that you do not listen to this commentary. It will have no meaning to you.

Holy Moses and Jesus Christ are undoubtedly the two most compelling moral figures of our current civilization, because they were chosen by God to deliver to the world His messages for the endurance of a good and ethical society. History records that after God created the world, He also created different civilizations to occupy it one at a time. Each civilization grew and evolved, and because of human lust and power, each gradually became so morally bankrupt that in disgust, God decided to discard them and start all over again. The present civilization is now showing unmistakable signs of so much moral decay that God may discard it also. He is very angry with us – witness the unusual and frequent abundant catastrophes our world is experiencing.

About six centuries ago, Moses was summoned by God to receive and disburse to His people, the Jews, His Ten Commandments, so that gradually all people would learn to worship

God by living productively and morally – i.e. not stealing, nor lying, nor killing, nor coveting, always honoring parents, etc. – in short, rules to live by to be good human beings. Our civilization presently is being assaulted by many people who have rejected religion, rejected the family unit, and who are trying vigorously to legalize same-sex marriage. These same people created legislation to allow pregnant 12-year-old girls to obtain abortions without the knowledge of their parents. Our society is going downhill rapidly. The wrong people are taking over, which does not bode well for the continued existence of this civilization.

Several centuries after God delivered to Moses His commandments, a very special human being was born. His name was Jesus. As a young adult, he wandered many places with a unique and simple message, which was "Love thy neighbor, and turn the other cheek." It is moot to argue whether Jesus was or was not divine. Suffice to say that His was a very special message because he offered the concept of goodness to a world that needed to hear it again. These teachings of Jesus were so new and so foreign to a dog-eat-dog, belligerent, and destructive world that many embraced them, and so Christianity was born.

About a couple of centuries ago, our nation, a democracy, was created by our forefathers and, in their wisdom, they combined the moral beliefs of both Judaism and Christianity as an ethical basis and mission statement for the incredible country. So from its inception, the United States has been, and always will be, a Judeo-Christian nation. We pray that our democracy will continue to prosper and endure despite the negative pressures of decadent, godless forces in our midst. So God, please continue to bless America!

5

(August 19, 2004) "A fool and his money are easily parted." That was an expression I used often when my children were growing up, and sometimes made foolish expenditures using their own money.

On a related subject, it was a creative idea cooked up by credit card issuers who saw a unique way to make more money. Even they didn't realize the enormity of their potential windfall. The plot involved them, retail businesses and the general public. It was a win-win situation for all involved. For the participating public, it was a nobrainer because for the first time, people could make purchases without paying up front. For retailers, it was worth up to 3% cost to get their money up front. Except for the always valuable and appreciated real estate mortgages and automobile loans, this scheme was new and exciting. For over 50 years now, public credit cards have become a way of life, and in retrospect one could believe it was liberating and good that the ordinary consumer lacking big savings no longer had to wait to acquire things they wanted. Impulse buying, especially big items, became easy, but there was and is a dark side to the new "buy now, pay later" idea. That little plastic card had the potential to seduce one into acquiring luxuries one might otherwise have done without or waited until one had the cash first. That same little plastic monster has made debtors out of many people who suddenly find they cannot ever seem to pay their monthly bills and this is where they get sucked into monetary quicksand for all the nebulous pleasure of acquiring more stuff. It's called 'Instant Gratification.' So often we let stuff own us.

The most dangerous time of year is the Christmas season when countless otherwise restrained people experience irrational exuberance and overextend themselves. They foolishly purchase much too much, then take months enslaved by outrageous interest rates, sometimes upwards of 25% on the unpaid balances and these rates are imposed by the credit card issuers. Some people don't' ever get out from under.

Now, for some motherly advice. For starters, our lawmakers should put reasonable ceilings on credit card interest rates, but that won't easily happen. Nothing will change until people stop overcharging on their credit cards and pay up their dangling balances once and for all. If that's not possible, then it's better to say, "Thanks but no thanks" to credit cards and live within your means on a case basis. You will then experience an indescribable peace of mind by not being in debt. It is well worth it.

6

(February 26, 2010) Breaking news: Suicide bombers in Britain are set to begin a three-day strike shortly.

They are in dispute over the number of virgins they are entitled to in the Afterlife. Emergency talks with Al Quaida management have so far failed to produce any agreement.

The unrest began last week when Al Quaida announced that the number of virgins a suicide bomber would receive after his death would be cut by 25% this month, from 72 to only 60. The rationale for the cut was the increase in recent years of the number of suicide bombings and a subsequent shortage of virgins in the Afterlife.

The Suicide Bombers Union, the British Organization of Occupational Martyrs (B.O.O.M.) responded with a statement that this was unacceptable to its members and immediately balloted for strike action.

General Secretary Abdul Amir told the press, "Our members are literally working themselves to death in the cause of Jihad. We do not ask for much in return but to be treated like this by management is a kick in the teeth."

Mr. Amir accepted the limited availability of virgins, but pointed out that the cutback was expected to be borne entirely by the workforce and not by the management.

Last Christmas Abu Hanza alone was awarded an annual bonus of 250,000 virgins complained Amir, and you can be sure they will all be pretty ones, too. How can Al Quaida afford that for members of the management, but not 72 for the people who do the real work?

Al Quaida Chief Executive Osama Bin Laden explained "We sympathize with our workers' concerns, but Al Quaida is simply not in the position to meet their demands. Thanks to western depravity, there is now a chronic shortage of virgins in the Afterlife. I do not like cutting wages, but I would hate to have to tell 3000 of my staff that they will not be able to blow themselves up."

Bin Laden defended management bonuses by claiming these were necessary to attract good fanatical clerics. "How am I supposed to attract the best people if I cannot compete with the private sector?"

Talks broke down this morning after management's last ditch proposal of a virgin-sharing scheme which was rejected outright after a failure to agree on allocation quotas. Certain virgins sign up to be available in the Afterlife to accommodate the honored suicide bombers. One virgin who refused to be named was quoted as saying "I will be compromised if I am agreeing to anything like that.... It is just too much to swallow."

Unless some sort of agreement is reached, suicide bombers will stop the explosives shortly.

The entire Australian continent stated that this situation would not affect their operations because there are no virgins in that area anyway.

Late news: Apparently the drop in the number of suicide bombings has been put down to the emergence of Susan Boyle – and now that bombers know what a virgin looks like, they are not so keen to go to Paradise.

For KSCO, this is Kay Zwerling.

7

(November 27, 2008) Perhaps the most destructive, life-changing aspect of American society in the past 50 years has been the advent of the liberalism-created philosophy of political correctness.

These arrogant rules of behavior have taken hold and have remained in our society for much too long. They are phony and should be discarded.

On the Internet, there are various descriptions of the meaning of "politically correct", also known as PC.

It is, eruption of social tyranny. It is also ugly, stupid truth about offending people and guarding the First Amendment. The thin skins of PC people make conversation a minefield. Also, PC is called cultural Marxism. It also is called the new communism. And finally, it's also responsible for stifling liberty and common sense. It is leftist bigotry. It's astonishing that these restrictive rules of behavior have been embraced and tolerated in our society – and even in all of Europe – for so many decades.

Now for the really destructive aspects of PC. As I mentioned before, it has made intellectual wimps of many elementary and high school students, because competition is stifled, and the achievement of excellence is a no-no because the egos of many students who can't measure up are damaged. Poor babies.

Worse than that – history is no longer factual. It's tampered with and changed so that nobody's feelings are hurt.

Now, with regard to the damage to our military. Note the difficulties with regard to fighting in Iraq. Many Americans feel it's immoral for our government to listen in on telephone calls originating from outside our country, where we could intercept any possible danger to our military by our enemies.

It's more important to that PC crowd of people to be sure that their First Amendment rights take precedence over our soldiers' safety in war. Another related topic is so-called torture. I believe that all war is torture. Waterboarding is called torture, though no one ever died or was permanently damaged by a few minutes of waterboarding. And very often, life-saving information is obtained.

I wonder at the liberal compassion for the enemy who slices off the heads of American soldiers and anyone else they don't like.

Waterboarding releases information that could save the lives of many soldiers. If it saves even one, I believe it should be used. Asking our military to fight with conditions is suicide. Waterboarding the enemy has proven to save many soldiers; to withhold it is crazy. And yes, the PC and their displaced compassion are idiotic. If a country is at war, it must fight to win and not fight with one hand tied behind.

How incongruous is the way of liberal displaced compassion, where those of the political left will show emotional concern for the perpetrator of evil, or the murderer, and yet minimize and ignore the pain or death of the victim. It's another form of callous political correctness.

8

(April 20, 2005) For some time, a primary irritation of mine has been the arrogant and stupid edict created by liberal extremists who, around 25 years ago, ordained that we all must abide by their rules of social behavior, which they call political correctness. I never bought into that rigid, humorless nonsense. And now, those of us who think with logic and not with selective feelings can see the destructive havoc political correctness has created, most of the damage to our children, many of whom are now bewildered and dependent adults, the ones that I said were cheated out of having any parameters.

Early in 2003, I wrote a commentary on political correctness. Recently I learned that my work on the subject is being aired on radio by unknown persons, and while imitation may be considered a form of flattery, I do resent my creation being attributed to Bill Gates of Microsoft or anyone else. If enough listeners would like an encore of that six or seven minute long commentary and call the radio station at 475-1080, it will be repeated sometime soon.

And now, how about a little chuckle time … .

9

While sitting in a doctor's waiting room recently, I reached for a magazine and four large words on the outside back cover jumped out at me. They were "Live happily ever now." I thought, wow – most of us, those deep and wise and those otherwise, tend to go through our allotted years thinking of the time when we can live happily ever after — if I get a better job, or if I get to own a house, or a nice car, or if I get to travel a lot, or maybe get a windfall of money, then I'll be happy. Not wise. After all, all we've each got is now. And, now is all we will ever have. So, let's try to live happily ever now.

About illegal immigration — provoking thought #2: A big, tall wall between the United States and Mexico must be built. Yesterday. Many Mexicans have had the blessing of their scoundrel leader, Vicente Fox, who encourages them to sneak into the United States, and with whom our president is playing footsie, probably because of Mexican oil. Why did we sit still so many years while Fox emptied his jails of the deadliest killers in Mexico and dumped them on us? Why was this allowed? And again, it will take the wisdom of a King Solomon to deal with the 11 million illegals living here.

The Democrats want to give amnesty to everybody. And just think of the extra votes for them, and how unfair for those who patiently waited years to come in legally. We should have learned after President Reagan ordered amnesty years ago – the illegal problem got much worse. Besides, if we do not respect and enforce our own laws, why then should any person or any nation respect us and our laws?

Final provoking thought: This is about Jewish humor and Jewish inebriation (that means getting drunk). Around the Middle Ages, Jews made sure to always remain sober and aware because they were the hated scapegoats for being money lenders, 1ike bankers today, and especially they were considered pariahs for rejecting Jesus as being divine and as being the Messiah. The Old Testament states that when the Messiah finally arrives, the world and everyone will be good, and peace will prevail. I still believe that Jesus was a special extraordinary human because he knew that love was the answer. Jews have suffered all sorts of indignities, and they learned early on that education was the most important because knowledge is power. And secondly, the hate they endured allowed them to survive because of another most important ingredient in life, and that is humor. If one can endure with humor, one can survive almost anything. The topic of humor is an excellent segue into a joke I'm going to tell you now.

A rabbi and a priest in the same town were friends. They met once a week to go bicycling together. One day, while the priest was waiting in their usual place, the rabbi came but without his bicycle. He told his friend the priest that it wasn't where he usually put it, so it was probably stolen. The priest paused a moment and then said to the rabbi, "I have an idea. This coming Friday night, when you deliver your sermon, why don't you make your subject the Ten Commandments, and when you get to the part where it says 'Thou shalt not steal', perhaps the thief will be listening and be remorseful and return your bike."

So the following week, when it was time for the buddies to meet, the rabbi arrived with his bike. Elated, the priest said, "See, I told you that when you read the commandment that said 'Thou shalt not steal,' it would work, and you'd get your bicycle back, and you did!" The rabbi replied, "Well, it wasn't exactly that way. I did give my sermon, but when I came to the part that says, 'Thou shalt not commit adultery,' I remembered where I'd left my bike."

10

To those listeners who do not believe in the existence of God, I respectfully suggest that you do not listen to this commentary. It will have no meaning for you.

Holy Moses and Jesus Christ – undoubtedly the two most compelling moral figures of our current civilization, because they were chosen by God to deliver to the world His messages for the endurance of a good and ethical society. History records that after God created the world, He also created different civilizations to occupy it one at a time. Each civilization grew and evolved, and because of human lust and power, each gradually became so morally bankrupt that in disgust God decided to discard them and start all over again. The present civilization is now showing unmistakable signs of so much moral decay that God may discard it, also. He is very angry with us – witness the unusual and frequent abundant catastrophes our world is experiencing. The latest catastrophe could be the announcement recently that 12-year-old boys in elementary school will be offered condoms.

About six centuries ago, Moses was summoned by God to receive and disburse to His people, the Jews, His Ten Commandments, so that gradually all people would learn to worship God by living productively and morally (like, not stealing, not lying, not killing, not coveting), always honoring parents, etc. – in short, rules to live by to be good human beings. Our civilization presently is being assaulted by many people who have rejected religion, rejected the family unit, are trying vigorously to legalize same-sex marriage. These same people created legislation to allow pregnant 12-year-old girls to obtain abortions without the knowledge of their parents. Our society is going downhill rapidly. The wrong people are taking over, which does not bode well for the continued existence of this civilization.

Several centuries after God delivered to Moses His Commandments, a very special human being was born, and His name was Jesus Christ. And, I love Jesus Christ. As a young adult, he wandered many places with a unique and simple message which was "Love they neighbor, and turn the other cheek." It is moot to argue whether Jesus was or was not divine. Suffice to say, that His was a very special message because He offered the concept of goodness to the world that needed to hear it. These teachings of Jesus were so new and so foreign to a dog-eat-dog belligerent and destructive world that many embraced his concept and so Christianity was born.

About a couple of centuries ago, our nation, a democracy, was created by our forefathers and in their wisdom they combined the moral beliefs of both Judaism and Christianity in an ethical basis and mission statement for the new incredible Country. So, from its inception the U.S. has been and always will be a Judeo Christian nation. We pray that our democracy will continue to prosper and endure despite the negative pressures of decadent godless forces in our midst. So, God, please continue to bless America.

For KSCO, this is Kay Zwerling.

11

(Spring 2010) This is called "If Israel is not evil, the world is in big trouble."

Kudos to Tammy Benjamin for sharing this current information, and I will add my thoughts, also. As an American Jewess, I am pained by the unfair twisting of the truth about Israel because of media omission.

Dear Friends,

As usual, Dennis Prager is the beacon of moral clarity in a sea of moral confusion. The last few sentences of his column of Tuesday, June 8, 2010, are the best and the most frightening, but you must wait for about three minutes to hear them.

With the exception of the United States, nearly all the world's nation, newspapers, radio, and TV news stations, the United Nations and the world's Leftists academics and organizations have condemned Israel over the Gaza flotilla incident. The characterizations of the Jewish State range from a society so evil that it should not be allowed to exist.

Well, let's hope the world is right.

Israel is almost totally isolated. A visitor from another planet would have every reason to report back home that the greatest problem on planet Earth was the planet's Jewish State. Though Israel is the size of the State of New Jersey, and smaller than El Salvador, and though its population is smaller than that of Sweden and Bolivia, it is the most censured country in United Nations' history. I must add, Israel can be traversed in a car from south to north in eight hours, and east to west in three hours. And, that is how small Israel is.

Let's hope the world is right.

Though Israel is a thriving liberal democracy for all its citizens, including the one out of five that is Arab (83% of whom are Muslim) with an independent judiciary and press, though it signed an agreement establishing an independent Palestinian State, at the same time Israel became a State, though it returned to Egypt every inch of the Sinai Peninsula, a land mass larger than Israel itself, with major oil reserves – the world deems Israel a villain.

Let's hope the world is right.

Though Hamas runs a theocratic police state in Gaza based on torture and terror with no freedom of speech, no freedom of any religious expression outside of radical Islam, seeks to annihilate the Jewish State and its State-controlled media depict Israelis and Jews as worthy of death, the world sees Israel, not Hamas, as the villain.

And, let's hope the world is right.

I say – the world media omits the vital information. Israel's only concern when regularly entering the ships, which go to Gaza with supplies, is to examine the ships so that bombs and explosives are not are not also sent to Gaza, which daily sends them to explode in Israel. The world media refuses to print that information.

It was routine for Israel's soldiers to enter the ships never expecting to be attacked and ambushed with metal pipes. They shot the nine attackers only in self-defense. But, the world media will not report that.

To conclude, the reason mankind has to hope that the world, its leaders, the newspapers, the so-called human rights organizations, and the United Nations are right about Israel is quite simple, if Israel is the decent party in its war with the Palestinian authority and Hamas and nearly all the world's countries, nearly all the world's media and the United Nations are morally wrong – what hope is there for humanity? If the world's moral compass is that broken, are we not sailing into a dark age?

For KSCO, this is Kay Zwerling.

12

(May 2010) Let's take a rest from daily stressful occurrences and bad world news, and just reminisce about the happier, simple past.

After a while, one realizes that everything in life is timing. Case in point – my two lifelong teen girlfriends and I planned to go to a party one Saturday night in 1936. I decided not to go, and told them to go without me. I was worrying then a lot about my dad's failing health. But, they coaxed me to go, and I did.

That party shaped my life – I met the young man – fleetingly – who was to become my husband, the father of my three children, and the love of my life for 58 years plus four years of courting. Sure – we bickered now and then.

If I had stayed home that Saturday night – we never would have met, and what a loss that would have been for us – and Louis, Regina, and MZ never would have happened.

Clearly, important life moments happen in unplanned times.

Also, during WW2, my husband Barry served in the Navy. Right after our Country conquered Germany, his group was ordered to San Francisco for several days in 1945 while en route to Japan, and as luck would have it VJ Day happened then, so this Navy contingent was not sent to Japan after all. See the unplanned good timing. My husband and his group remained in San Francisco for one year until they were released from the Navy, during which time he discovered how beautiful California was, and decided we should try to live here.

That was a good thought – we didn't want to remain in New York, and the timing made California an option.

If you have a moment to think, you will discover that some inconsequential incidences may have shaped your whole life, also. Think about it.

Another prophetic incident – after our little family of four (MZ had not yet entered this world), on Labor Day 1947, we arrived in Santa Cruz from New York. That happened to be the day that KSCO came on the air for the first time. Little did we know then how important it would become in our lives.

When we arrived in Santa Cruz in September 1947, Barry planned to meet a certain retiring optometrist who wrote to us several times in Brooklyn about how wonderful life was in Santa Cruz, then population 12,500. He said he went fishing several times a week, and convinced us to come and look at his practice which he wanted to sell.

The morning after we arrived, Barry visited with the retiring optometrist for several hours, and became convinced that we should stay here in Santa Cruz, and purchase his practice.

In retrospect, it was a wonderful move, and a great place to raise our family. MZ joined us in 1951, and we were all thrilled with his arrival.

At that time, the early '50s, we had intercoms, and I woke the children every morning with KGO, that big San Francisco station that initiated the new format of interactive newstalk in the late '50s.

The rest is history. In his teens, MZ would go to San Francisco often on a bus for an afternoon just to watch the celebrities enter and leave the KGO building. As a teenager, also, he hosted a weekly high school program on KSCO until he was fired by the boss, Mr. Berlin, for making a fart noise with his mouth on the air. Decades later, when we purchased KSCO, Mr. Berlin, the original engineer owner, and MZ became very good friends.

Wouldn't this be a good script for a movie?

This waxing sentimental must end for the time being. Thanks for listening, and yes you must agree that unplanned timing often changes the direction of our lives in an unusual or exciting way.

For KSCO, this is Kay Zwerling.

13

(May 2010) This bewilders me that I have lived so long, but never heard of the Paradoxical Commandments until recently when my friend Marcia told me about them.

Here's the story – evidently the Paradoxical Commandments were written by an 18-year-old named Kent Keith, a freshman at Harvard in 1968. He is probably 60 years old now. The Commandments were later found posted on Mother Teresa's wall in India.

One wonders how an 18-year-old could have the wisdom and depth of understanding of human nature to be so right-on and so humanly generous as Kent Keith had to be to come up with those mature thoughts. It is like finding meaning in a crazy world, and how many of us humans achieve such wisdom? I wonder, also, how can an 18-year-old have become so disenchanted so early in his life? That is a paradox, too. And, maybe there was a little bit of paranoia in him, also. Here are the Paradoxical Commandments:

People are illogical, unreasonable, and self-centered – Love them anyway. If you do good, people will accuse you of selfish ulterior motives – Do good anyway. If you are successful, you will win false friends and true enemies – Succeed anyway. The good you do today will be forgotten tomorrow – Do good anyway. Honesty and frankness make you vulnerable – Be honest and frank anyway. The biggest men and women with the biggest ideas can be shot down by the smallest men and women with the smallest minds – Think big anyway. People favor underdogs but follow only top dogs – Fight for a few underdogs anyway. What you spend years building may be destroyed overnight – Build anyway. People really need help but may attack you if you do help them – Help people anyway. And finally – Give the world the best you have and you'll get kicked in the teeth – Give the world the best you have anyway.

So much for the Paradoxical Commandments.

There is another little gem that I think fits in here because of the strength of its honest unsolicited loving kindness.

At the heart of medicine, we find soul medicine.

I once met a Jewish patient who happened to be a medical doctor. He told me how he practiced medicine. He said "Whenever a patient would come to me, before I would do any examination, I would place my hand on the patient's shoulder and say 'I offer you Racamonos'."

Racamonos is a Yiddish word which means loving kindness or compassion. It occurred to me that loving kindness is the primary medicine, the first medicine that we can offer. It is soul medicine. To offer loving kindness to our patients and clients verbally and nonverbally supports the atmosphere for every other service we do. Loving kindness creates hospitality and welcome. It creates comfort and safety. Loving kindness offers a relationship in humility; it encourages receptivity and openness for the wellbeing of those who serve. Loving kindness softens and opens the heart of the one who offers it. I thanked the Jewish doctor for the gift of his words to me. May the soul medicine of Racamonos be a healing bomb in your heart. And, this was quoted from Dominican Hospital Scanner in July 2004.

For KSCO, this is Kay Zwerling.

14

(May 2010) This is another little gem from listener Gene Sanden. It is called "God is busy". If you do not know God, do not make stupid remarks.

A United States Marine was attending some college courses between assignments. He had complete missions in Iraq and Afghanistan. One of the courses had a professor who was an avowed atheist and member of ACLU. One day the professor shocked the class when he came in. He looked to the ceiling and flatly stated "God, if You are real, then I want You to knock me off this platform. I will give You exactly 15 minutes." The lecture room fell silent. You could hear a pin drop. Ten minutes went by, and the professor proclaimed "Here I am, God. I am still waiting." It got down to the last couple minutes, when the Marine got out of his chair, went up to the professor, and cold-cocked him, knocking him off the platform. The professor was out cold. The Marine went back to his seat, and sat there silently. The other students were shocked, stunned, and sat there looking on in silence. The professor eventually came to, noticeably shaken, looked at the Marine and asked "What in the world is the matter with you? Why did you do that?" The Marine calmly replied "God was too busy today protecting American soldiers who are protecting you and your right to say stupid stuff and act like an idiot. So, He sent me." The classroom erupted in cheers.

This is good. Keep it going. Amen.

Live simply, love generously, care deeply, speak kindly. Now go in peace, and serve the Lord.

Sincerely,

For KSCO, this is Kay Zwerling.

15

(Jan 2010) Despite the several compelling issues ready to be discussed, let just opt to remind ourselves early on in 2010, about things we should remember to make life better and happier for ourselves, our loved ones, and friends.

About HEALTH:

Drink plenty of water.

Eat foods that grow on trees and plants.

Eat less food that is manufactured in plants.

Live with the three E's: Energy, Enthusiasm, Empathy.

Make time to pray.

Play more games.

Read more books than you did in 2009.

Sit in silence for at least ten minutes everyday.

Sleep for seven hours.

Take a 10-30 minute walk daily. While you walk, smile.

Now on PERSONALITY:

Do not compare your life to others. You have no idea what their journey is all about!

Do not have negative thoughts of things you cannot control. Instead, invest your energy in the positive present moment.

Do not overdo. Keep your limits.

Do not take yourself so seriously. No one else does!

Do not waste your precious energy on gossip.

Dream more while you are awake.

Envy is a waste of time. You already have all you need.

Forget issues of the past.

Do not remind your partner of his or her mistakes of the past. That will ruin your present happiness.

Life is too short to waste time hating anyone. Do not hate others.

Make peace with your past so it will not spoil your present.

No one is in charge of your happiness except you.

Realize that life is a school, and you are here to learn. Problems are simply part of the curriculum that appear and fade away, but the lessons you learn will last a lifetime.

Smile and laugh more.

You do not have to win every argument. Agree to disagree.

About SOCIETY:

Call your family often.

Each day give something good to others.

Forgive everyone for everything.

Spend time with people over the age of 70, and under the age of six.

Try to make at least three people smile each day.

Whatever people think of you is none of your business.

Your job will not take care of you when you are sick. Your friends will. Stay in touch.

And finally, on LIFE:

Do the right thing.

Get rid of everything that is not useful, beautiful, or joyful.

Remember that God heals everything!

However good or bad a situation is, it will change.

No matter how you feel, get up, dress up, and show up.

The best is yet to come.

When you awake, arise in the morning, thank God for it.

Your innermost is always happy, so be happy.

For KSCO, this is Kay Zwerling.

16

(Fall 2009) The title is "This is an insult".

This is an insult. Read all of this and weep, folks. This is what our elected officials have done to you and me. A great thank you to all of us.

From an Emergency Room doctor – I live and work in a border State overrun with illegals. They make more money having kids than we earn working fulltime. Today, I had a 25-year-old with eight kids. That's right. Eight. All illegal anchor babies, and she had the nicest nails, cellphone, handbag, clothing, etc. She makes about $1500 monthly for each. Do the math.

I used to say "We are the dumbest nation on earth." Now, I must say, and sadly admit, "You are the dumbest people on earth, and that includes me, for we elected the idiot idea foolishly who have passed the Bills that allow this." Sorry, we need a Revolution. Vote them all out in 2010!

Remember – in November 2010, we have a golden opportunity to clean out the entire House and one-third of the Senate. This is an insult and a kick in the butt to all of us.

Get mad, and pass it on.

I do not know how, but maybe some good will come of this travesty.

If an immigrant is over 65, they can apply for SSI and Medicaid and get more than a woman on Social Security, who worked from 1944 til 2004. She is only getting $791 per month because she was born in 1924 and there is a Catch 22. It is interesting that the federal government provides a single refugee with a monthly allowance of $1,890. Each can also obtain an additional $580 in social assistance, for a total of $2,470 a month. This compares to a single pensioner, who after contributing to the growth and development of America for 40-50 years, can only receive a monthly maximum of $1,012 in old age pension and Guaranteed Income Supplement. Maybe our pensioners should apply as refugees!

Consider sending this to all your American friends, so we can all be ticked off and maybe get the refugees cut back to $1,012 and the pensioners up to $2,470. Then we can enjoy some of the money we were forced to submit to the Government over the last 40, 50, 60 years.

Please forward to every American to expose what our elected politicians have been doing over the past 11 years to the overtaxed American. Send this to every American taxpayer you know.

For KSCO, this is Kay Zwerling.

5

Photos

KSCO

KSCO